OF THE GALAXIES

BEST STORY EVER

GUARDIANS OF THE GALAXY

BEST STORY EVER

GUARDIANS OF THE GALAXY: BEST STORY EVER #1

WRITER: **TIM SEELEY**

STORYBOARDS: **REILLY BROWN**

FINISHERS: **IBAN COELLO & JACOPO CAMAGNI**

COLORIST: **JIM CHARALAMPIDIS**

LETTERER: **VC'S CORY PETIT**

COVER ART: **TIM SEELEY**

EDITORS: **JORDAN D. WHITE & XANDER JAROWEY**

GROUP EDITOR: **MIKE MARTS**

GUARDIANS OF THE GALAXY: GALAXY'S MOST WANTED #1

WRITER: **WILL CORONA PILGRIM**

ARTIST: **ANDREA DI VITO**

COLORIST: **LAURA VILLARI**

COVER ART: **JEE-HYUNG LEE**

ASSISTANT EDITOR: **MARK BASSO**

EDITOR: **BILL ROSEMANN**

MARVEL STUDIOS:

VP PRODUCTION & DEVELOPMENT: **JONATHAN SCHWARTZ**

SVP PRODUCTION & DEVELOPMENT: **JEREMY LATCHAM**

PRESIDENT: **KEVIN FEIGE**

GUARDIANS OF THE GALAXY: TOMORROW'S AVENGERS #1

WRITER: **BRIAN MICHAEL BENDIS**

DRAX

ARTIST: **MICHAEL AVON OEMING**

COLORIST: **RAIN BEREDO**

ROCKET RACCOON

ARTIST: **MING DOYLE**

COLORIST: **JAVIER RODRIGUEZ**

GAMORA & GROOT

ARTIST: **MIKE DEL MUNDO**

LETTERER: **VC'S JOE CARAMAGNA**

COVER ARTIST: **MING DOYLE**

EDITOR: **SANA AMANAT**

SENIOR EDITOR: **STEVE WACKER**

FREE COMIC BOOK DAY 2014 (ROCKET RACCOON) #1

WRITER: **JOE CARAMAGNA**

ARTIST: **ADAM ARCHER**

COLORIST: **JOHN RAUCH**

LETTERER: **VIRTUAL CALLIGRAPHY**

COVER ART: **SKOTTIE YOUNG**

ASSISTANT EDITOR: **JON MOISAN**

EDITOR: **MARK PANICCIA**

THOR #314

WRITER: **DOUG MOENCH**

LAYOUTS & COVER ART: **KEITH POLLARD**

FINISHERS: **DAN GREEN & PABLO MARCOS**

COLORIST: **GEORGE ROUSSOS**

LETTERER: **JANICE CHIANG**

EDITOR: **JIM SALICRUP**

LOGAN'S RUN #6

WRITER: **SCOTT EDELMAN**

ARTIST: **MIKE ZECK**

COLORIST: **PETRA GOLDBERG**

LETTERER: **SUSAN FOX**

EDITOR: **ARCHIE GOODWIN**

MARVEL HOLIDAY SPECIAL #2

WRITER: **JIM STARLIN**

PENCILER: **RON LIM**

INKER: **TERRY AUSTIN**

COLORIST: **TOM VINCENT**

LETTERER: **BRAD JOYCE**

EDITOR: **RENEE WITTERSTAETTER**

COLLECTION EDITOR: **SARAH BRUNSTAD**

ASSOCIATE MANAGING EDITOR: **ALEX STARBUCK**

EDITORS, SPECIAL PROJECTS: **JENNIFER GRÜNWALD & MARK D. BEAZLEY**

SENIOR EDITOR, SPECIAL PROJECTS: **JEFF YOUNGQUIST**

SVP PRINT, SALES & MARKETING: **DAVID GABRIEL**

EDITOR IN CHIEF: **AXEL ALONSO**

CHIEF CREATIVE OFFICER: **JOE QUESADA**

PUBLISHER: **DAN BUCKLEY**

EXECUTIVE PRODUCER: **ALAN FINE**

GUARDIANS OF THE GALAXY: BEST STORY EVER. Contains material originally published in magazine form as GUARDIANS OF THE GALAXY: BEST STORY EVER #1, GUARDIANS OF THE GALAXY: TOMORROW'S AVENGERS #1, FREE COMIC BOOK DAY (2014) ROCKET RACCOON #1, GUARDIANS OF THE GALAXY: GALAXY'S MOST WANTED #1, THOR #314, LOGAN'S RUN #6 and MARVEL HOLIDAY SPECIAL #2. First printing 2015. ISBN# 978-0-7851-9797-3. Published by MARVEL WORLDWIDE, INC., a subsidiary of MARVEL ENTERTAINMENT, LLC. OFFICE OF PUBLICATION: 135 West 50th Street, New York, NY 10020. Copyright © 2015 MARVEL No similarity between any of the names, characters, persons, and/or institutions in this magazine with those of any living or dead person or institution is intended, and any such similarity which may exist is purely coincidental. **Printed in Canada.** ALAN FINE, President, Marvel Entertainment; DAN BUCKLEY, President, TV, Publishing and Brand Management; JOE QUESADA, Chief Creative Officer; TOM BREVOORT, SVP of Publishing; DAVID BOGART, SVP of Operations & Procurement, Publishing; C.B. CEBULSKI, VP of International Development & Brand Management; DAVID GABRIEL, SVP Print, Sales & Marketing; JIM O'KEEFE, VP of Operations & Logistics; DAN CARR, Executive Director of Publishing Technology; SUSAN CRESPI, Editorial Operations Manager; ALEX MORALES, Publishing Operations Manager; STAN LEE, Chairman Emeritus. For information regarding advertising in Marvel Comics or on Marvel.com, please contact Jonathan Rheingold, VP of Custom Solutions Ad Sales, at jrheingold@marvel.com. For Marvel subscription inquiries, please call 800-217-9158. Manufactured between 6/26/2015 and 8/3/2015 by SOLISCO PRINTERS, SCOTT, QC, CANAD

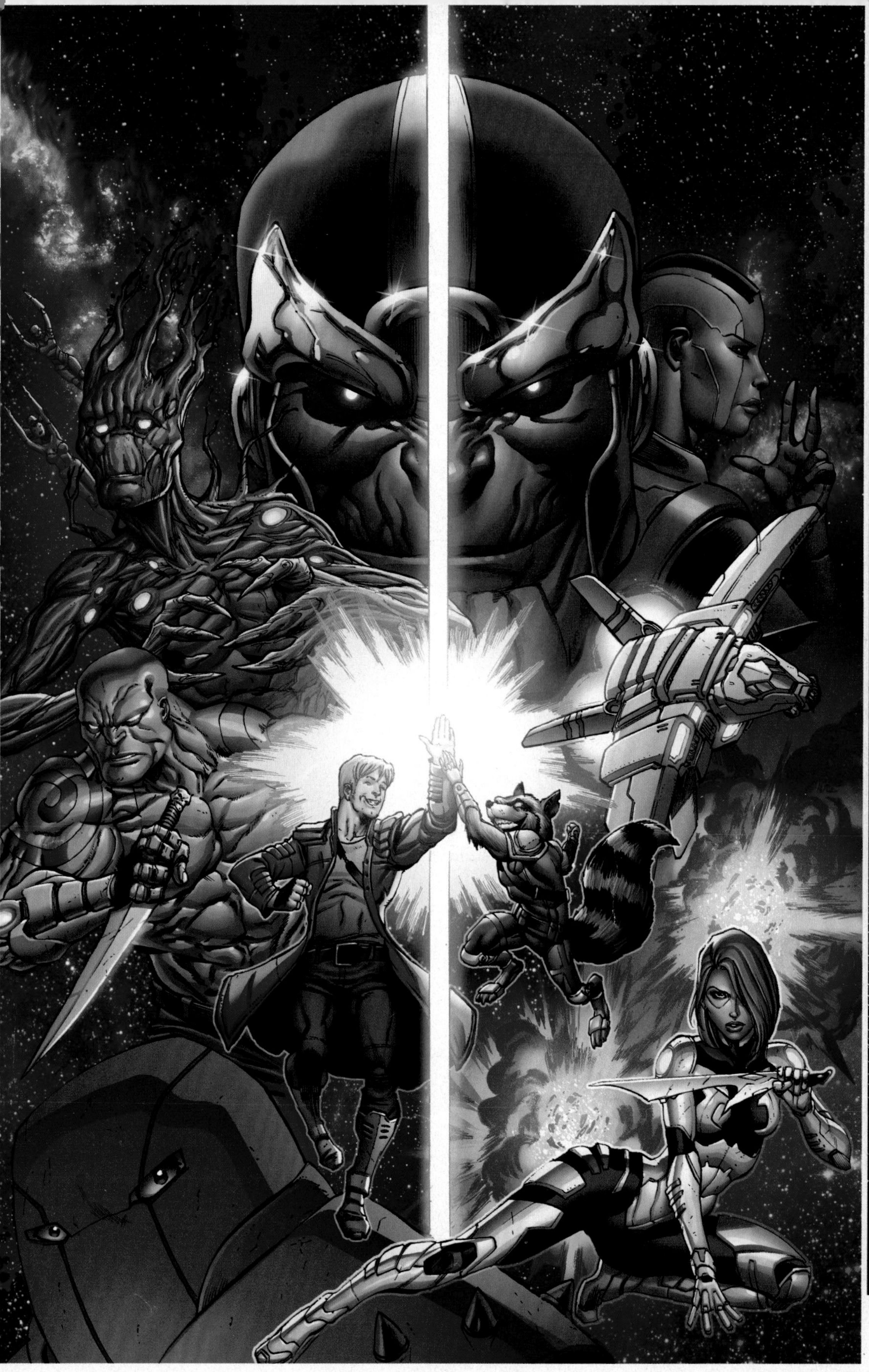

GUARDIANS OF THE GALAXY: BEST STORY EVER #1

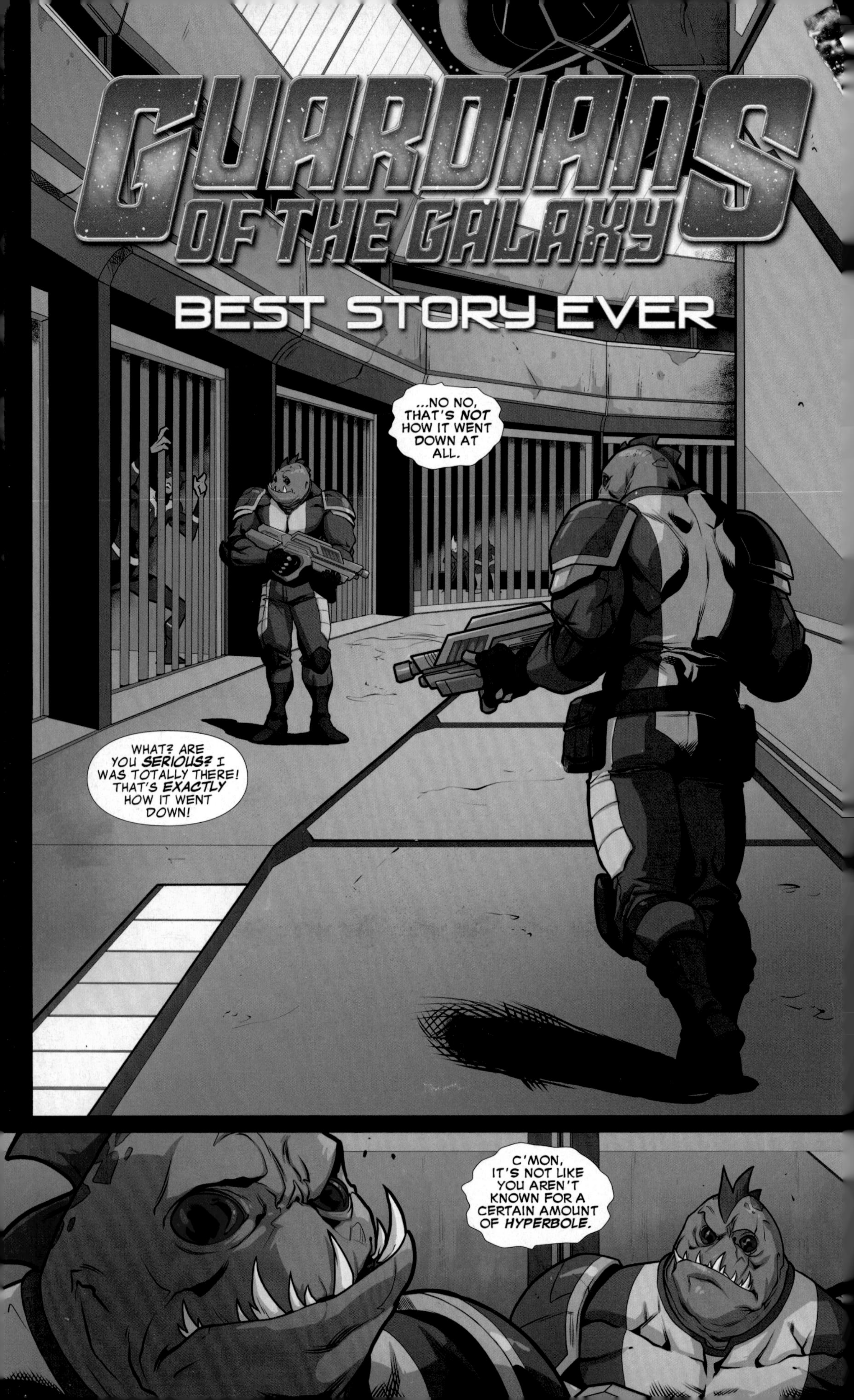
GUARDIANS OF THE GALAXY
BEST STORY EVER
...NO NO, THAT'S NOT HOW IT WENT DOWN AT ALL.
WHAT? ARE YOU SERIOUS? I WAS TOTALLY THERE! THAT'S EXACTLY HOW IT WENT DOWN!
C'MON, IT'S NOT LIKE YOU AREN'T KNOWN FOR A CERTAIN AMOUNT OF HYPERBOLE.

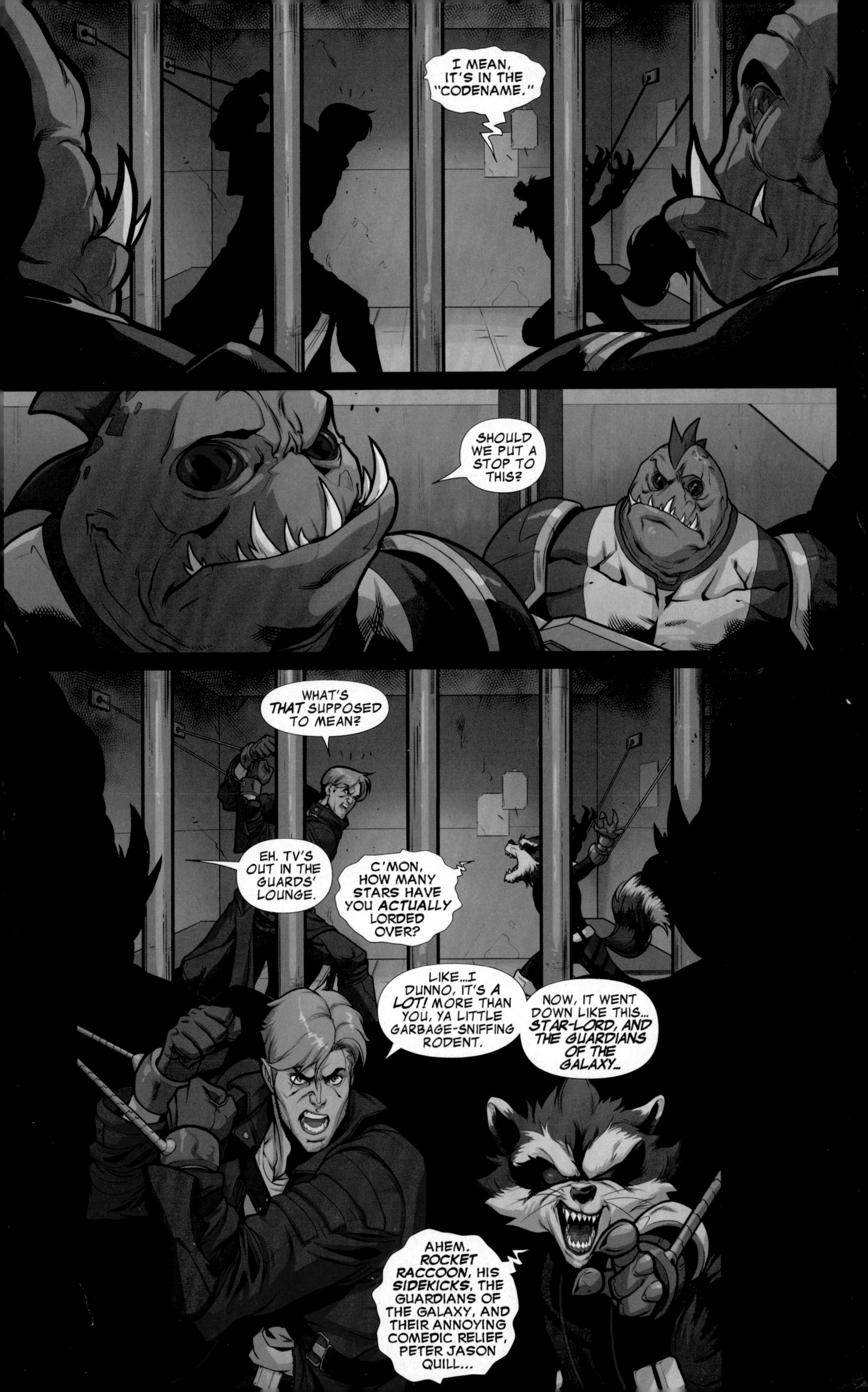
I MEAN, IT'S IN THE "CODENAME."
SHOULD WE PUT A STOP TO THIS?
WHAT'S THAT SUPPOSED TO MEAN?
EH. TV'S OUT IN THE GUARDS' LOUNGE.
C'MON, HOW MANY STARS HAVE YOU ACTUALLY LORDED OVER?
LIKE...I DUNNO, IT'S A LOT! MORE THAN YOU, YA LITTLE GARBAGE-SNIFFING RODENT.
NOW, IT WENT DOWN LIKE THIS... STAR-LORD, AND THE GUARDIANS OF THE GALAXY...
AHEM. ROCKET RACCOON, HIS SIDEKICKS, THE GUARDIANS OF THE GALAXY, AND THEIR ANNOYING COMEDIC RELIEF, PETER JASON QUILL...

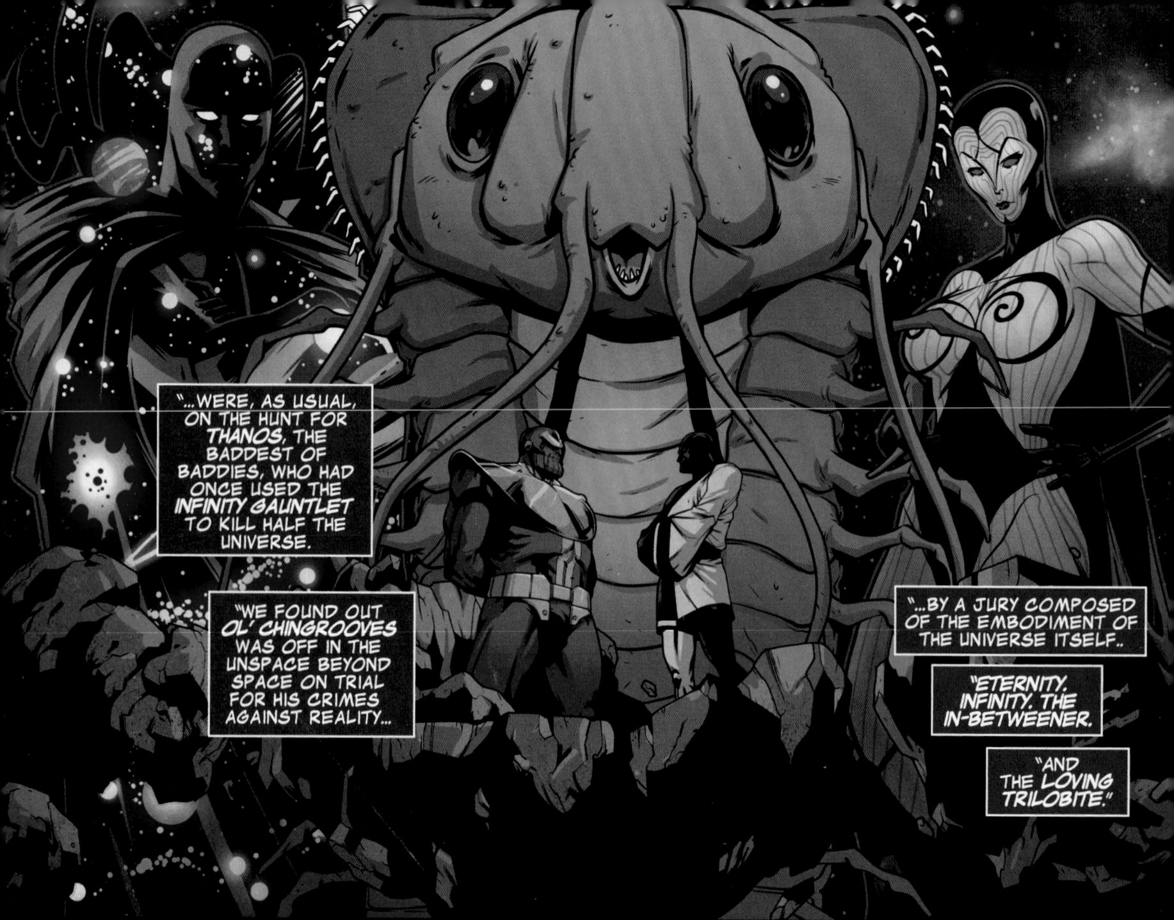
"...WERE, AS USUAL, ON THE HUNT FOR THANOS, THE BADDEST OF BADDIES, WHO HAD ONCE USED THE INFINITY GAUNTLET TO KILL HALF THE UNIVERSE.
"WE FOUND OUT OL' CHINGROOVES WAS OFF IN THE UNSPACE BEYOND SPACE ON TRIAL FOR HIS CRIMES AGAINST REALITY...
"...BY A JURY COMPOSED OF THE EMBODIMENT OF THE UNIVERSE ITSELF..
"ETERNITY. INFINITY. THE IN-BETWEENER.
"AND THE LOVING TRILOBITE."
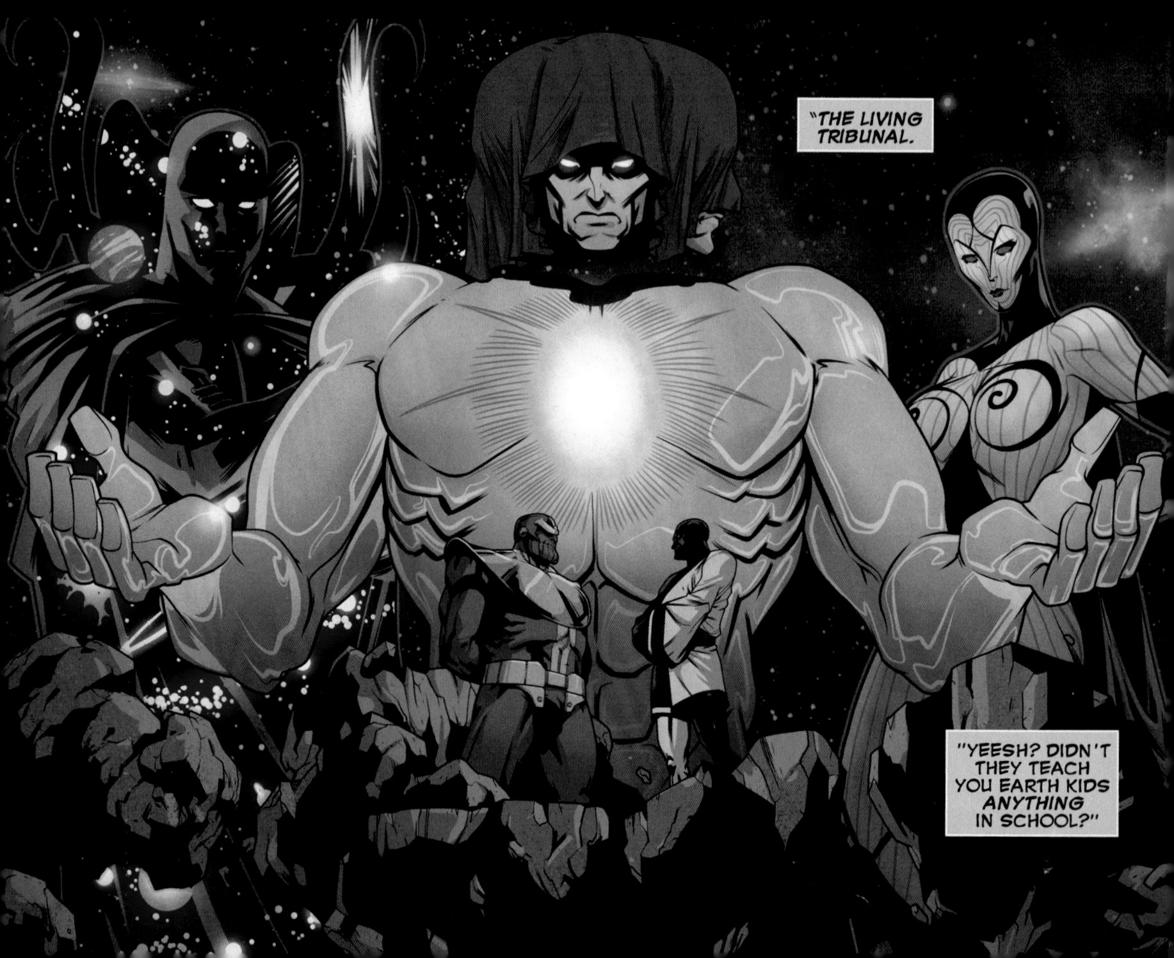
"THE LIVING TRIBUNAL.
"YEESH? DIDN'T THEY TEACH YOU EARTH KIDS ANYTHING IN SCHOOL?"

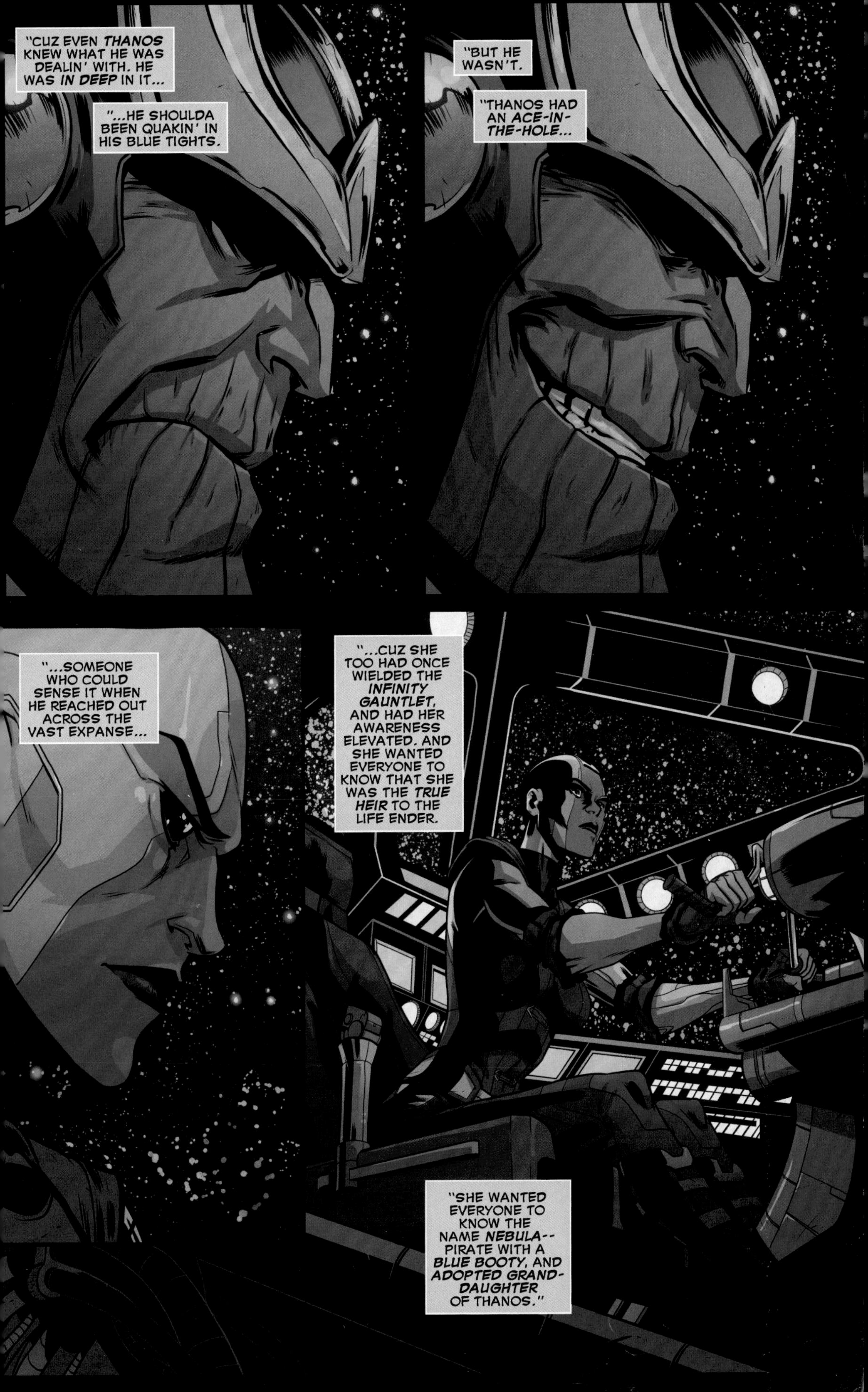
"CUZ EVEN THANOS KNEW WHAT HE WAS DEALIN' WITH. HE WAS IN DEEP IN IT...
"...HE SHOULDA BEEN QUAKIN' IN HIS BLUE TIGHTS.
"BUT HE WASN'T.
"THANOS HAD AN ACE-IN-THE-HOLE...
"...SOMEONE WHO COULD SENSE IT WHEN HE REACHED OUT ACROSS THE VAST EXPANSE...
"...CUZ SHE TOO HAD ONCE WIELDED THE INFINITY GAUNTLET, AND HAD HER AWARENESS ELEVATED. AND SHE WANTED EVERYONE TO KNOW THAT SHE WAS THE TRUE HEIR TO THE LIFE ENDER.
"SHE WANTED EVERYONE TO KNOW THE NAME NEBULA--PIRATE WITH A BLUE BOOTY, AND ADOPTED GRAND-DAUGHTER OF THANOS."

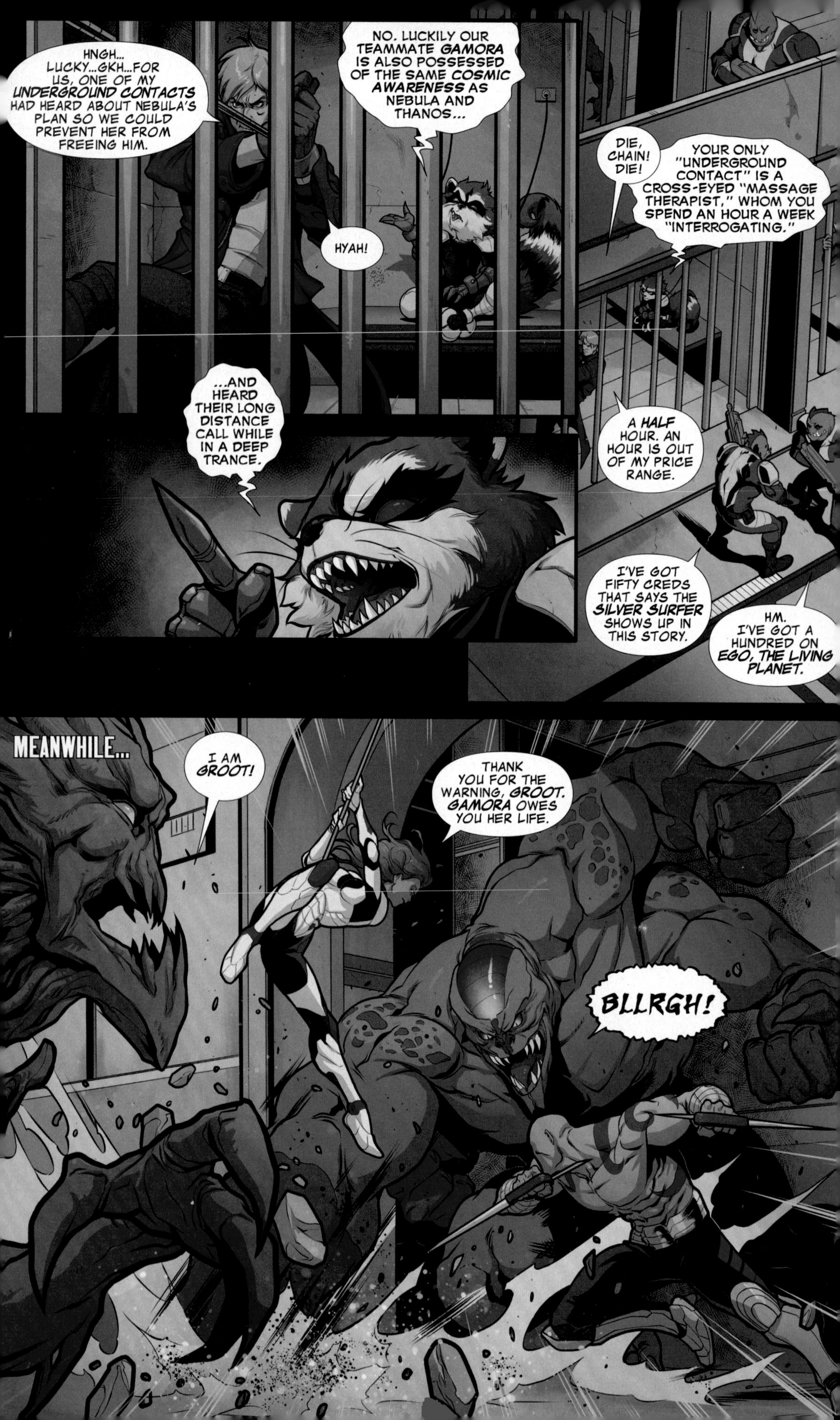
HNGH... LUCKY...GKH...FOR US, ONE OF MY UNDERGROUND CONTACTS HAD HEARD ABOUT NEBULA'S PLAN SO WE COULD PREVENT HER FROM FREEING HIM.
NO. LUCKILY OUR TEAMMATE GAMORA IS ALSO POSSESSED OF THE SAME COSMIC AWARENESS AS NEBULA AND THANOS...
HYAH!
...AND HEARD THEIR LONG DISTANCE CALL WHILE IN A DEEP TRANCE.
DIE, CHAIN! DIE!
YOUR ONLY "UNDERGROUND CONTACT" IS A CROSS-EYED "MASSAGE THERAPIST," WHOM YOU SPEND AN HOUR A WEEK "INTERROGATING."
A HALF HOUR. AN HOUR IS OUT OF MY PRICE RANGE.
I'VE GOT FIFTY CREDS THAT SAYS THE SILVER SURFER SHOWS UP IN THIS STORY.
HM. I'VE GOT A HUNDRED ON EGO, THE LIVING PLANET.
MEANWHILE...
I AM GROOT!
THANK YOU FOR THE WARNING, GROOT. GAMORA OWES YOU HER LIFE.
BLLRGH!

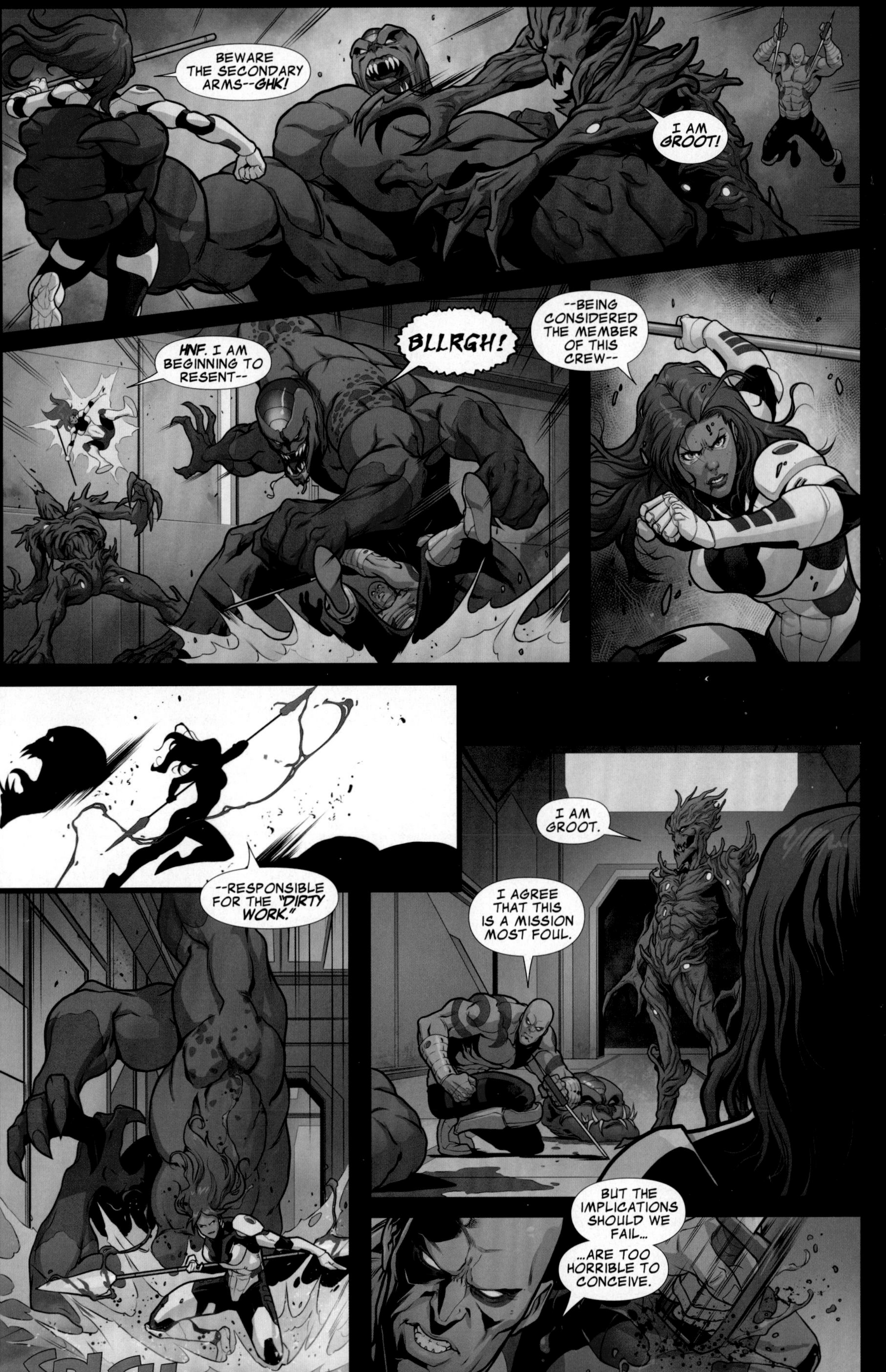
BEWARE THE SECONDARY ARMS--GHK!
I AM GROOT!
HNF. I AM BEGINNING TO RESENT--
BLLRGH!
--BEING CONSIDERED THE MEMBER OF THIS CREW--
--RESPONSIBLE FOR THE "DIRTY WORK."
SPLSH
I AM GROOT.
I AGREE THAT THIS IS A MISSION MOST FOUL.
BUT THE IMPLICATIONS SHOULD WE FAIL...
...ARE TOO HORRIBLE TO CONCEIVE.

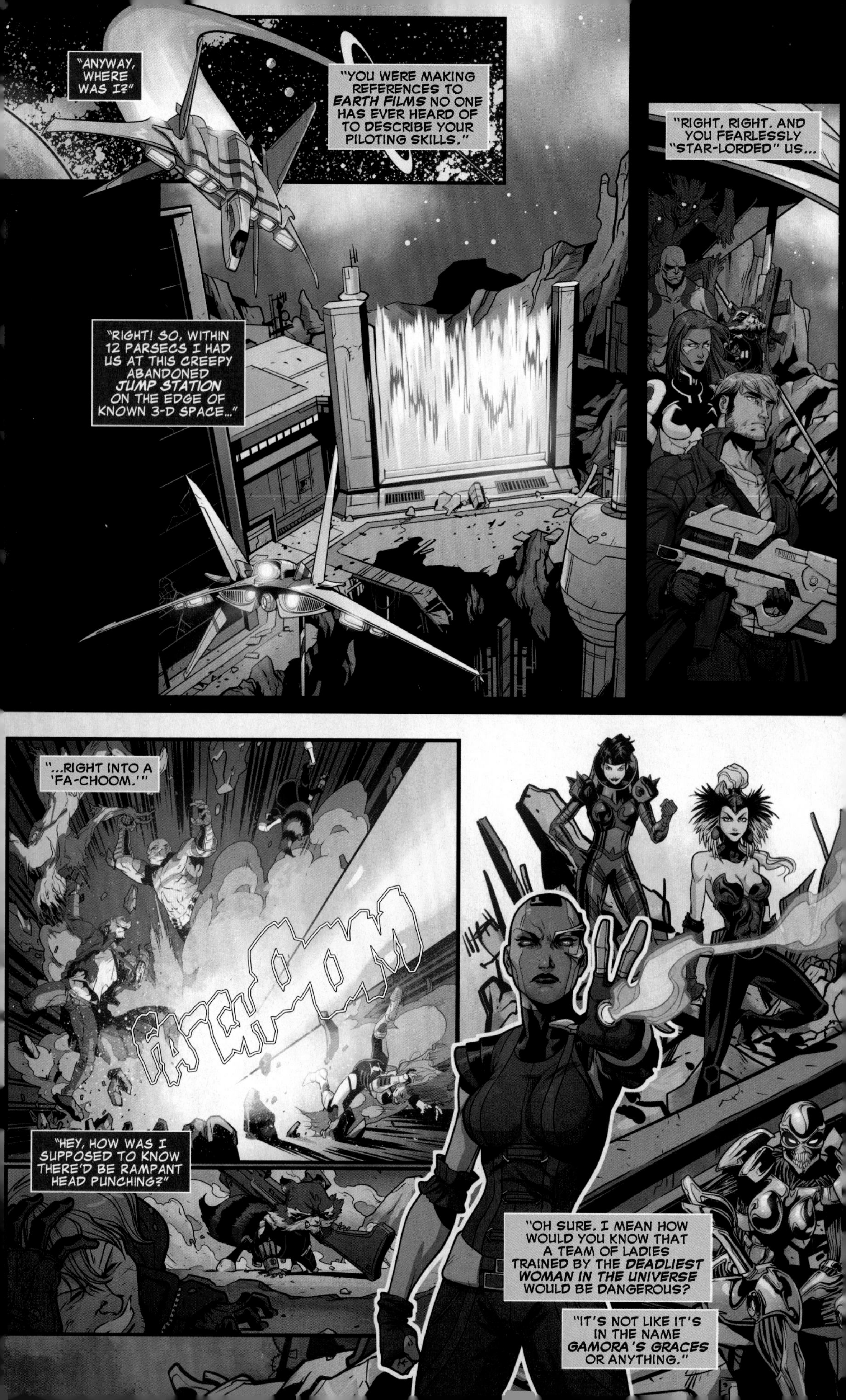
"ANYWAY, WHERE WAS I?"
"YOU WERE MAKING REFERENCES TO *EARTH FILMS* NO ONE HAS EVER HEARD OF TO DESCRIBE YOUR PILOTING SKILLS."
"RIGHT! SO, WITHIN 12 PARSECS I HAD US AT THIS CREEPY ABANDONED *JUMP STATION* ON THE EDGE OF KNOWN 3-D SPACE..."
"RIGHT, RIGHT. AND YOU FEARLESSLY "STAR-LORDED" US...
"...RIGHT INTO A 'FA-CHOOM.'"
FA-CHOOM
"HEY, HOW WAS I SUPPOSED TO KNOW THERE'D BE RAMPANT HEAD PUNCHING?"
"OH SURE. I MEAN HOW WOULD YOU KNOW THAT A TEAM OF LADIES TRAINED BY THE *DEADLIEST WOMAN IN THE UNIVERSE* WOULD BE DANGEROUS?
"IT'S NOT LIKE IT'S IN THE NAME *GAMORA'S GRACES* OR ANYTHING."

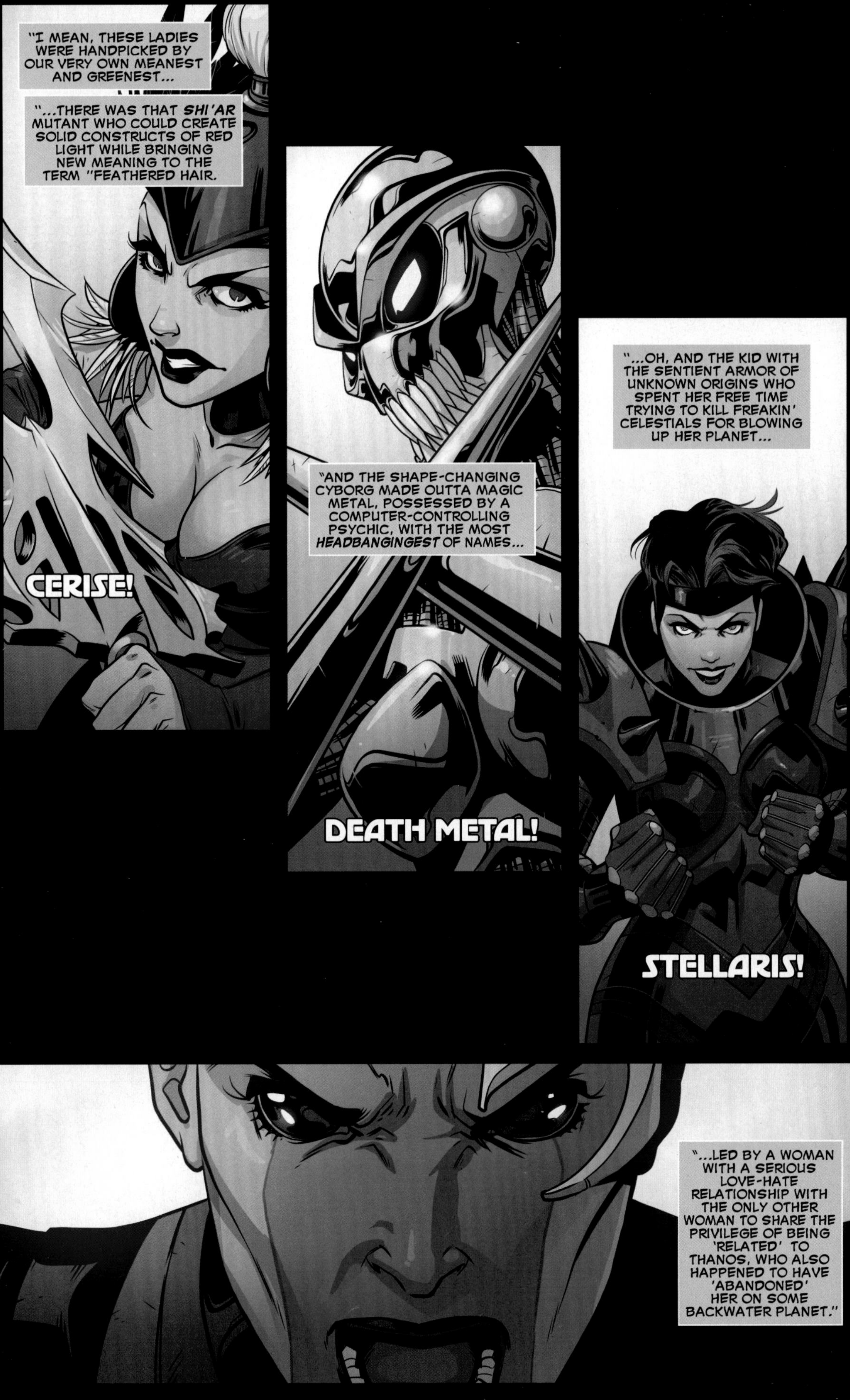
"I MEAN, THESE LADIES WERE HANDPICKED BY OUR VERY OWN MEANEST AND GREENEST...
"...THERE WAS THAT SHI'AR MUTANT WHO COULD CREATE SOLID CONSTRUCTS OF RED LIGHT WHILE BRINGING NEW MEANING TO THE TERM "FEATHERED HAIR.
CERISE!
"AND THE SHAPE-CHANGING CYBORG MADE OUTTA MAGIC METAL, POSSESSED BY A COMPUTER-CONTROLLING PSYCHIC, WITH THE MOST HEADBANGINGEST OF NAMES...
DEATH METAL!
"...OH, AND THE KID WITH THE SENTIENT ARMOR OF UNKNOWN ORIGINS WHO SPENT HER FREE TIME TRYING TO KILL FREAKIN' CELESTIALS FOR BLOWING UP HER PLANET...
STELLARIS!
"...LED BY A WOMAN WITH A SERIOUS LOVE-HATE RELATIONSHIP WITH THE ONLY OTHER WOMAN TO SHARE THE PRIVILEGE OF BEING 'RELATED' TO THANOS, WHO ALSO HAPPENED TO HAVE 'ABANDONED' HER ON SOME BACKWATER PLANET."

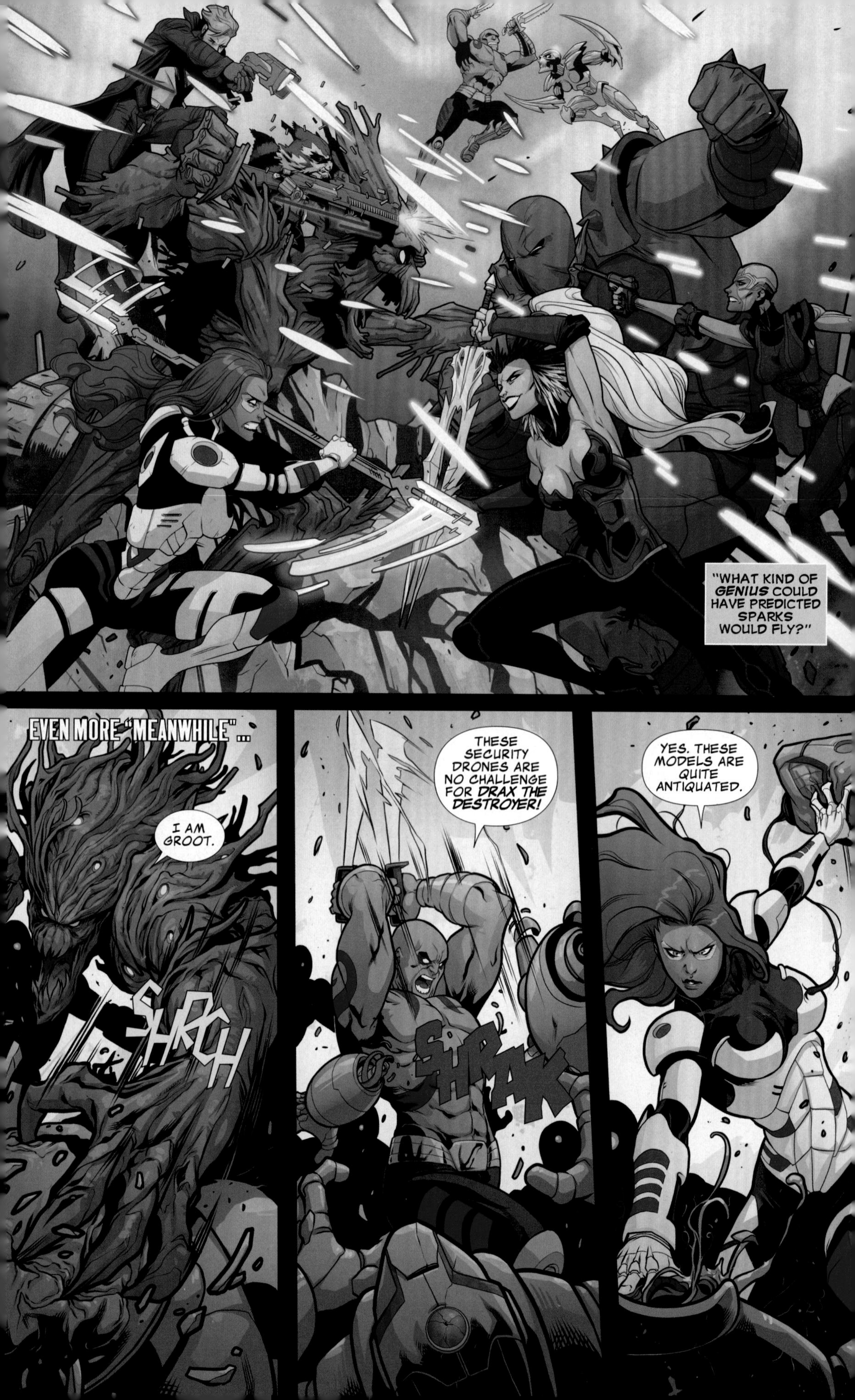
"WHAT KIND OF GENIUS COULD HAVE PREDICTED SPARKS WOULD FLY?"
EVEN MORE "MEANWHILE"...
I AM GROOT.
SHRCH
THESE SECURITY DRONES ARE NO CHALLENGE FOR DRAX THE DESTROYER!
SHRAK
YES. THESE MODELS ARE QUITE ANTIQUATED.

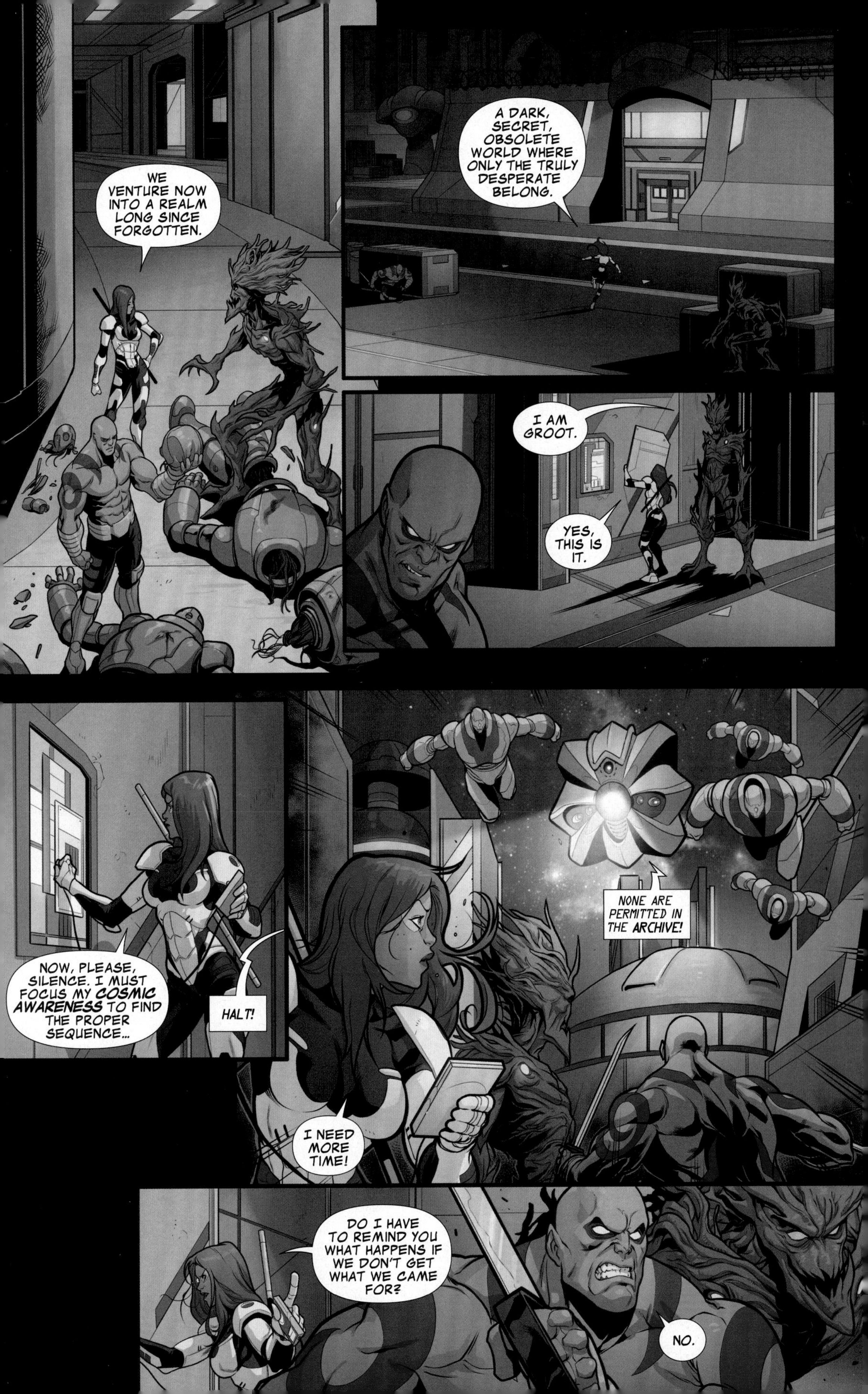
WE VENTURE NOW INTO A REALM LONG SINCE FORGOTTEN.
A DARK, SECRET, OBSOLETE WORLD WHERE ONLY THE TRULY DESPERATE BELONG.
I AM GROOT.
YES, THIS IS IT.
NOW, PLEASE, SILENCE. I MUST FOCUS MY COSMIC AWARENESS TO FIND THE PROPER SEQUENCE...
HALT!
NONE ARE PERMITTED IN THE ARCHIVE!
I NEED MORE TIME!
DO I HAVE TO REMIND YOU WHAT HAPPENS IF WE DON'T GET WHAT WE CAME FOR?
NO.

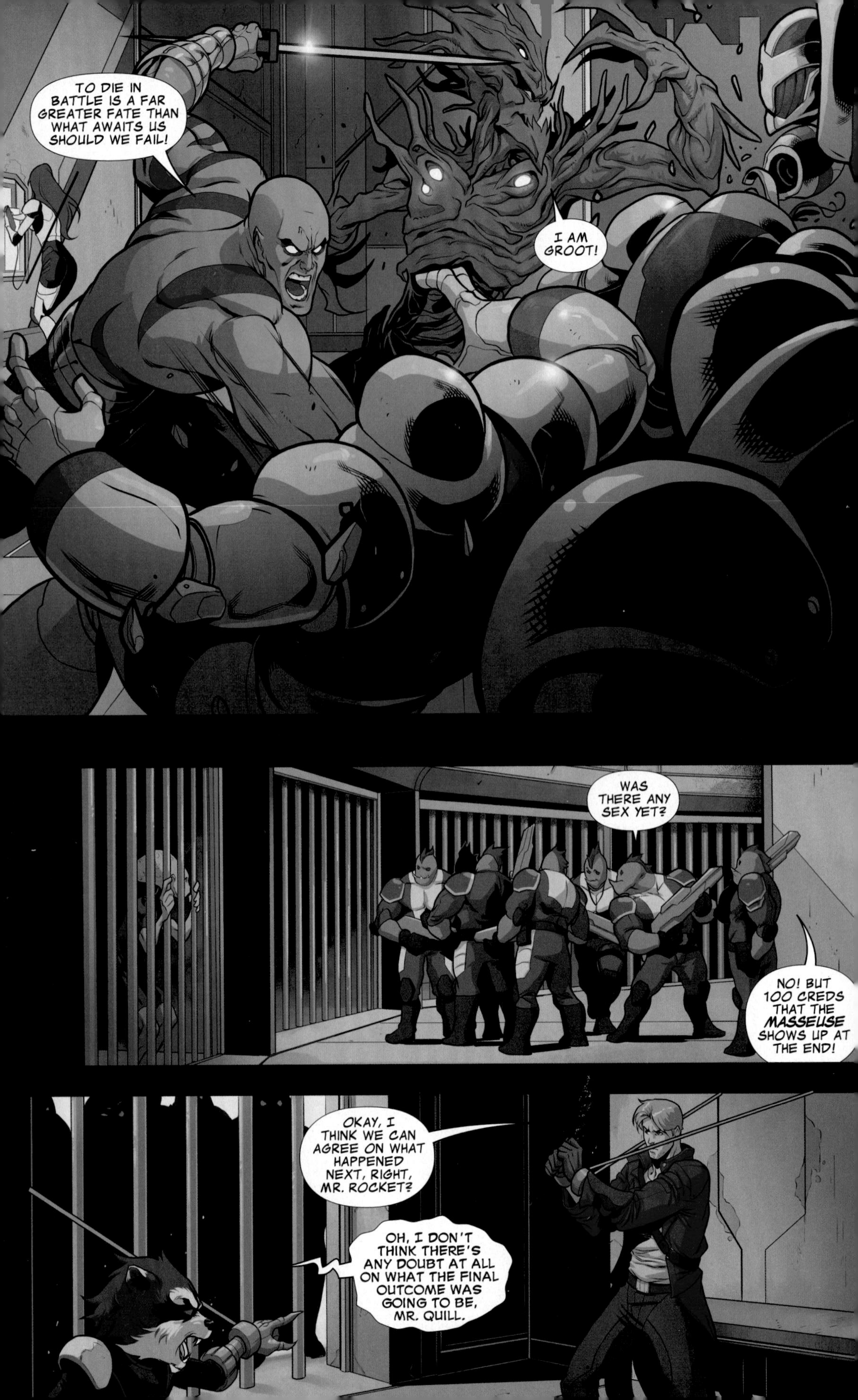
TO DIE IN BATTLE IS A FAR GREATER FATE THAN WHAT AWAITS US SHOULD WE FAIL!
I AM GROOT!
WAS THERE ANY SEX YET?
NO! BUT 100 CREDS THAT THE MASSEUSE SHOWS UP AT THE END!
OKAY, I THINK WE CAN AGREE ON WHAT HAPPENED NEXT, RIGHT, MR. ROCKET?
OH, I DON'T THINK THERE'S ANY DOUBT AT ALL ON WHAT THE FINAL OUTCOME WAS GOING TO BE, MR. QUILL.

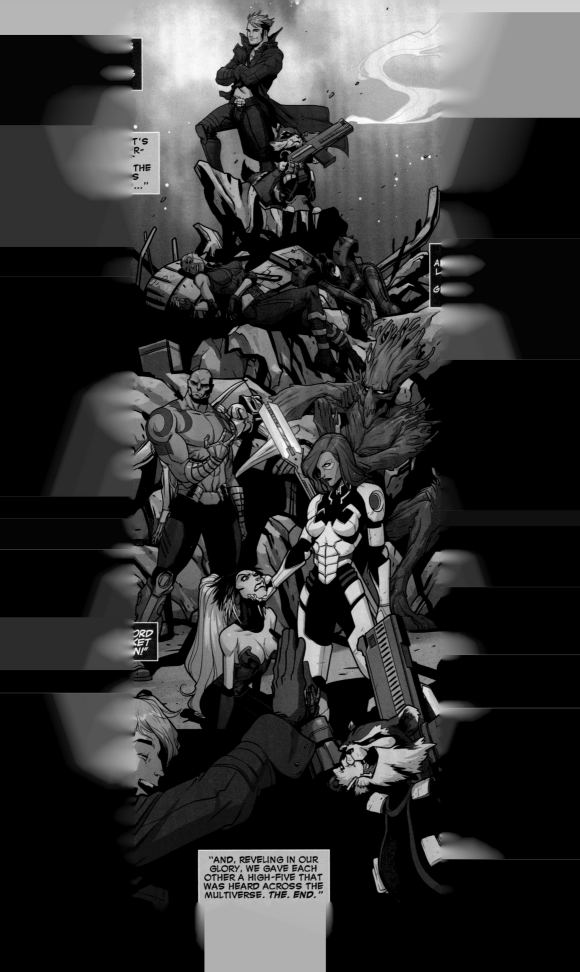

"...R- THE S..."

"AND, REVELING IN OUR GLORY, WE GAVE EACH OTHER A HIGH-FIVE THAT WAS HEARD ACROSS THE MULTIVERSE. *THE. END.*"

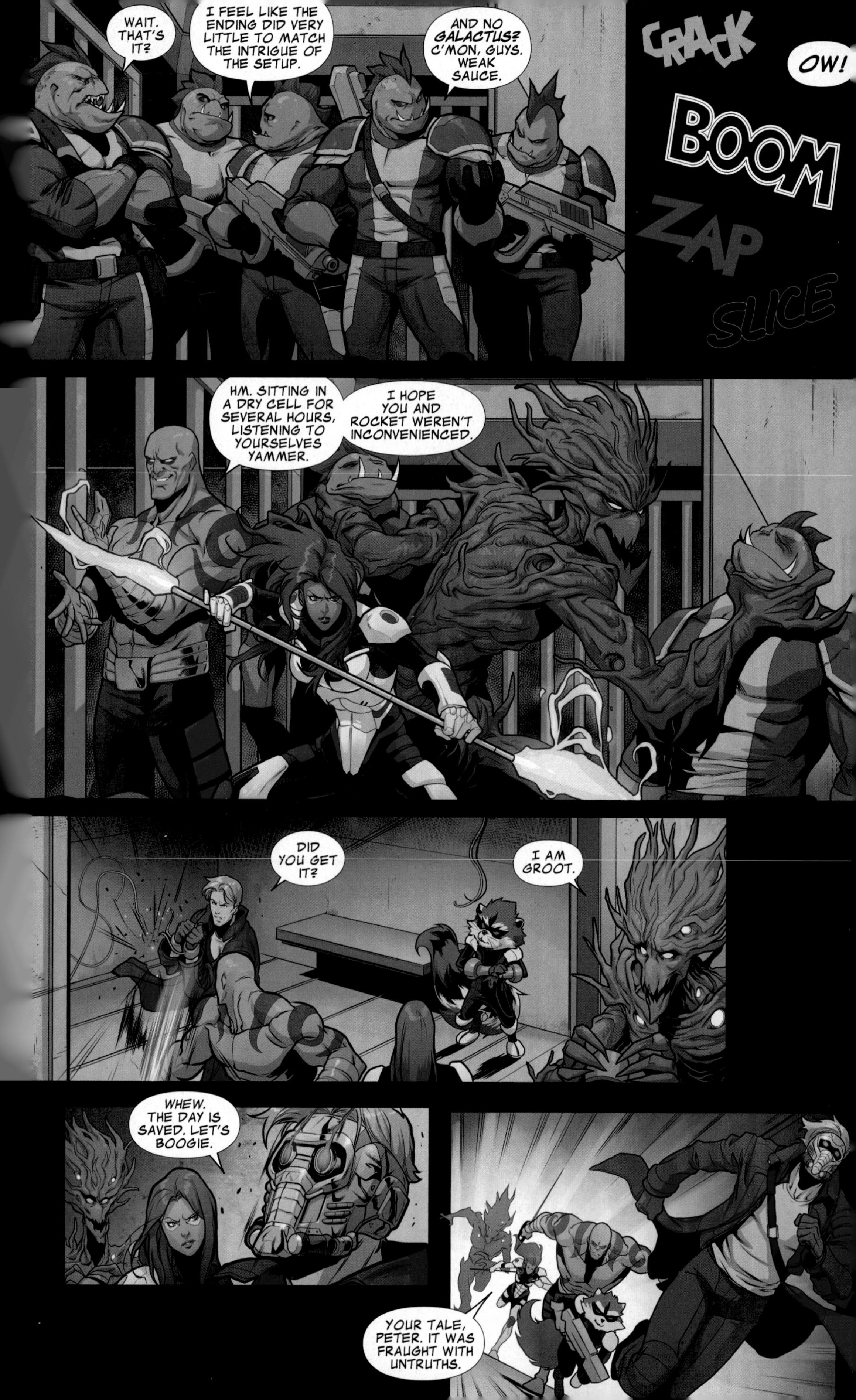
WAIT. THAT'S IT?
I FEEL LIKE THE ENDING DID VERY LITTLE TO MATCH THE INTRIGUE OF THE SETUP.
AND NO GALACTUS? C'MON, GUYS. WEAK SAUCE.
CRACK
OW!
BOOM
ZAP
SLICE
HM. SITTING IN A DRY CELL FOR SEVERAL HOURS, LISTENING TO YOURSELVES YAMMER.
I HOPE YOU AND ROCKET WEREN'T INCONVENIENCED.
DID YOU GET IT?
I AM GROOT.
WHEW. THE DAY IS SAVED. LET'S BOOGIE.
YOUR TALE, PETER. IT WAS FRAUGHT WITH UNTRUTHS.

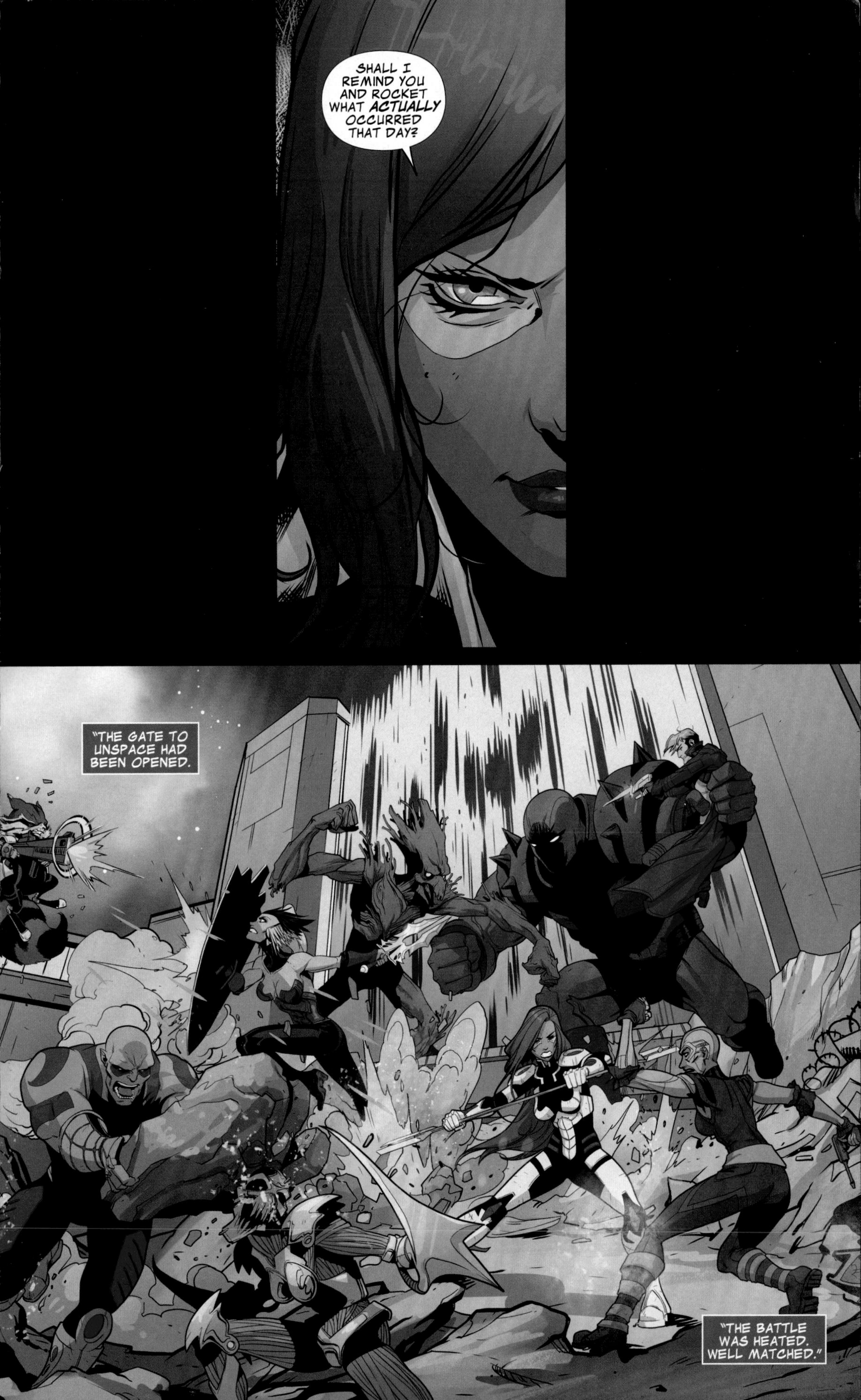
SHALL I REMIND YOU AND ROCKET WHAT ACTUALLY OCCURRED THAT DAY?
"THE GATE TO UNSPACE HAD BEEN OPENED.
"THE BATTLE WAS HEATED. WELL MATCHED."

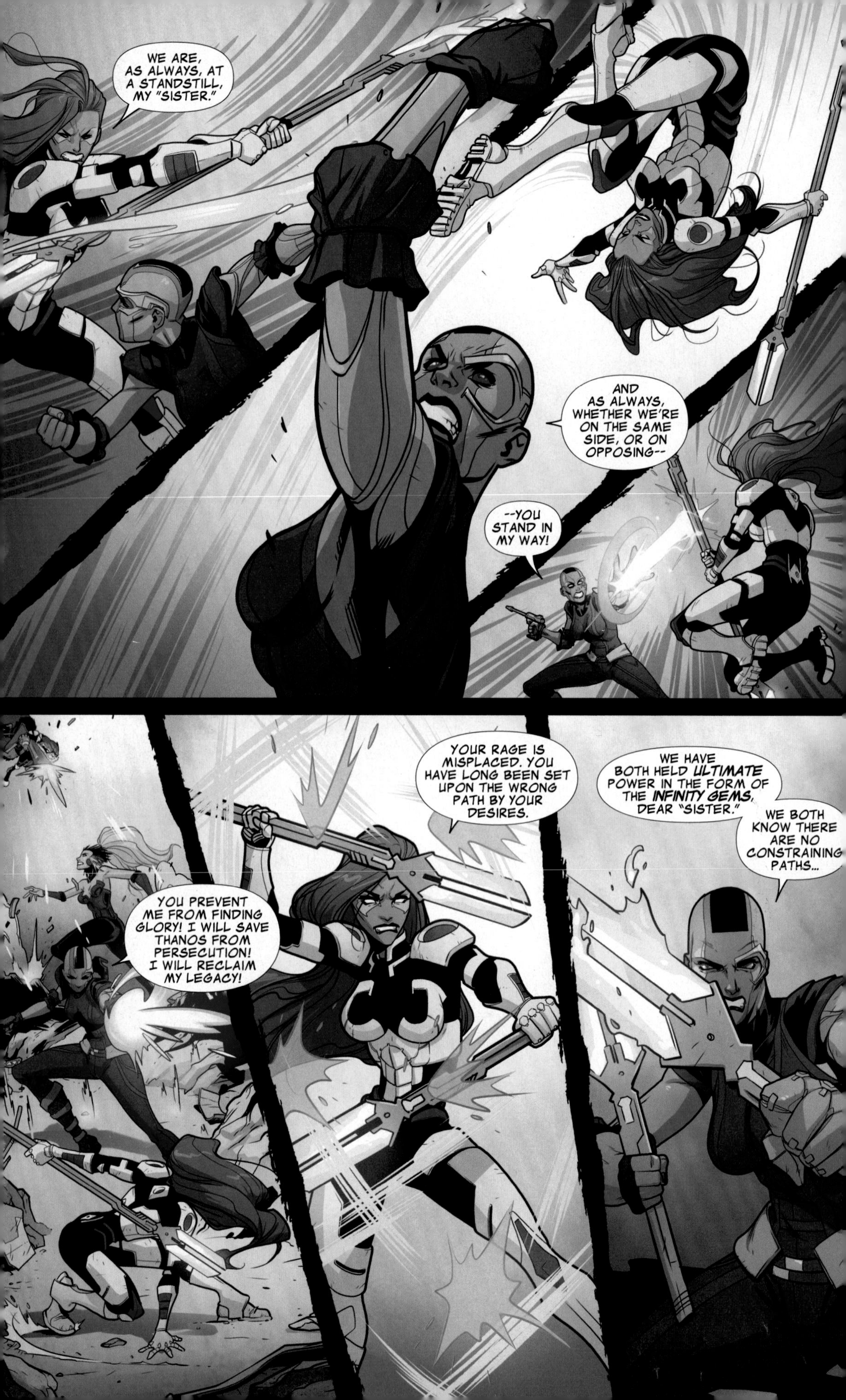
WE ARE, AS ALWAYS, AT A STANDSTILL, MY "SISTER."
AND AS ALWAYS, WHETHER WE'RE ON THE SAME SIDE, OR ON OPPOSING--
--YOU STAND IN MY WAY!
YOU PREVENT ME FROM FINDING GLORY! I WILL SAVE THANOS FROM PERSECUTION! I WILL RECLAIM MY LEGACY!
YOUR RAGE IS MISPLACED. YOU HAVE LONG BEEN SET UPON THE WRONG PATH BY YOUR DESIRES.
WE HAVE BOTH HELD ULTIMATE POWER IN THE FORM OF THE INFINITY GEMS, DEAR "SISTER."
WE BOTH KNOW THERE ARE NO CONSTRAINING PATHS...

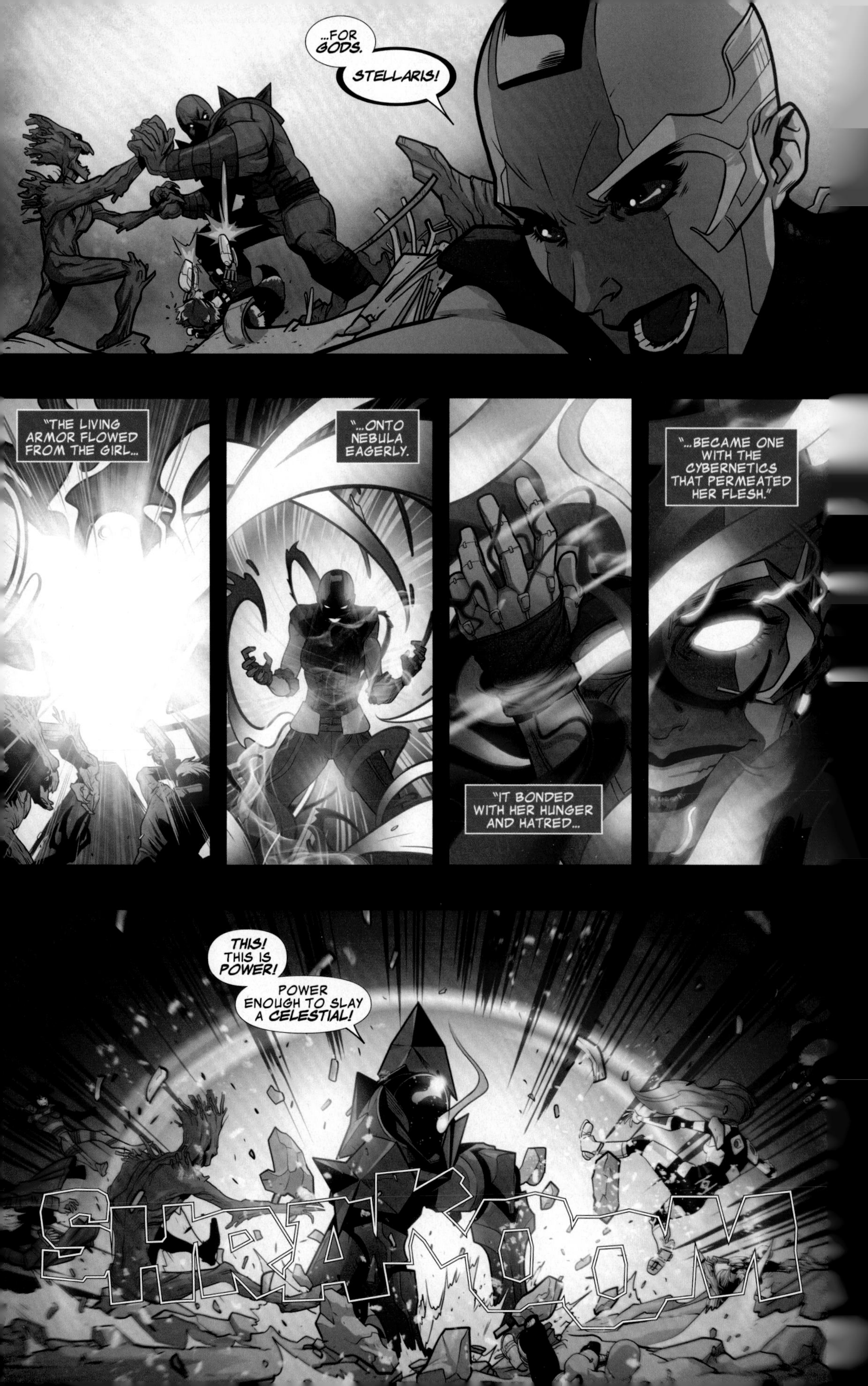
...FOR GODS.
STELLARIS!
"THE LIVING ARMOR FLOWED FROM THE GIRL...
"...ONTO NEBULA EAGERLY.
"IT BONDED WITH HER HUNGER AND HATRED...
"...BECAME ONE WITH THE CYBERNETICS THAT PERMEATED HER FLESH."
THIS! THIS IS POWER!
POWER ENOUGH TO SLAY A CELESTIAL!
SHRAKOOM

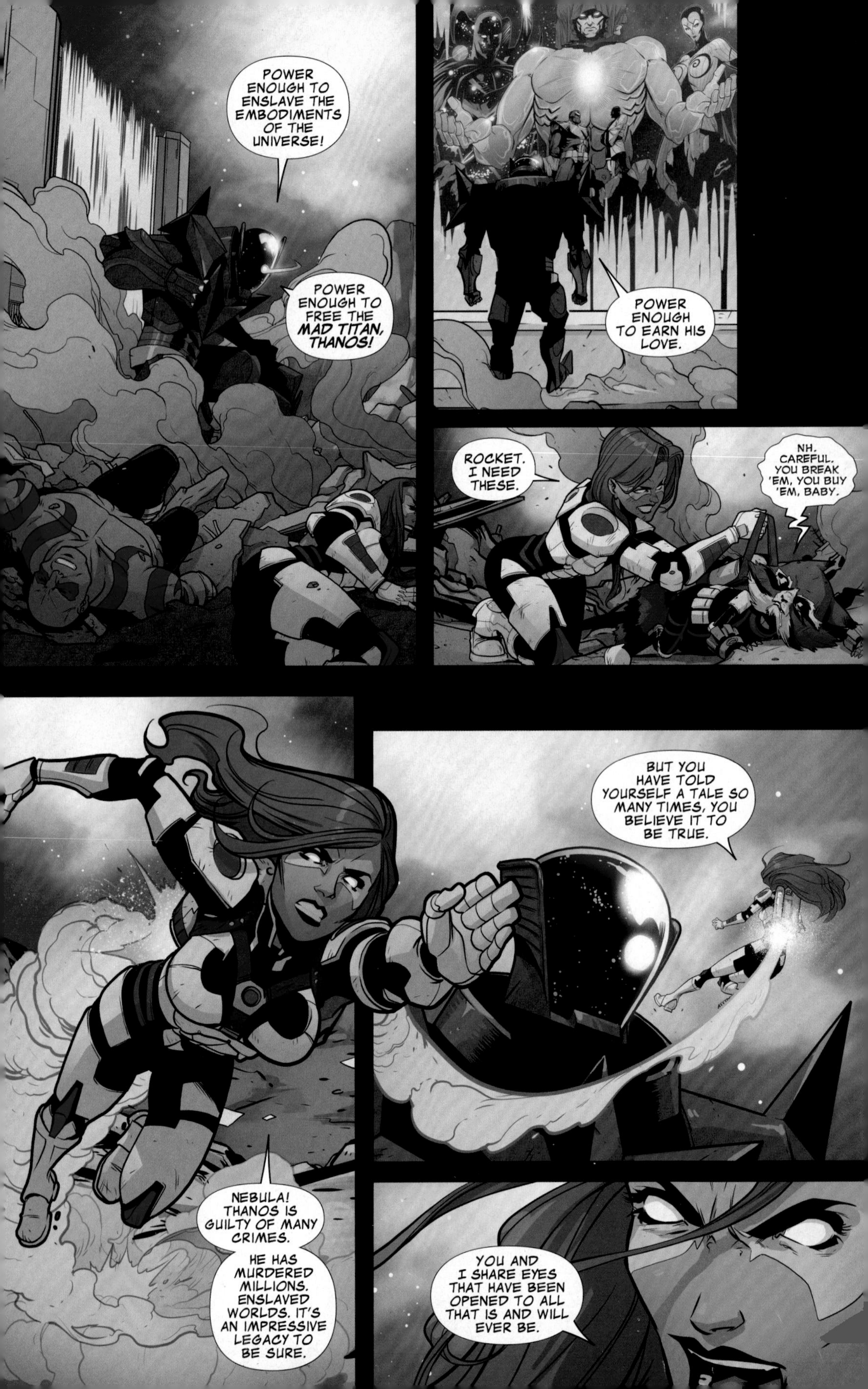
POWER ENOUGH TO ENSLAVE THE EMBODIMENTS OF THE UNIVERSE!
POWER ENOUGH TO FREE THE MAD TITAN, THANOS!
POWER ENOUGH TO EARN HIS LOVE.
ROCKET. I NEED THESE.
NH. CAREFUL. YOU BREAK 'EM, YOU BUY 'EM, BABY.
NEBULA! THANOS IS GUILTY OF MANY CRIMES.
HE HAS MURDERED MILLIONS. ENSLAVED WORLDS. IT'S AN IMPRESSIVE LEGACY TO BE SURE.
BUT YOU HAVE TOLD YOURSELF A TALE SO MANY TIMES, YOU BELIEVE IT TO BE TRUE.
YOU AND I SHARE EYES THAT HAVE BEEN OPENED TO ALL THAT IS AND WILL EVER BE.

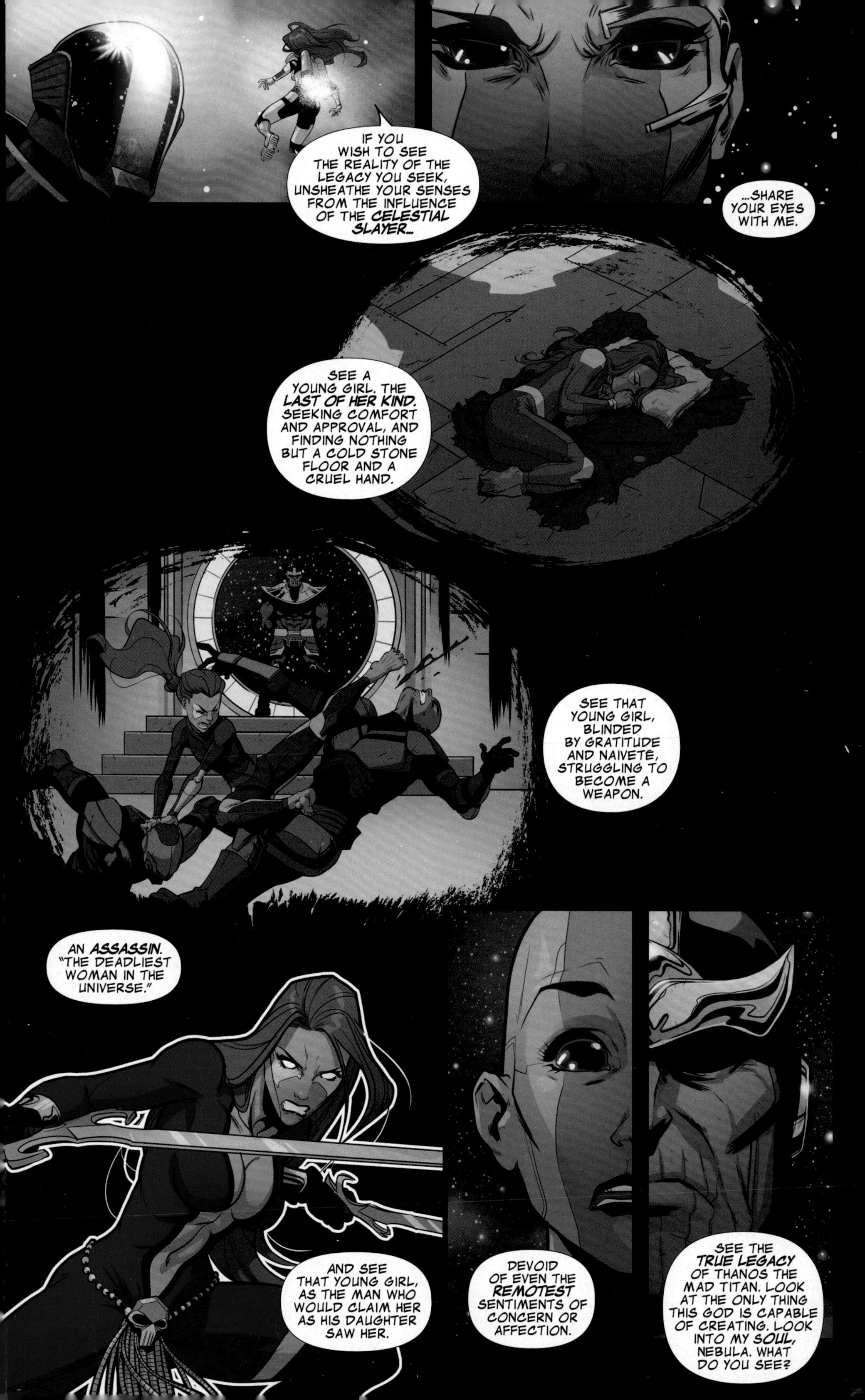

IF YOU WISH TO SEE THE REALITY OF THE LEGACY YOU SEEK, UNSHEATHE YOUR SENSES FROM THE INFLUENCE OF THE CELESTIAL SLAYER...
...SHARE YOUR EYES WITH ME.
SEE A YOUNG GIRL. THE LAST OF HER KIND. SEEKING COMFORT AND APPROVAL, AND FINDING NOTHING BUT A COLD STONE FLOOR AND A CRUEL HAND.
SEE THAT YOUNG GIRL, BLINDED BY GRATITUDE AND NAIVETE, STRUGGLING TO BECOME A WEAPON.
AN ASSASSIN. "THE DEADLIEST WOMAN IN THE UNIVERSE."
AND SEE THAT YOUNG GIRL, AS THE MAN WHO WOULD CLAIM HER AS HIS DAUGHTER SAW HER.
DEVOID OF EVEN THE REMOTEST SENTIMENTS OF CONCERN OR AFFECTION.
SEE THE TRUE LEGACY OF THANOS THE MAD TITAN. LOOK AT THE ONLY THING THIS GOD IS CAPABLE OF CREATING. LOOK INTO MY SOUL, NEBULA. WHAT DO YOU SEE?

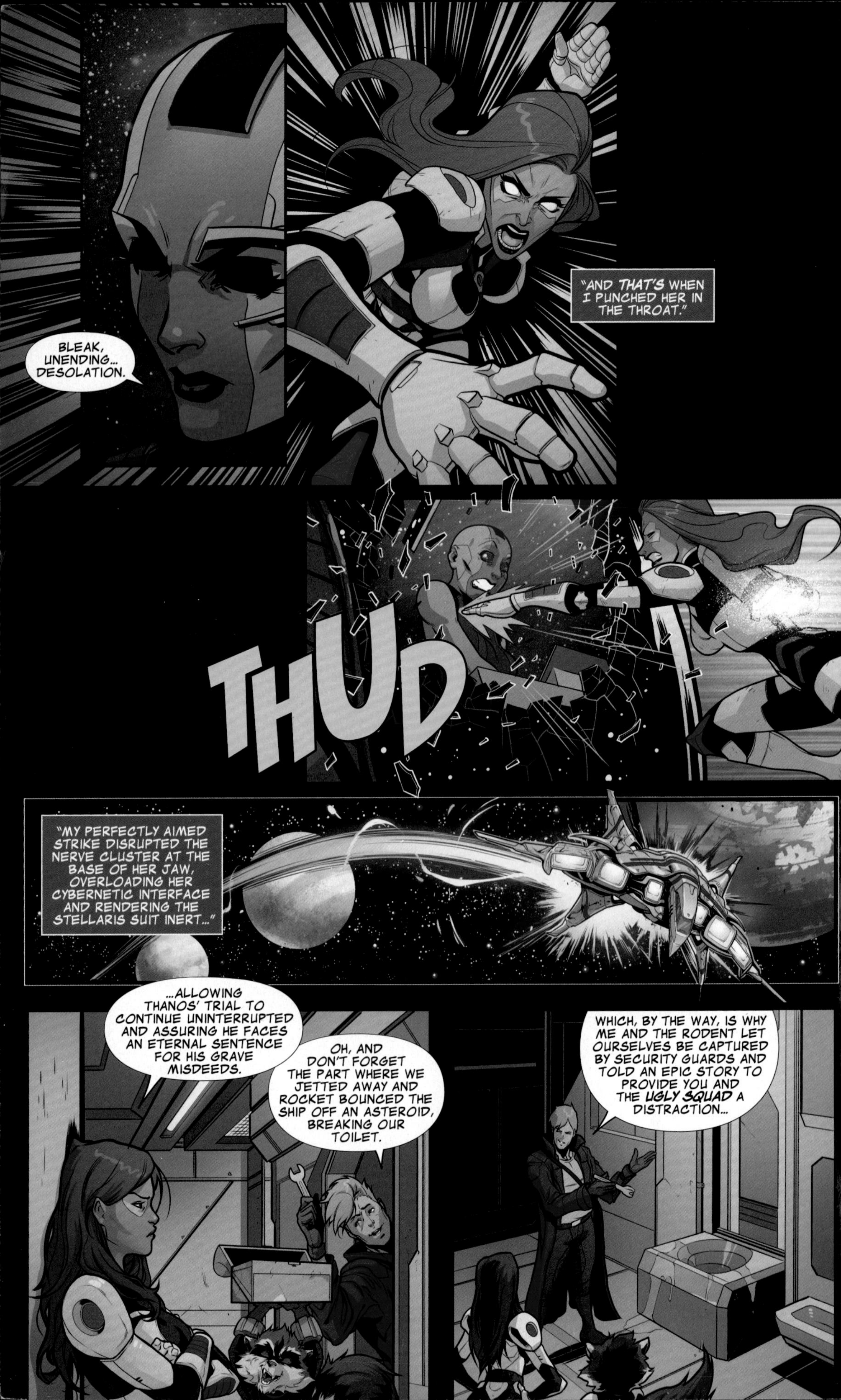
BLEAK, UNENDING... DESOLATION.
"AND THAT'S WHEN I PUNCHED HER IN THE THROAT."
THUD
"MY PERFECTLY AIMED STRIKE DISRUPTED THE NERVE CLUSTER AT THE BASE OF HER JAW, OVERLOADING HER CYBERNETIC INTERFACE AND RENDERING THE STELLARIS SUIT INERT..."
...ALLOWING THANOS' TRIAL TO CONTINUE UNINTERRUPTED AND ASSURING HE FACES AN ETERNAL SENTENCE FOR HIS GRAVE MISDEEDS.
OH, AND DON'T FORGET THE PART WHERE WE JETTED AWAY AND ROCKET BOUNCED THE SHIP OFF AN ASTEROID, BREAKING OUR TOILET.
WHICH, BY THE WAY, IS WHY ME AND THE RODENT LET OURSELVES BE CAPTURED BY SECURITY GUARDS AND TOLD AN EPIC STORY TO PROVIDE YOU AND THE UGLY SQUAD A DISTRACTION...

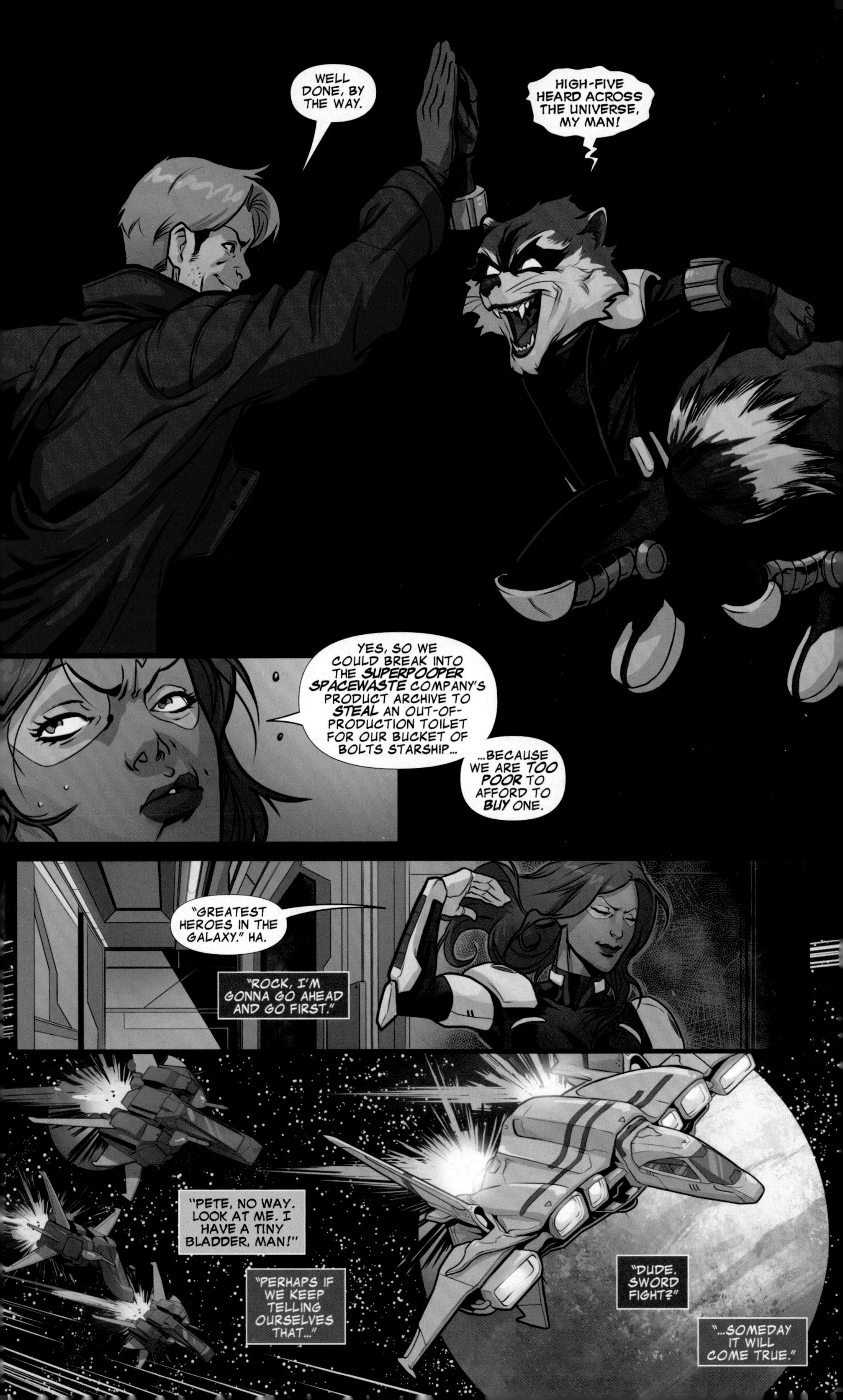
WELL DONE, BY THE WAY.
HIGH-FIVE HEARD ACROSS THE UNIVERSE, MY MAN!
YES, SO WE COULD BREAK INTO THE SUPERPOOPER SPACEWASTE COMPANY'S PRODUCT ARCHIVE TO STEAL AN OUT-OF-PRODUCTION TOILET FOR OUR BUCKET OF BOLTS STARSHIP...
...BECAUSE WE ARE TOO POOR TO AFFORD TO BUY ONE.
"GREATEST HEROES IN THE GALAXY." HA.
"ROCK, I'M GONNA GO AHEAD AND GO FIRST."
"PETE, NO WAY. LOOK AT ME. I HAVE A TINY BLADDER, MAN!"
"PERHAPS IF WE KEEP TELLING OURSELVES THAT..."
"DUDE. SWORD FIGHT?"
"...SOMEDAY IT WILL COME TRUE."

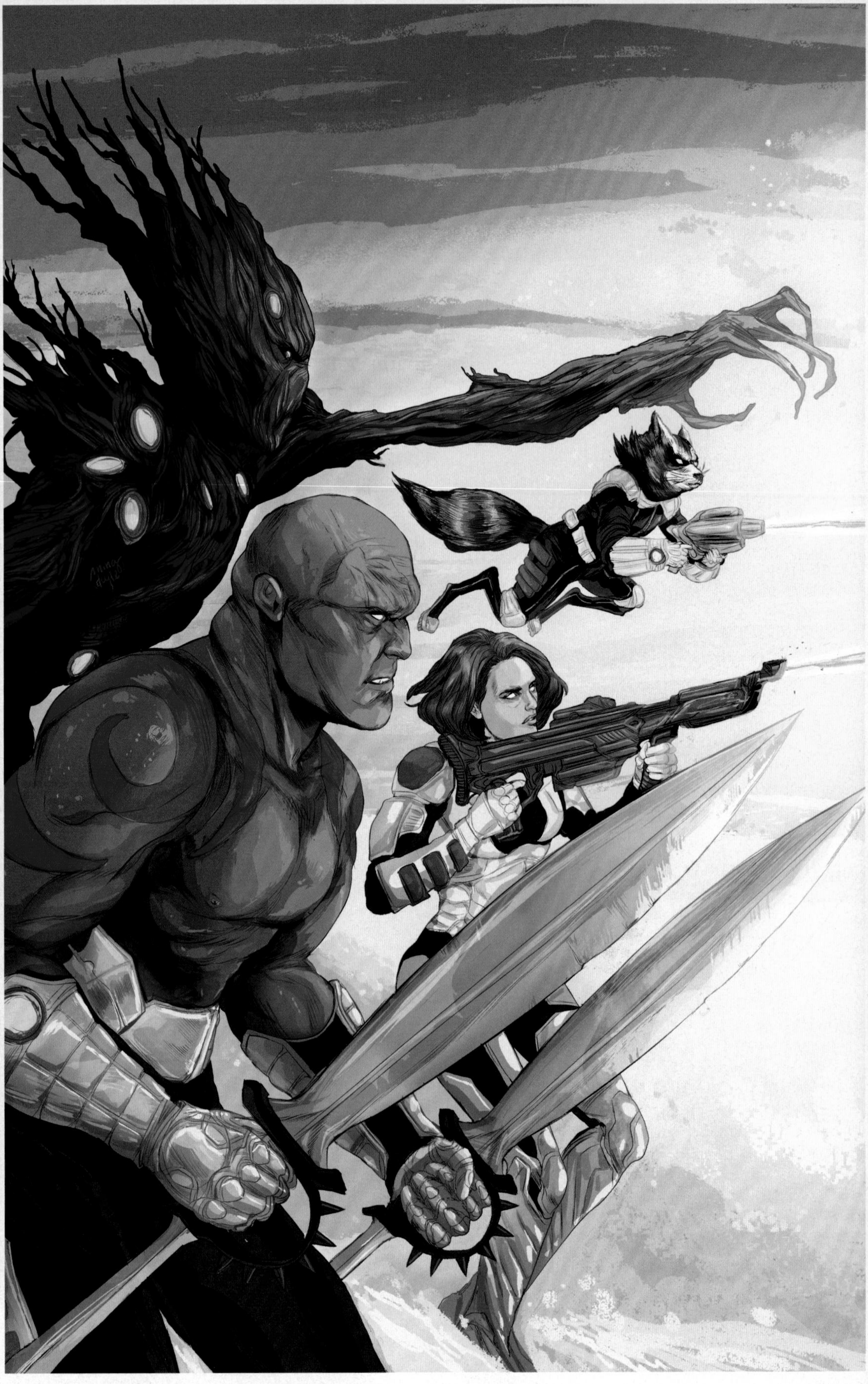

GUARDIANS OF THE GALAXY: TOMORROW'S AVENGERS #1

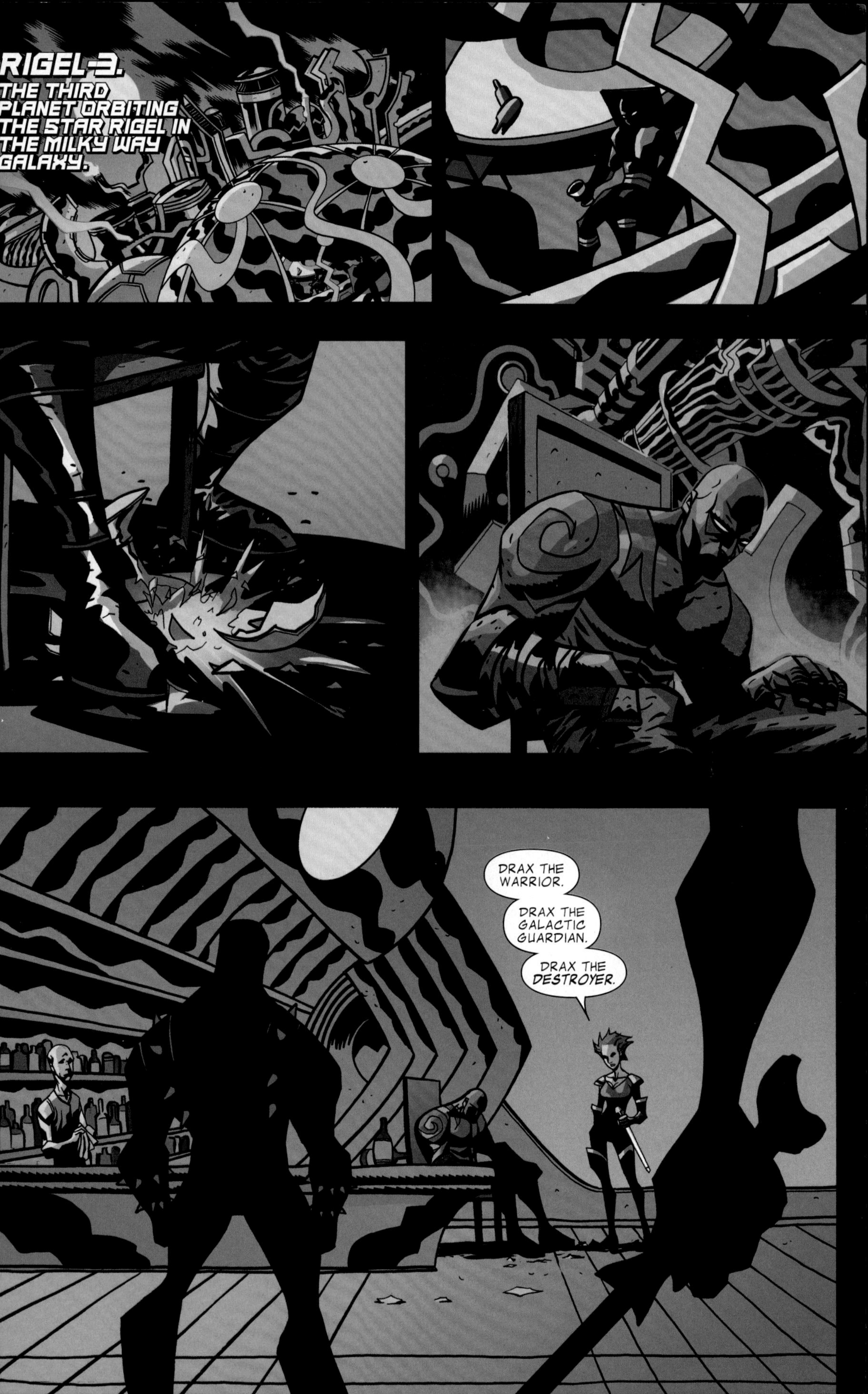
RIGEL-3.
THE THIRD PLANET ORBITING THE STAR RIGEL IN THE MILKY WAY GALAXY.
DRAX THE WARRIOR.
DRAX THE GALACTIC GUARDIAN.
DRAX THE DESTROYER.

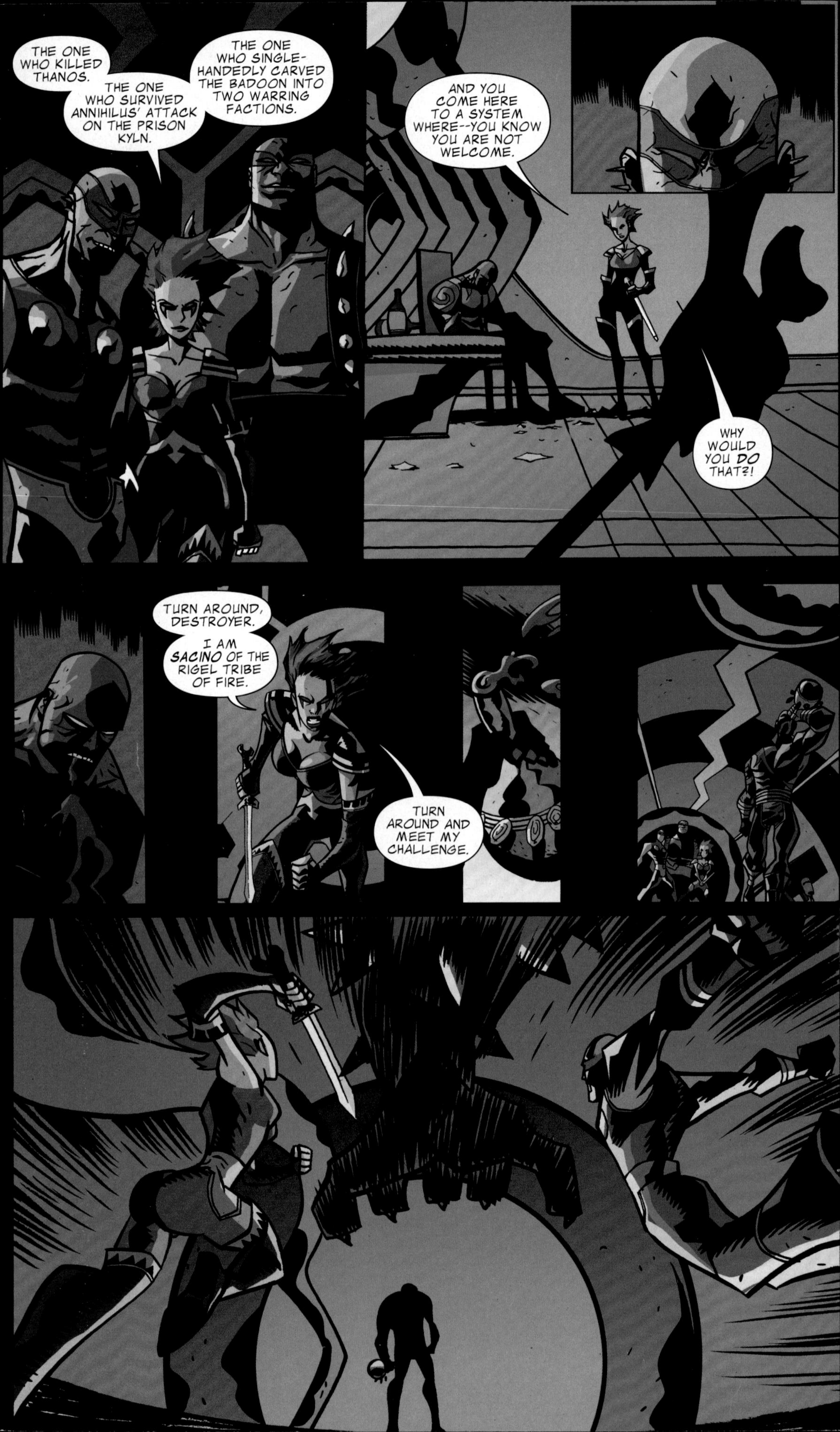
THE ONE WHO KILLED THANOS.
THE ONE WHO SURVIVED ANNIHILUS' ATTACK ON THE PRISON KYLN.
THE ONE WHO SINGLE-HANDEDLY CARVED THE BADOON INTO TWO WARRING FACTIONS.
AND YOU COME HERE TO A SYSTEM WHERE--YOU KNOW YOU ARE NOT WELCOME.
WHY WOULD YOU **DO** THAT?!
TURN AROUND, DESTROYER.
I AM **SACINO** OF THE RIGEL TRIBE OF FIRE.
TURN AROUND AND MEET MY CHALLENGE.

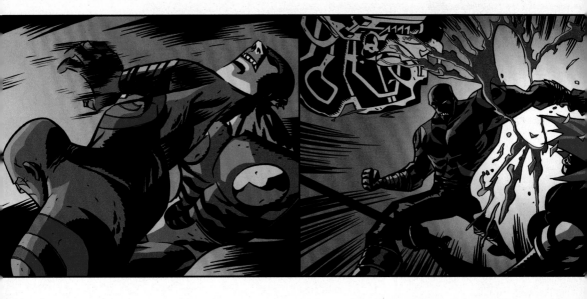

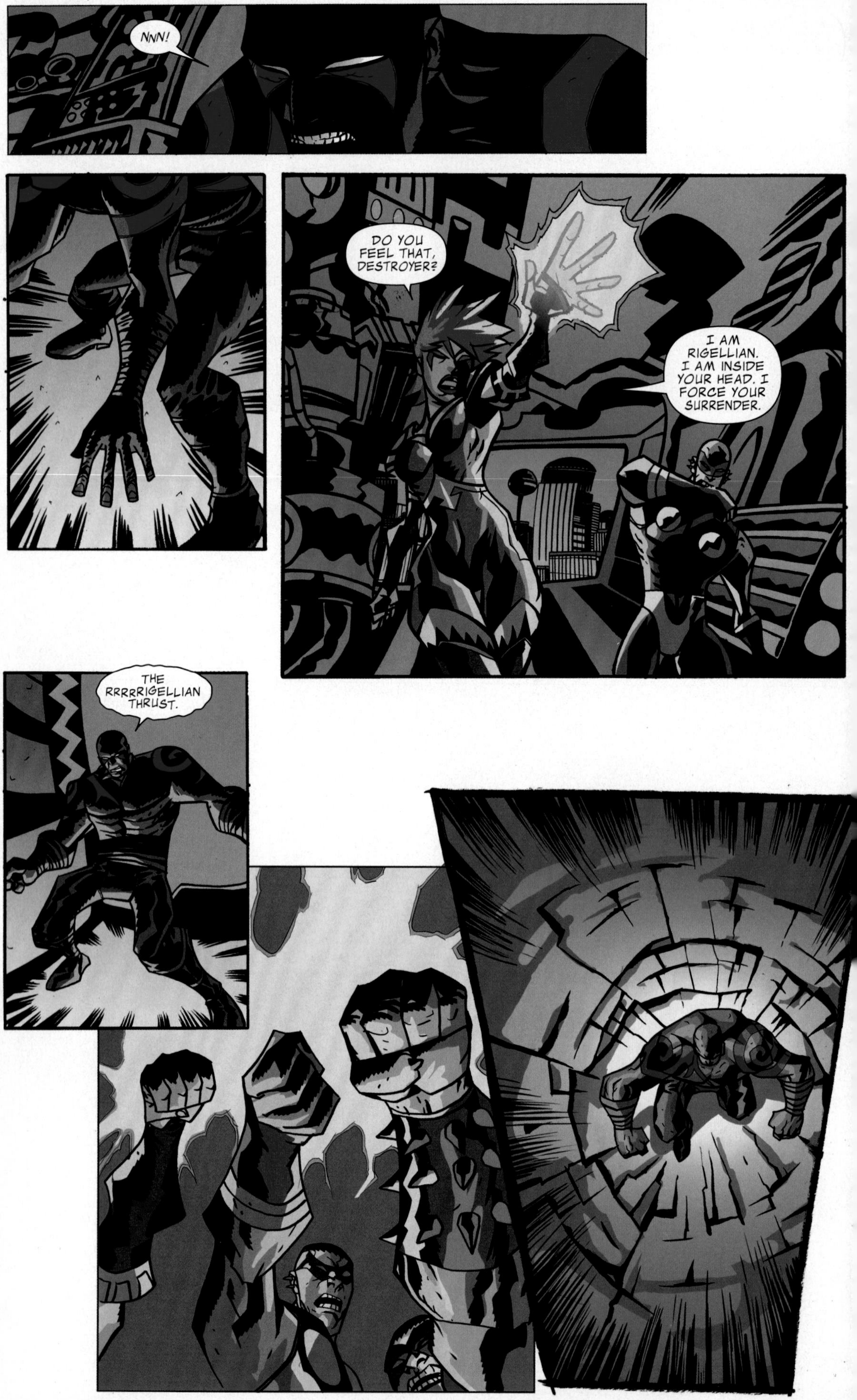
NNN!
DO YOU FEEL THAT, DESTROYER?
I AM RIGELLIAN. I AM INSIDE YOUR HEAD. I FORCE YOUR SURRENDER.
THE RRRRRIGELLIAN THRUST.

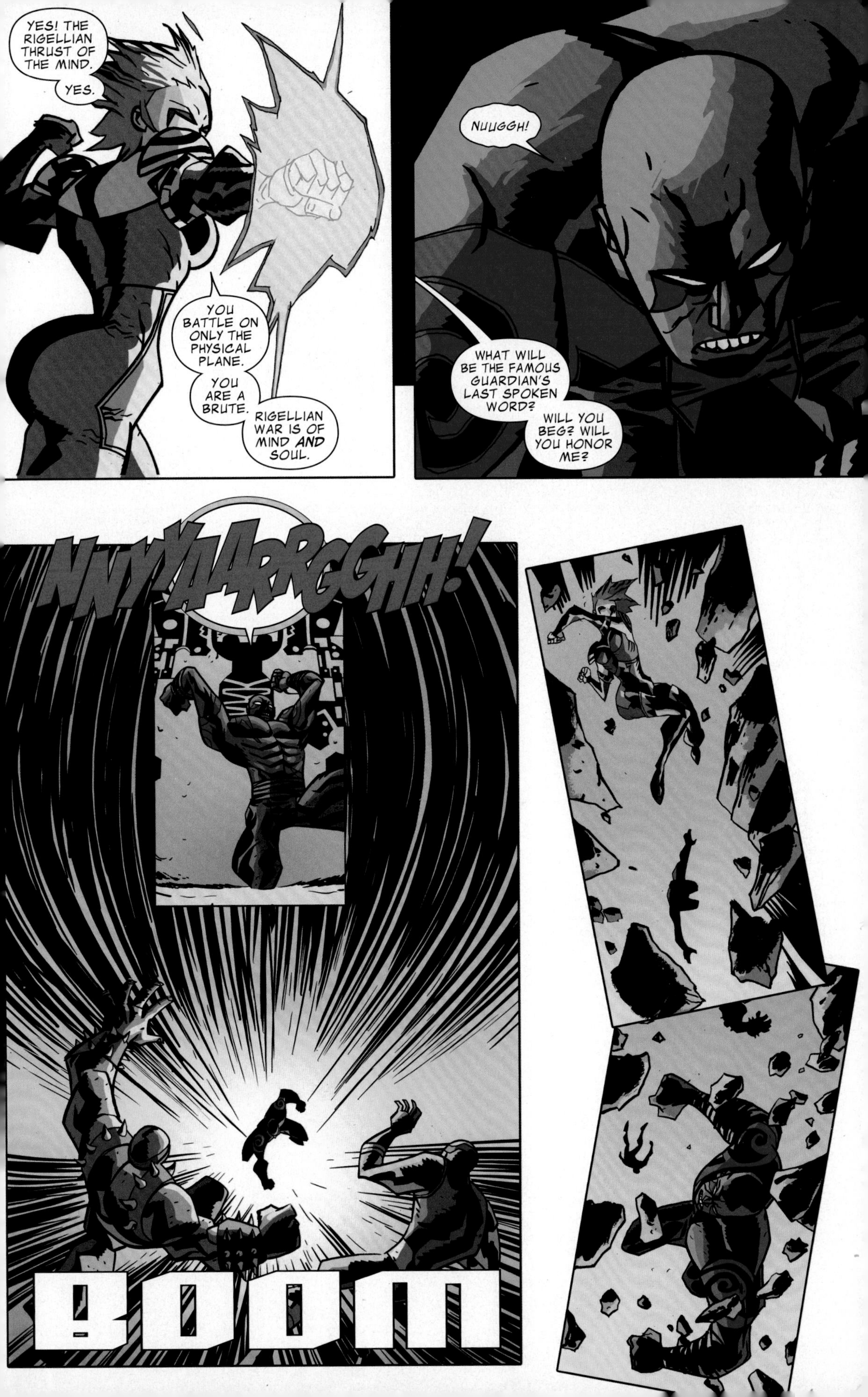
YES! THE RIGELLIAN THRUST OF THE MIND.
YES.
YOU BATTLE ON ONLY THE PHYSICAL PLANE.
YOU ARE A BRUTE.
RIGELLIAN WAR IS OF MIND AND SOUL.
NUUGGH!
WHAT WILL BE THE FAMOUS GUARDIAN'S LAST SPOKEN WORD?
WILL YOU BEG? WILL YOU HONOR ME?
NNYYAARRGGHH!
BOOM

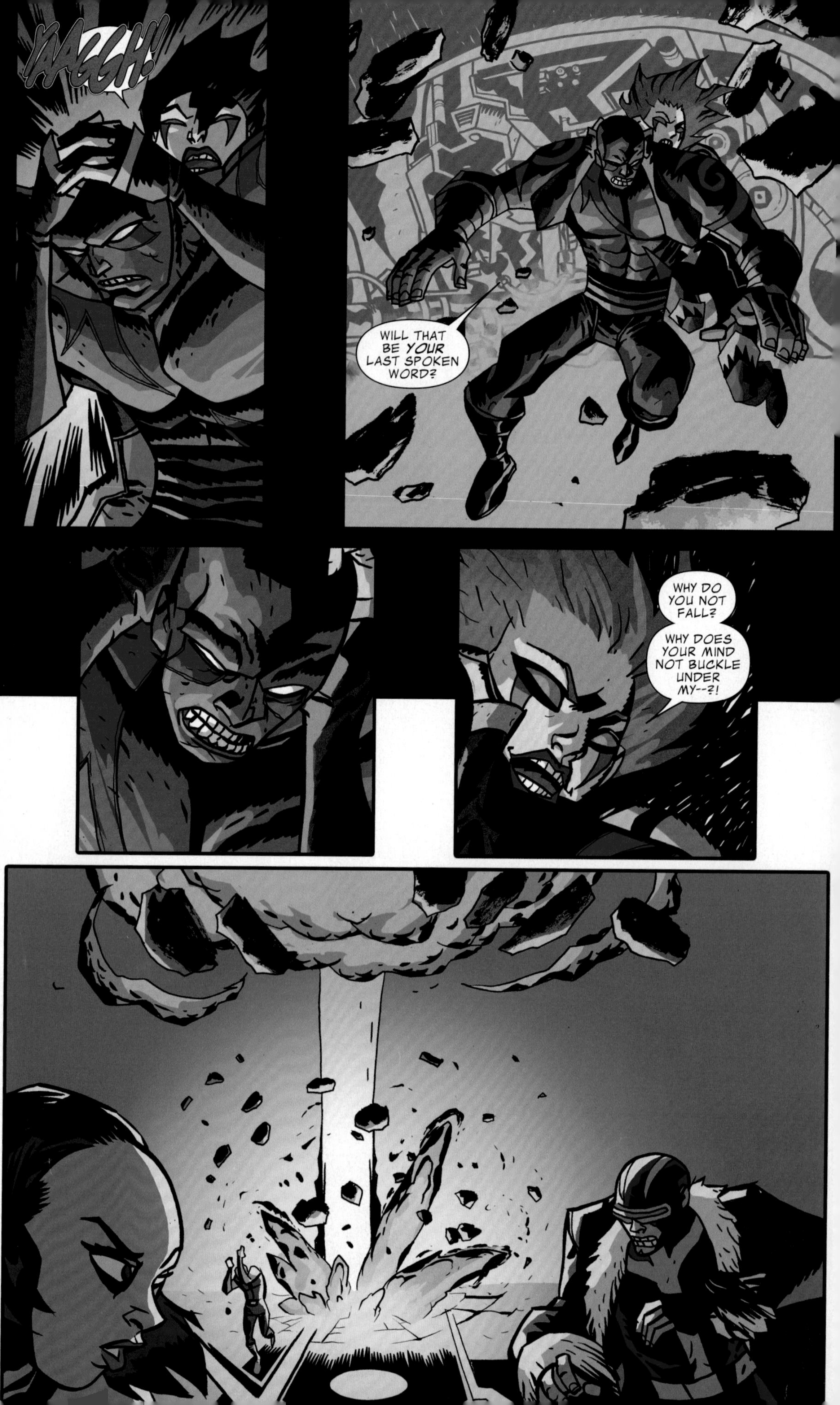
YAAGGH!
WILL THAT BE YOUR LAST SPOKEN WORD?
WHY DO YOU NOT FALL?
WHY DOES YOUR MIND NOT BUCKLE UNDER MY--?!

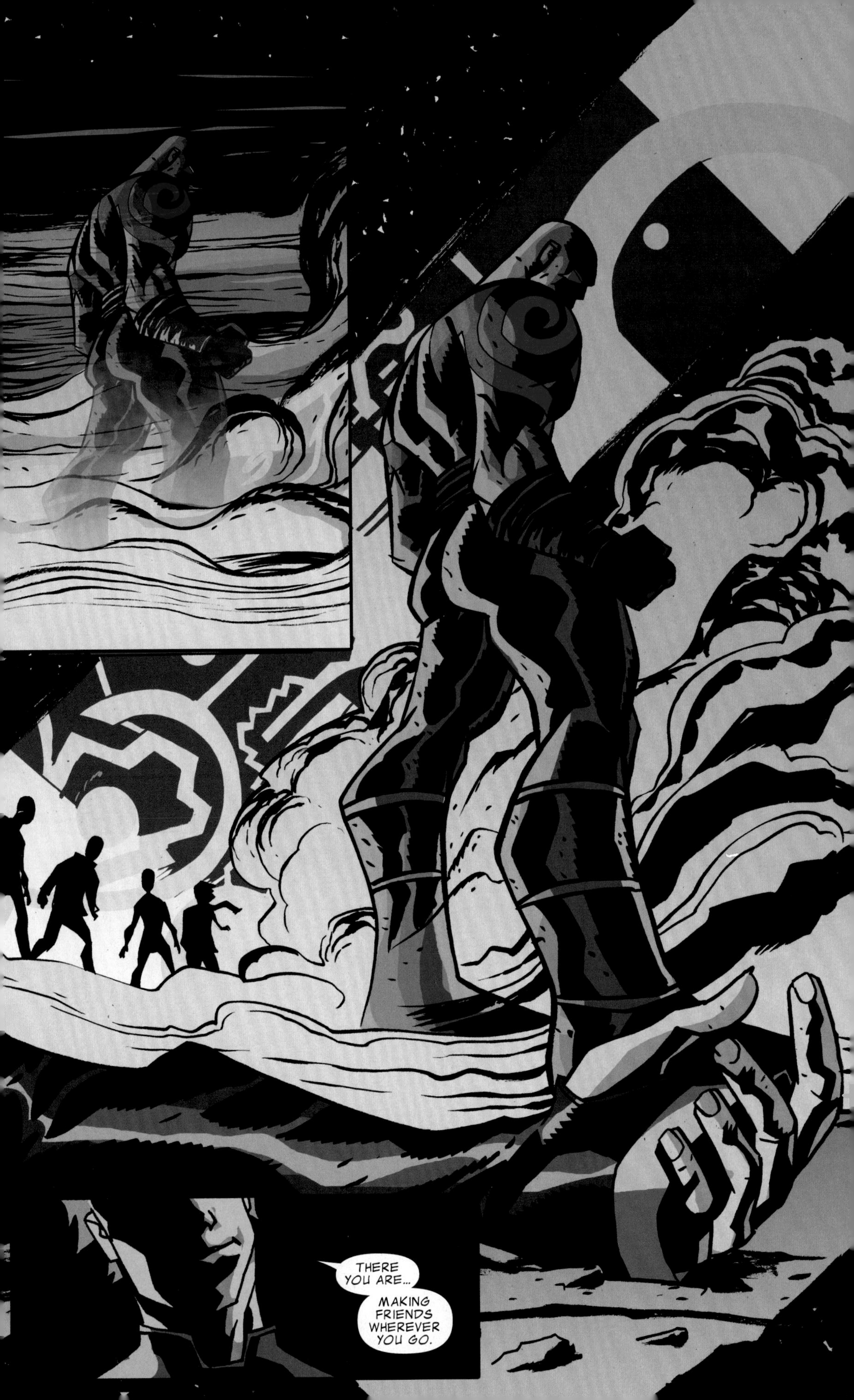
THERE YOU ARE...
MAKING FRIENDS WHEREVER YOU GO.

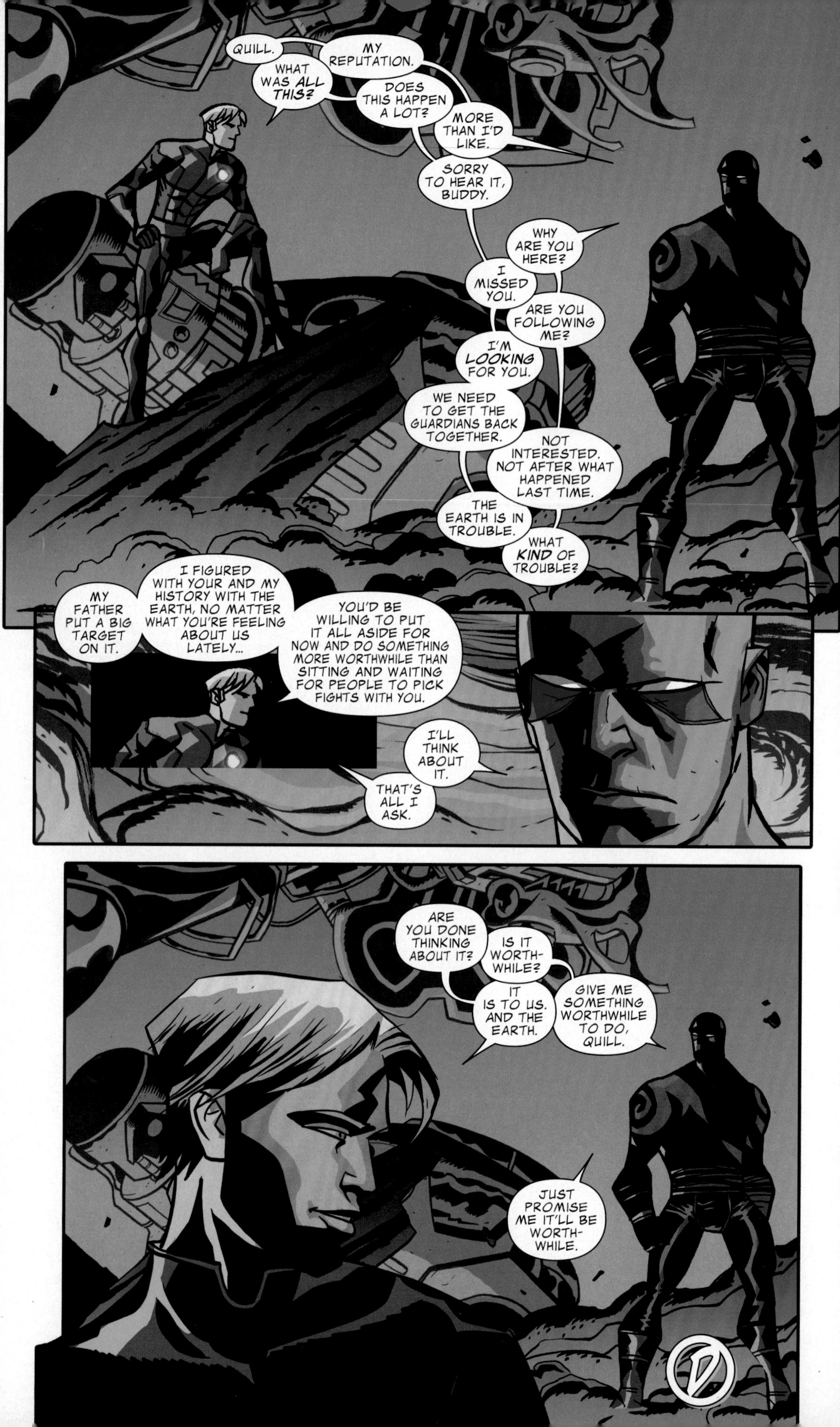
QUILL.
MY REPUTATION.
WHAT WAS ALL THIS?
DOES THIS HAPPEN A LOT?
MORE THAN I'D LIKE.
SORRY TO HEAR IT, BUDDY.
WHY ARE YOU HERE?
I MISSED YOU.
ARE YOU FOLLOWING ME?
I'M LOOKING FOR YOU.
WE NEED TO GET THE GUARDIANS BACK TOGETHER.
NOT INTERESTED. NOT AFTER WHAT HAPPENED LAST TIME.
THE EARTH IS IN TROUBLE.
WHAT KIND OF TROUBLE?
MY FATHER PUT A BIG TARGET ON IT.
I FIGURED WITH YOUR AND MY HISTORY WITH THE EARTH, NO MATTER WHAT YOU'RE FEELING ABOUT US LATELY...
YOU'D BE WILLING TO PUT IT ALL ASIDE FOR NOW AND DO SOMETHING MORE WORTHWHILE THAN SITTING AND WAITING FOR PEOPLE TO PICK FIGHTS WITH YOU.
I'LL THINK ABOUT IT.
THAT'S ALL I ASK.
ARE YOU DONE THINKING ABOUT IT?
IS IT WORTH-WHILE?
IT IS TO US. AND THE EARTH.
GIVE ME SOMETHING WORTHWHILE TO DO, QUILL.
JUST PROMISE ME IT'LL BE WORTH-WHILE.

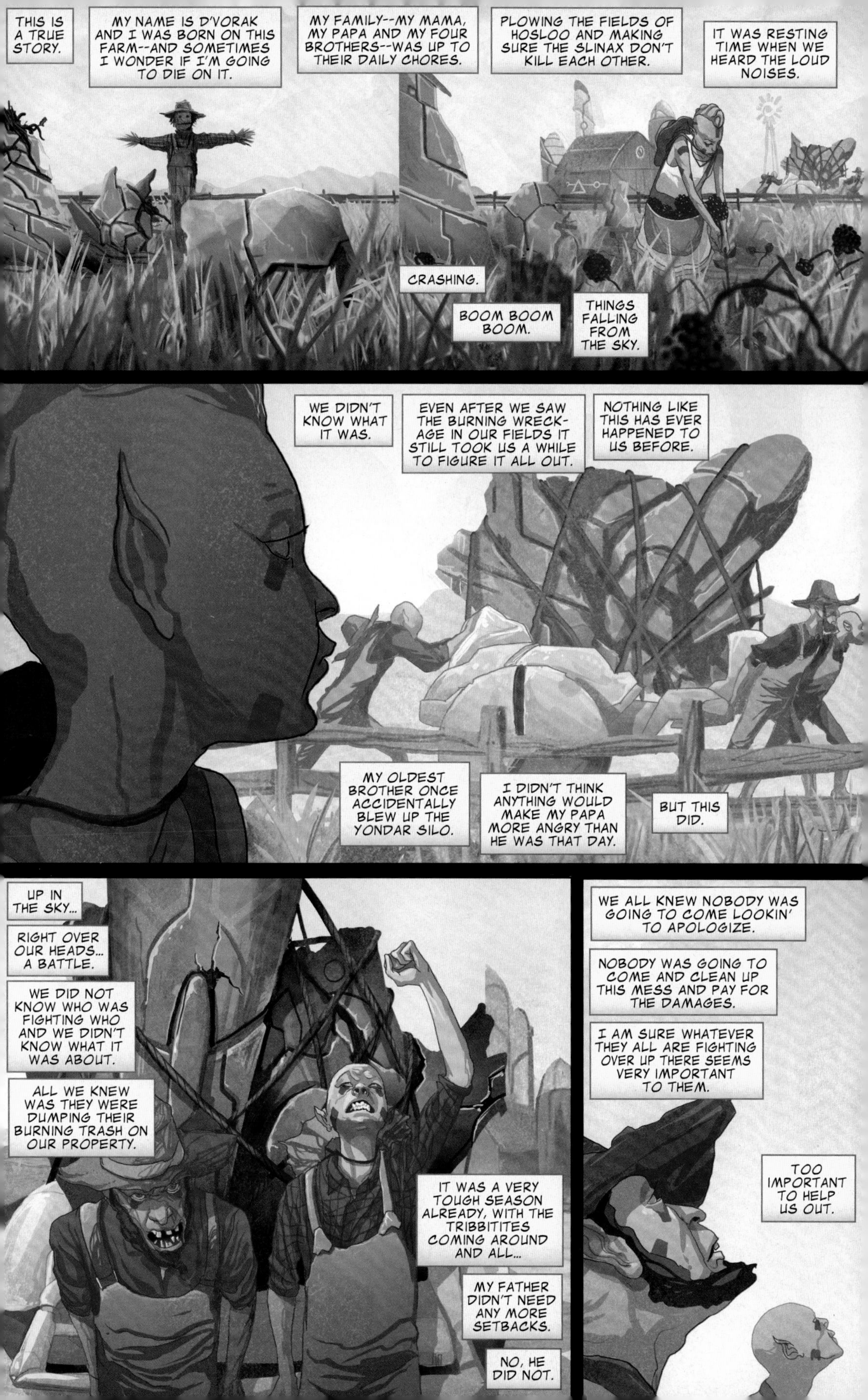

THIS IS A TRUE STORY.
MY NAME IS D'VORAK AND I WAS BORN ON THIS FARM--AND SOMETIMES I WONDER IF I'M GOING TO DIE ON IT.
MY FAMILY--MY MAMA, MY PAPA AND MY FOUR BROTHERS--WAS UP TO THEIR DAILY CHORES.
PLOWING THE FIELDS OF HOSLOO AND MAKING SURE THE SLINAX DON'T KILL EACH OTHER.
IT WAS RESTING TIME WHEN WE HEARD THE LOUD NOISES.
CRASHING.
BOOM BOOM BOOM.
THINGS FALLING FROM THE SKY.
WE DIDN'T KNOW WHAT IT WAS.
EVEN AFTER WE SAW THE BURNING WRECK-AGE IN OUR FIELDS IT STILL TOOK US A WHILE TO FIGURE IT ALL OUT.
NOTHING LIKE THIS HAS EVER HAPPENED TO US BEFORE.
MY OLDEST BROTHER ONCE ACCIDENTALLY BLEW UP THE YONDAR SILO.
I DIDN'T THINK ANYTHING WOULD MAKE MY PAPA MORE ANGRY THAN HE WAS THAT DAY.
BUT THIS DID.
UP IN THE SKY...
RIGHT OVER OUR HEADS... A BATTLE.
WE DID NOT KNOW WHO WAS FIGHTING WHO AND WE DIDN'T KNOW WHAT IT WAS ABOUT.
ALL WE KNEW WAS THEY WERE DUMPING THEIR BURNING TRASH ON OUR PROPERTY.
IT WAS A VERY TOUGH SEASON ALREADY, WITH THE TRIBBITITES COMING AROUND AND ALL...
MY FATHER DIDN'T NEED ANY MORE SETBACKS.
NO, HE DID NOT.
WE ALL KNEW NOBODY WAS GOING TO COME LOOKIN' TO APOLOGIZE.
NOBODY WAS GOING TO COME AND CLEAN UP THIS MESS AND PAY FOR THE DAMAGES.
I AM SURE WHATEVER THEY ALL ARE FIGHTING OVER UP THERE SEEMS VERY IMPORTANT TO THEM.
TOO IMPORTANT TO HELP US OUT.

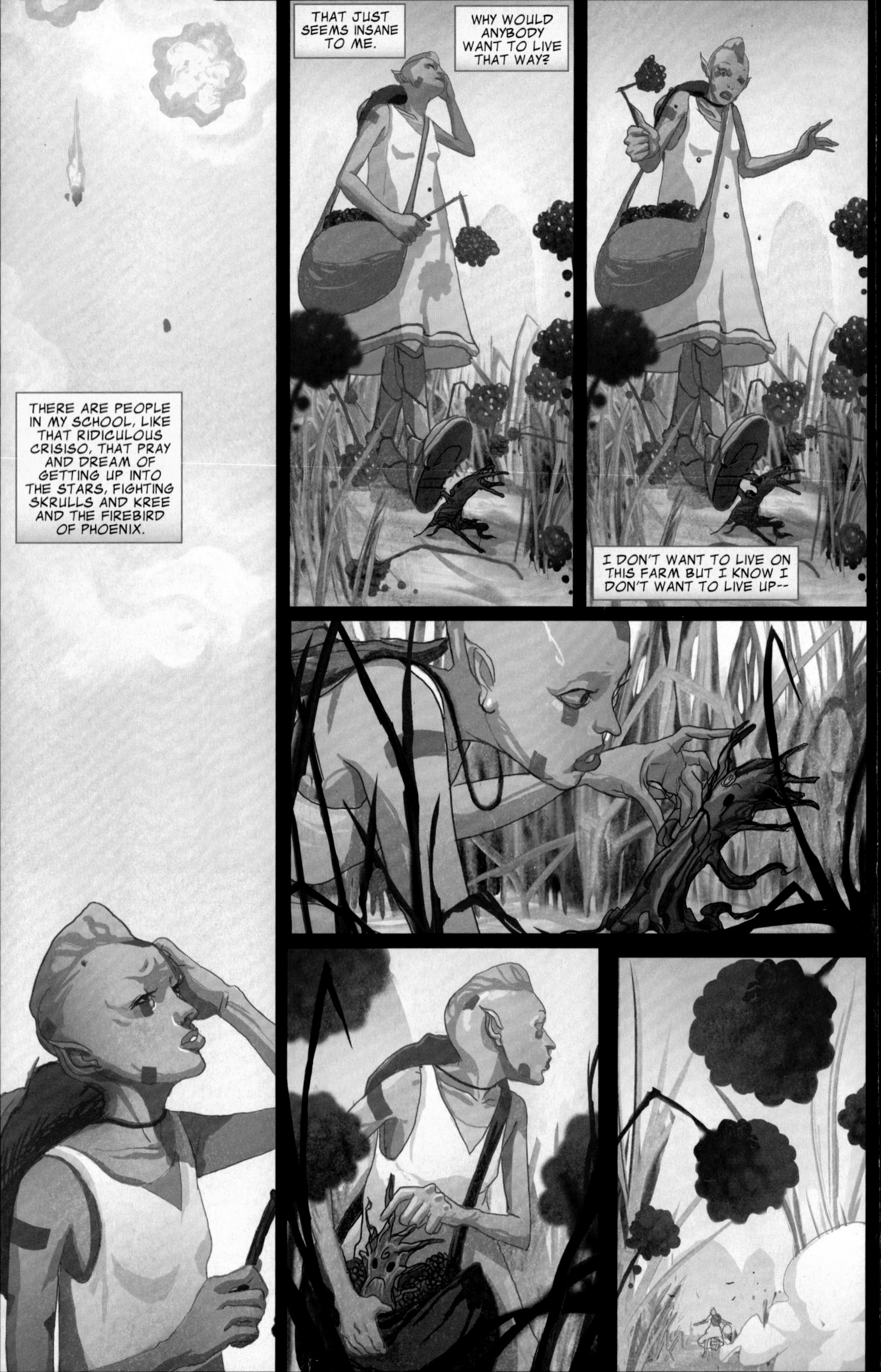

THERE ARE PEOPLE IN MY SCHOOL, LIKE THAT RIDICULOUS CRISISO, THAT PRAY AND DREAM OF GETTING UP INTO THE STARS, FIGHTING SKRULLS AND KREE AND THE FIREBIRD OF PHOENIX.
THAT JUST SEEMS INSANE TO ME.
WHY WOULD ANYBODY WANT TO LIVE THAT WAY?
I DON'T WANT TO LIVE ON THIS FARM BUT I KNOW I DON'T WANT TO LIVE UP--

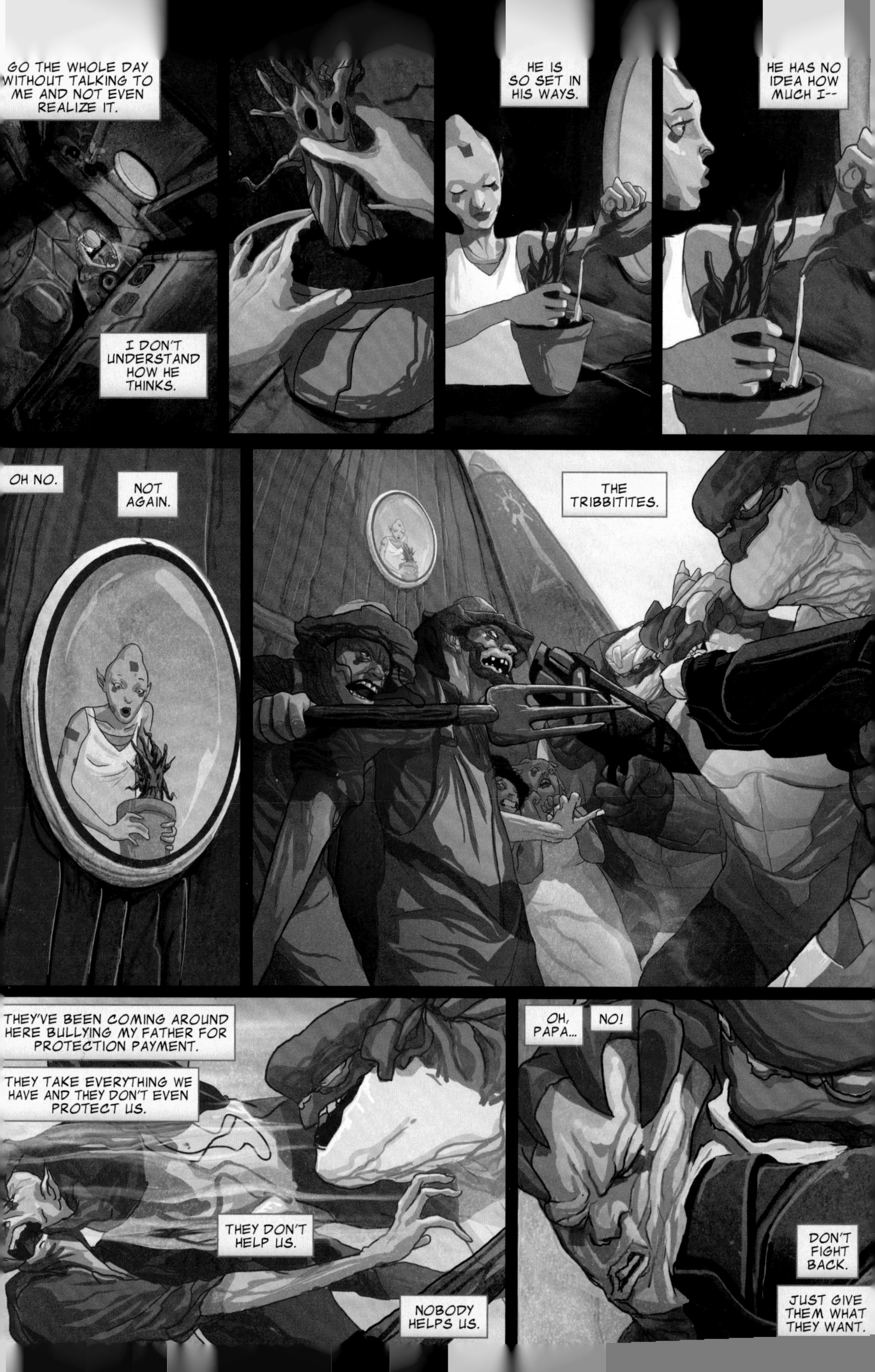
GO THE WHOLE DAY WITHOUT TALKING TO ME AND NOT EVEN REALIZE IT.
I DON'T UNDERSTAND HOW HE THINKS.
HE IS SO SET IN HIS WAYS.
HE HAS NO IDEA HOW MUCH I--
OH NO.
NOT AGAIN.
THE TRIBBITITES.
THEY'VE BEEN COMING AROUND HERE BULLYING MY FATHER FOR PROTECTION PAYMENT.
THEY TAKE EVERYTHING WE HAVE AND THEY DON'T EVEN PROTECT US.
THEY DON'T HELP US.
NOBODY HELPS US.
OH, PAPA...
NO!
DON'T FIGHT BACK.
JUST GIVE THEM WHAT THEY WANT.

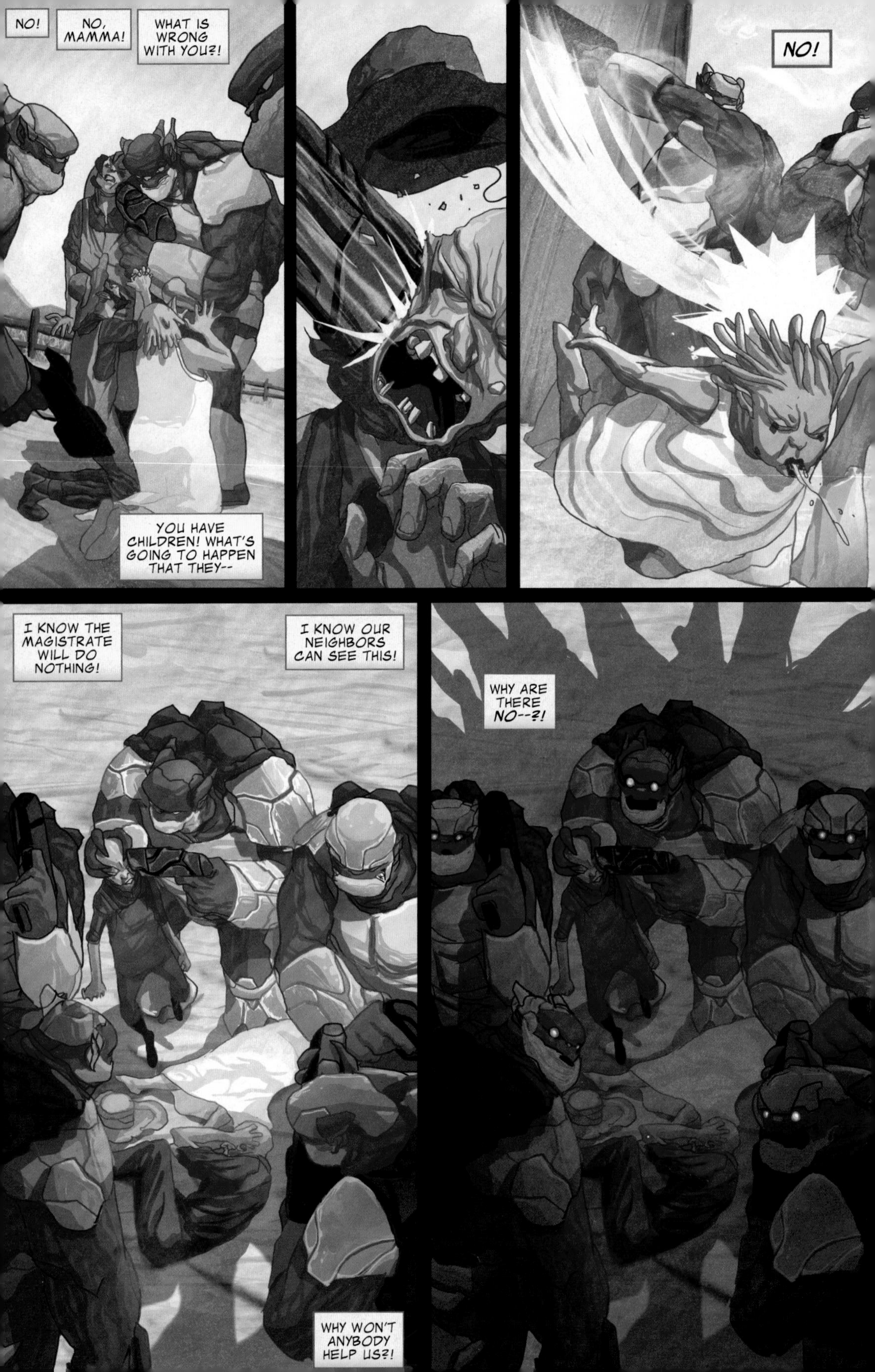
NO!
NO, MAMMA!
WHAT IS WRONG WITH YOU?!
YOU HAVE CHILDREN! WHAT'S GOING TO HAPPEN THAT THEY--
NO!
I KNOW THE MAGISTRATE WILL DO NOTHING!
I KNOW OUR NEIGHBORS CAN SEE THIS!
WHY WON'T ANYBODY HELP US?!
WHY ARE THERE NO--?!

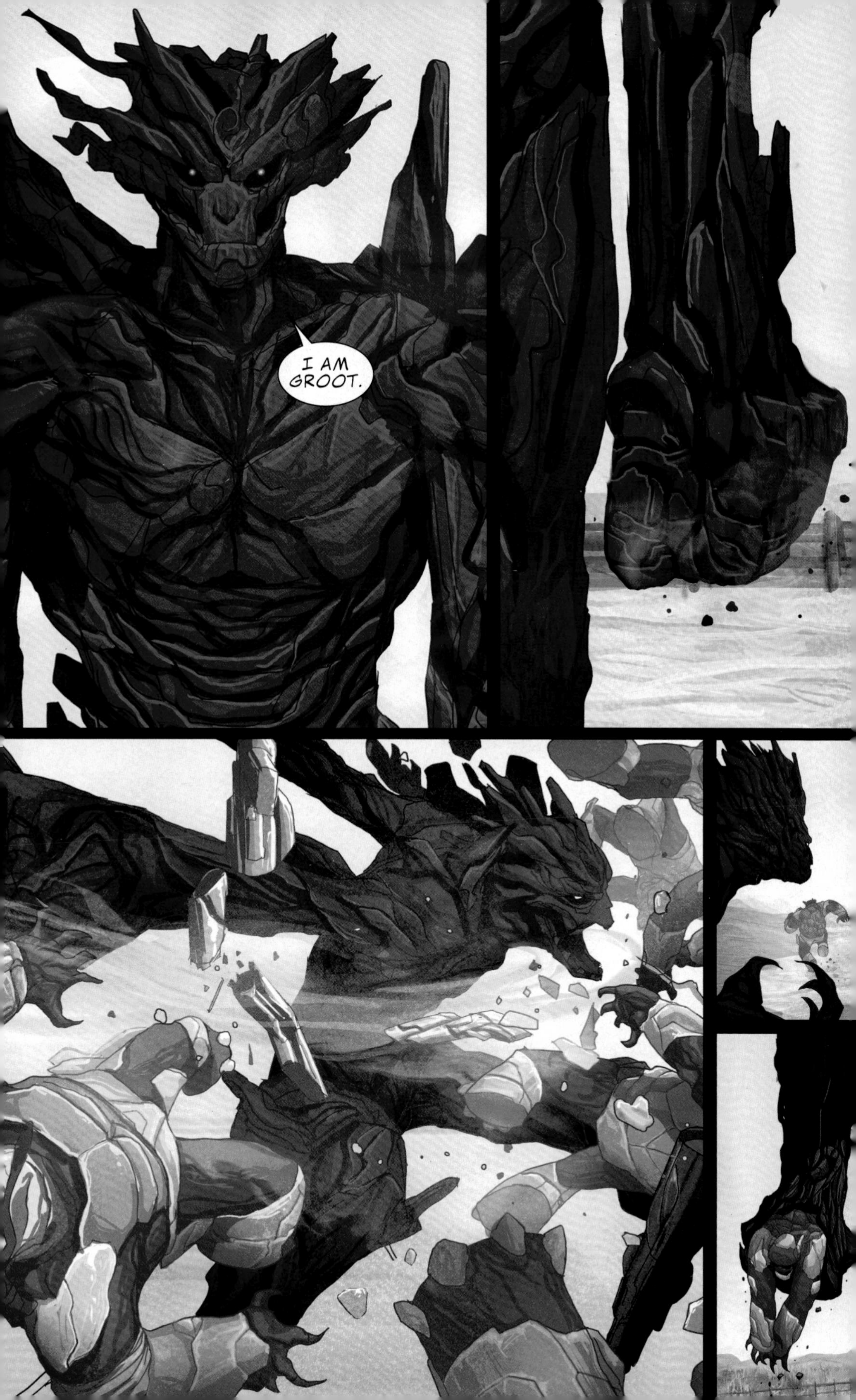
I AM GROOT.

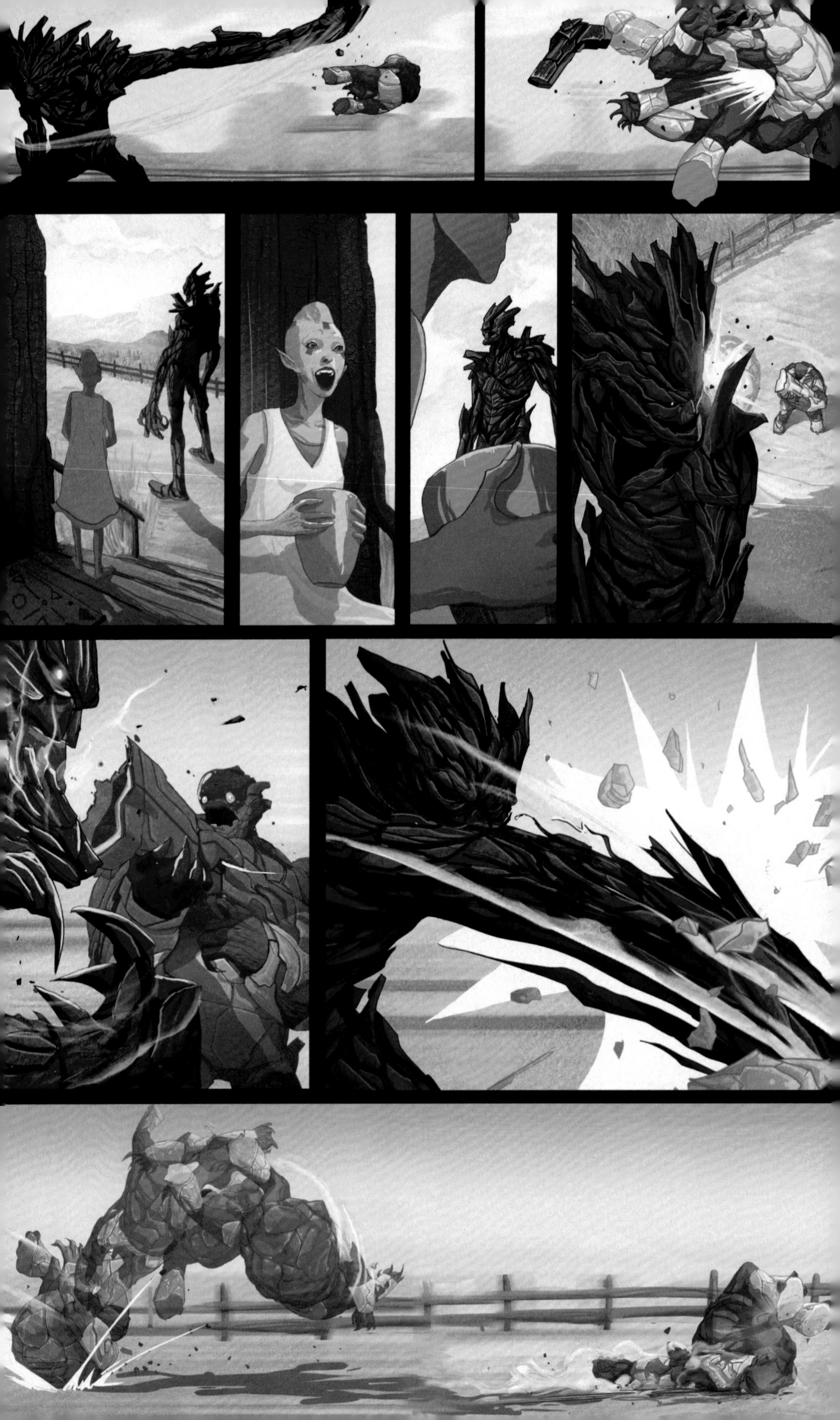

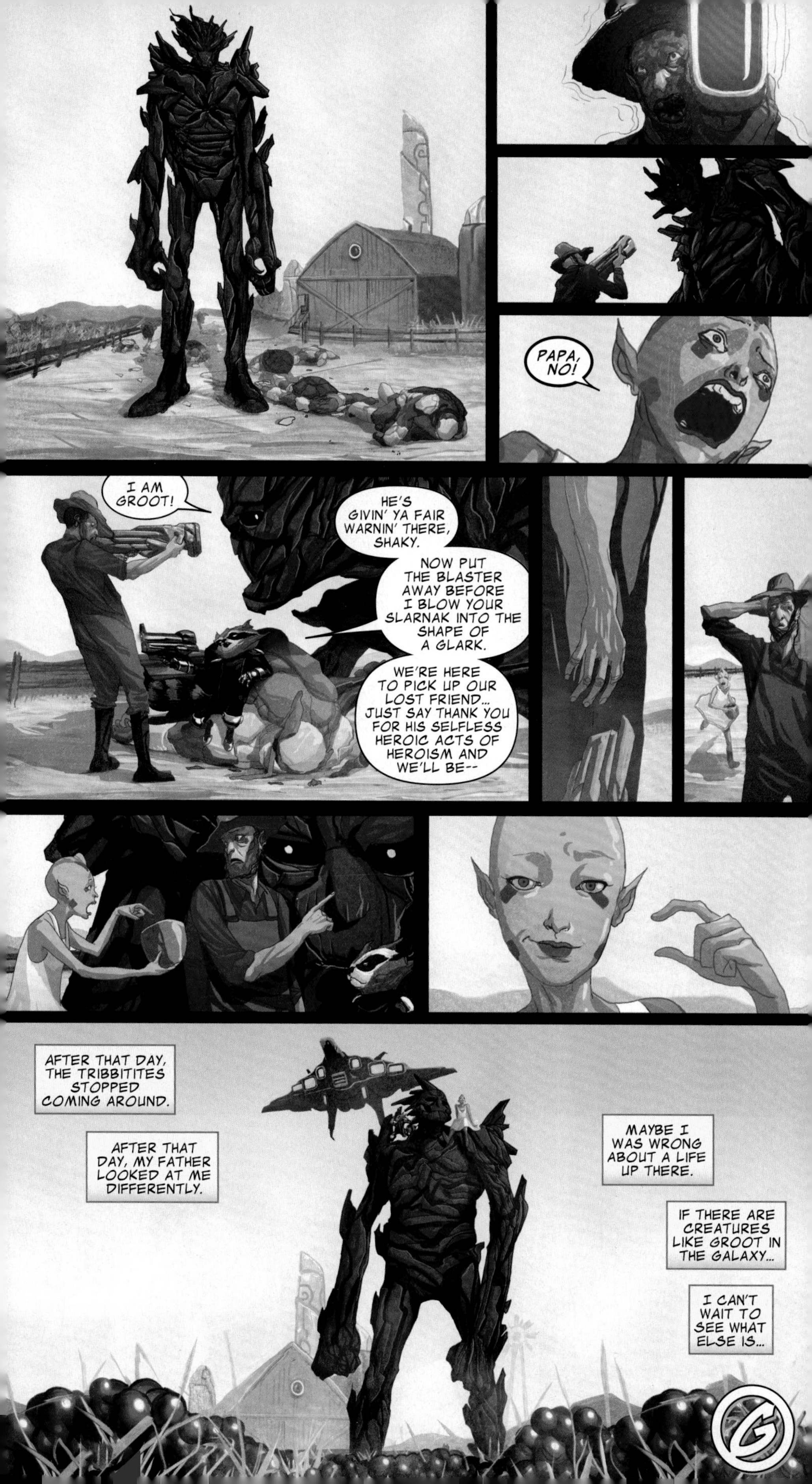
PAPA, NO!
I AM GROOT!
HE'S GIVIN' YA FAIR WARNIN' THERE, SHAKY.
NOW PUT THE BLASTER AWAY BEFORE I BLOW YOUR SLARNAK INTO THE SHAPE OF A GLARK.
WE'RE HERE TO PICK UP OUR LOST FRIEND... JUST SAY THANK YOU FOR HIS SELFLESS HEROIC ACTS OF HEROISM AND WE'LL BE--
AFTER THAT DAY, THE TRIBBITITES STOPPED COMING AROUND.
AFTER THAT DAY, MY FATHER LOOKED AT ME DIFFERENTLY.
MAYBE I WAS WRONG ABOUT A LIFE UP THERE.
IF THERE ARE CREATURES LIKE GROOT IN THE GALAXY...
I CAN'T WAIT TO SEE WHAT ELSE IS...

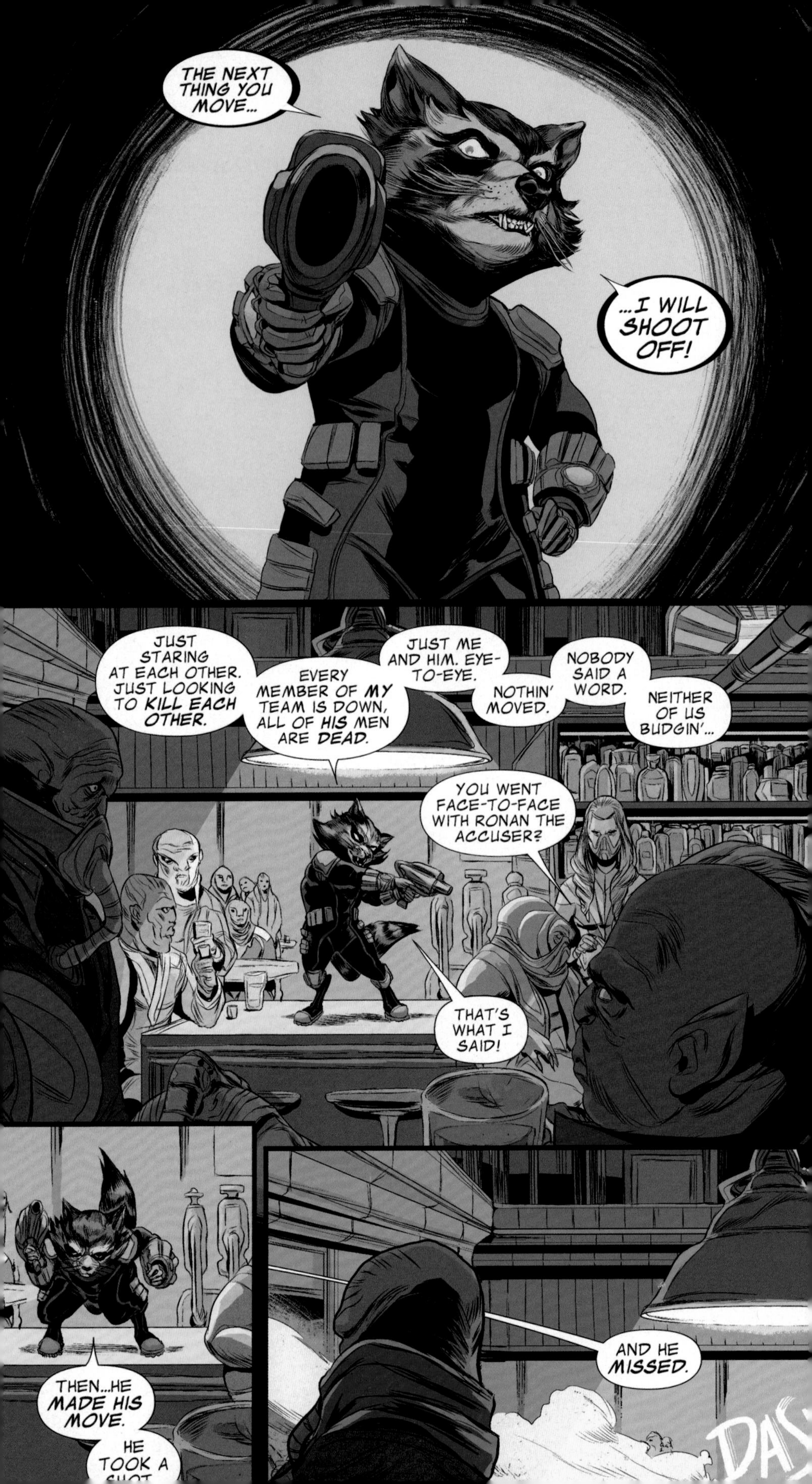
THE NEXT THING YOU MOVE...
...I WILL SHOOT OFF!
JUST STARING AT EACH OTHER. JUST LOOKING TO KILL EACH OTHER.
EVERY MEMBER OF MY TEAM IS DOWN, ALL OF HIS MEN ARE DEAD.
JUST ME AND HIM. EYE-TO-EYE.
NOTHIN' MOVED.
NOBODY SAID A WORD.
NEITHER OF US BUDGIN'...
YOU WENT FACE-TO-FACE WITH RONAN THE ACCUSER?
THAT'S WHAT I SAID!
THEN...HE MADE HIS MOVE.
HE TOOK A
AND HE MISSED.

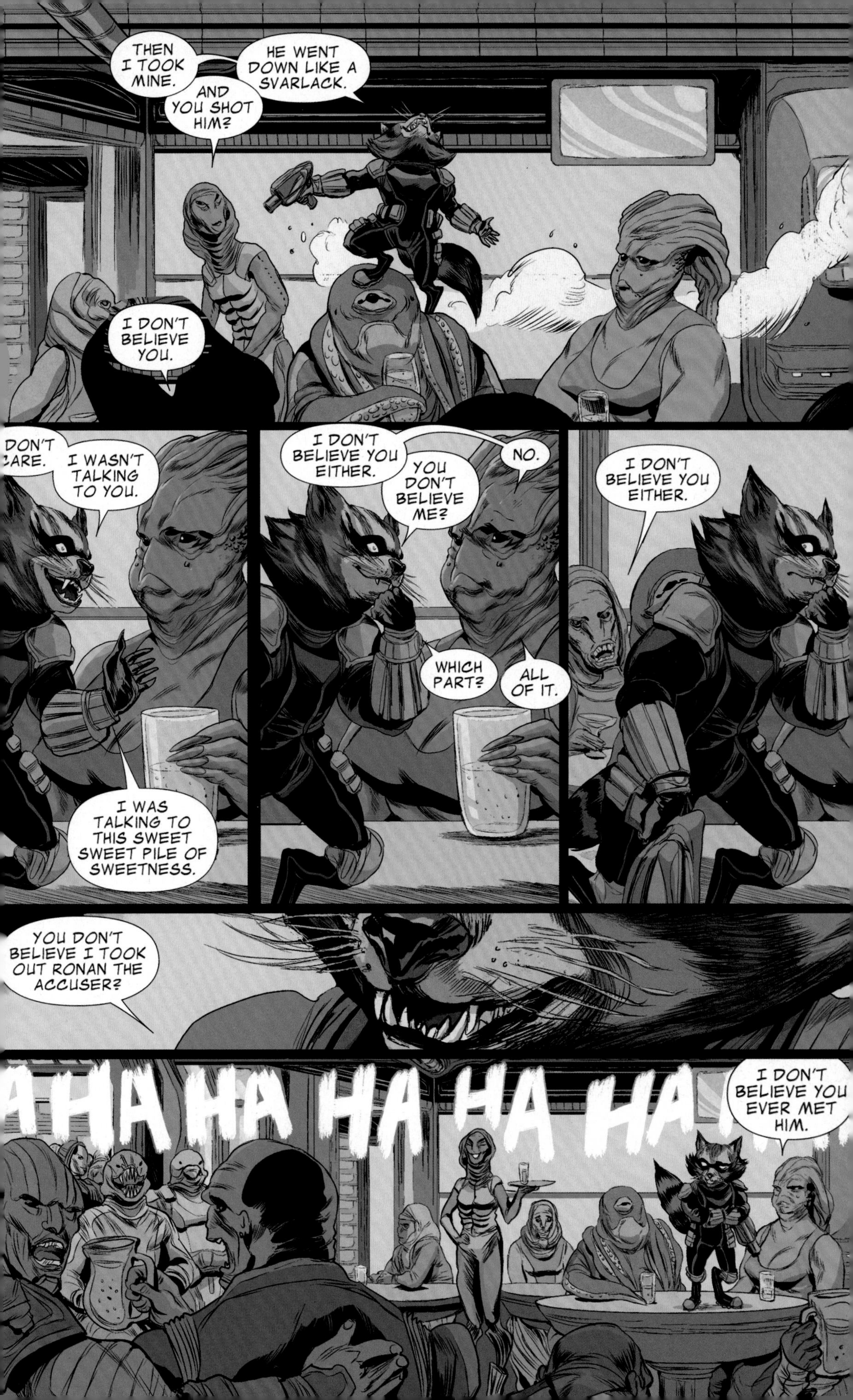
THEN I TOOK MINE.
HE WENT DOWN LIKE A SVARLACK.
AND YOU SHOT HIM?
I DON'T BELIEVE YOU.
DON'T CARE.
I WASN'T TALKING TO YOU.
I WAS TALKING TO THIS SWEET SWEET PILE OF SWEETNESS.
I DON'T BELIEVE YOU EITHER.
NO.
YOU DON'T BELIEVE ME?
WHICH PART?
ALL OF IT.
I DON'T BELIEVE YOU EITHER.
YOU DON'T BELIEVE I TOOK OUT RONAN THE ACCUSER?
HA HA HA HA HA HA HA
I DON'T BELIEVE YOU EVER MET HIM.

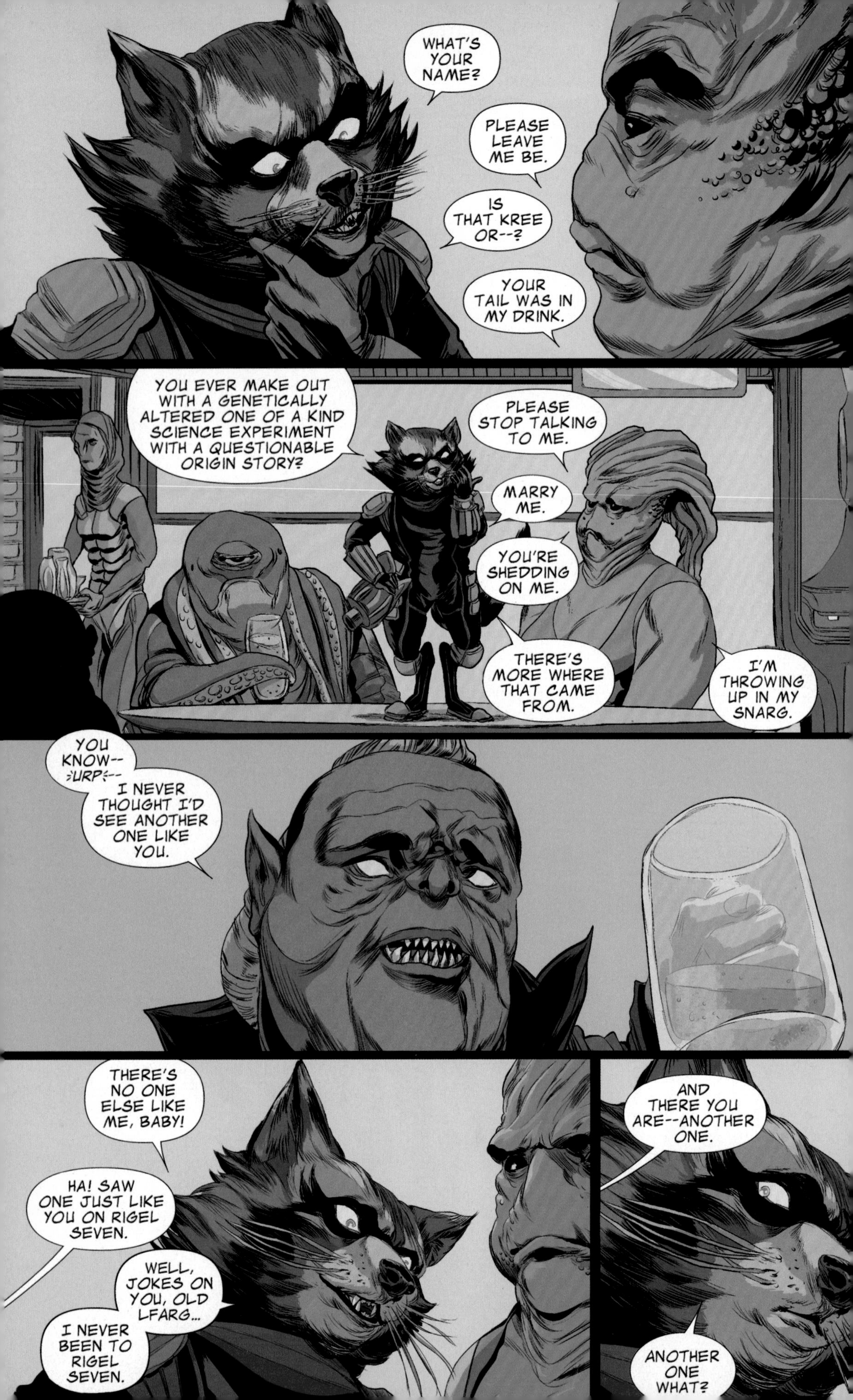
WHAT'S YOUR NAME?
PLEASE LEAVE ME BE.
IS THAT KREE OR--?
YOUR TAIL WAS IN MY DRINK.
YOU EVER MAKE OUT WITH A GENETICALLY ALTERED ONE OF A KIND SCIENCE EXPERIMENT WITH A QUESTIONABLE ORIGIN STORY?
PLEASE STOP TALKING TO ME.
MARRY ME.
YOU'RE SHEDDING ON ME.
THERE'S MORE WHERE THAT CAME FROM.
I'M THROWING UP IN MY SNARG.
YOU KNOW-- *URP*-- I NEVER THOUGHT I'D SEE ANOTHER ONE LIKE YOU.
THERE'S NO ONE ELSE LIKE ME, BABY!
HA! SAW ONE JUST LIKE YOU ON RIGEL SEVEN.
WELL, JOKES ON YOU, OLD LFARG...
I NEVER BEEN TO RIGEL SEVEN.
AND THERE YOU ARE--ANOTHER ONE.
ANOTHER ONE WHAT?

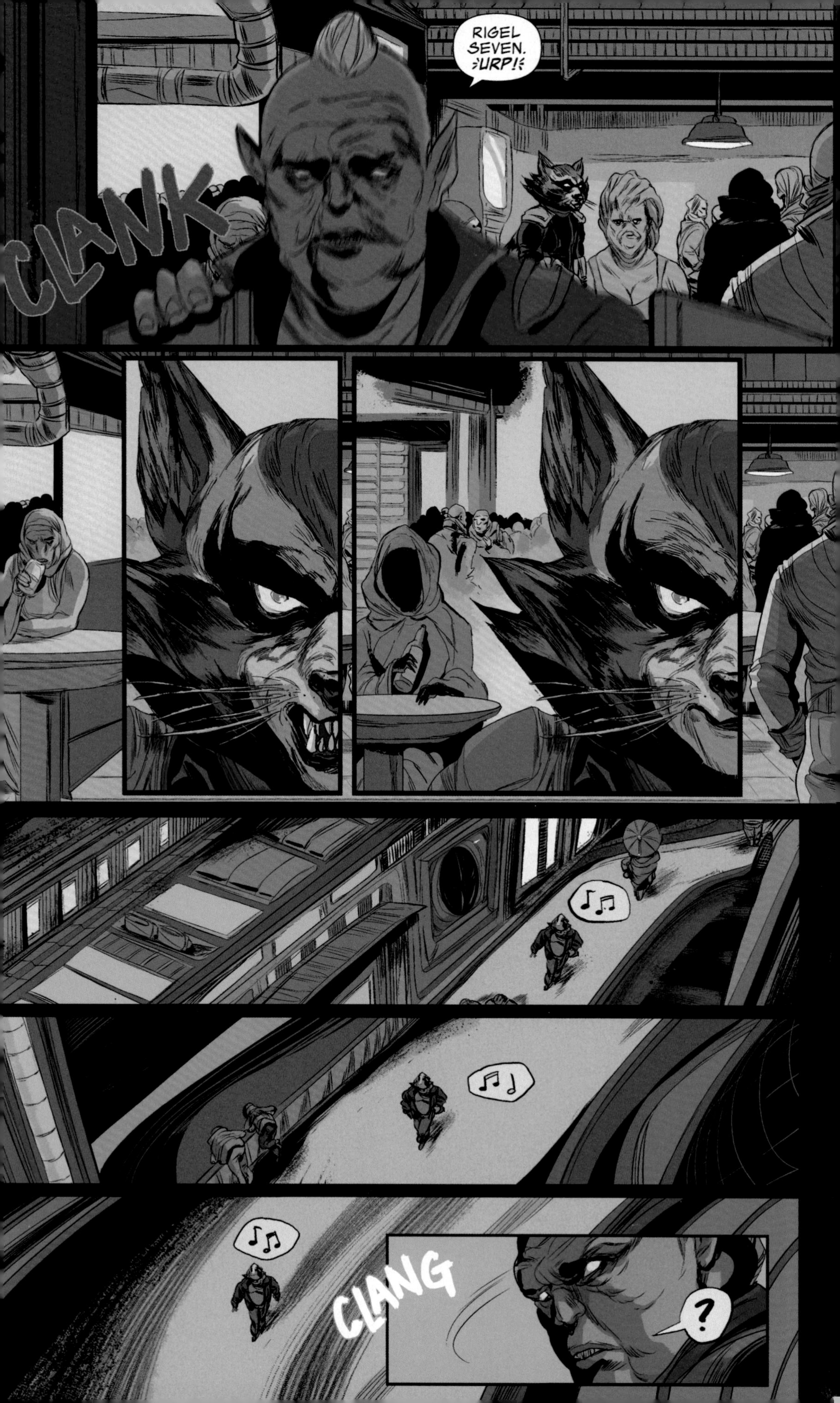

CLANK
RIGEL SEVEN. URP!
♫♫
♫♪
♫♫
CLANG
?

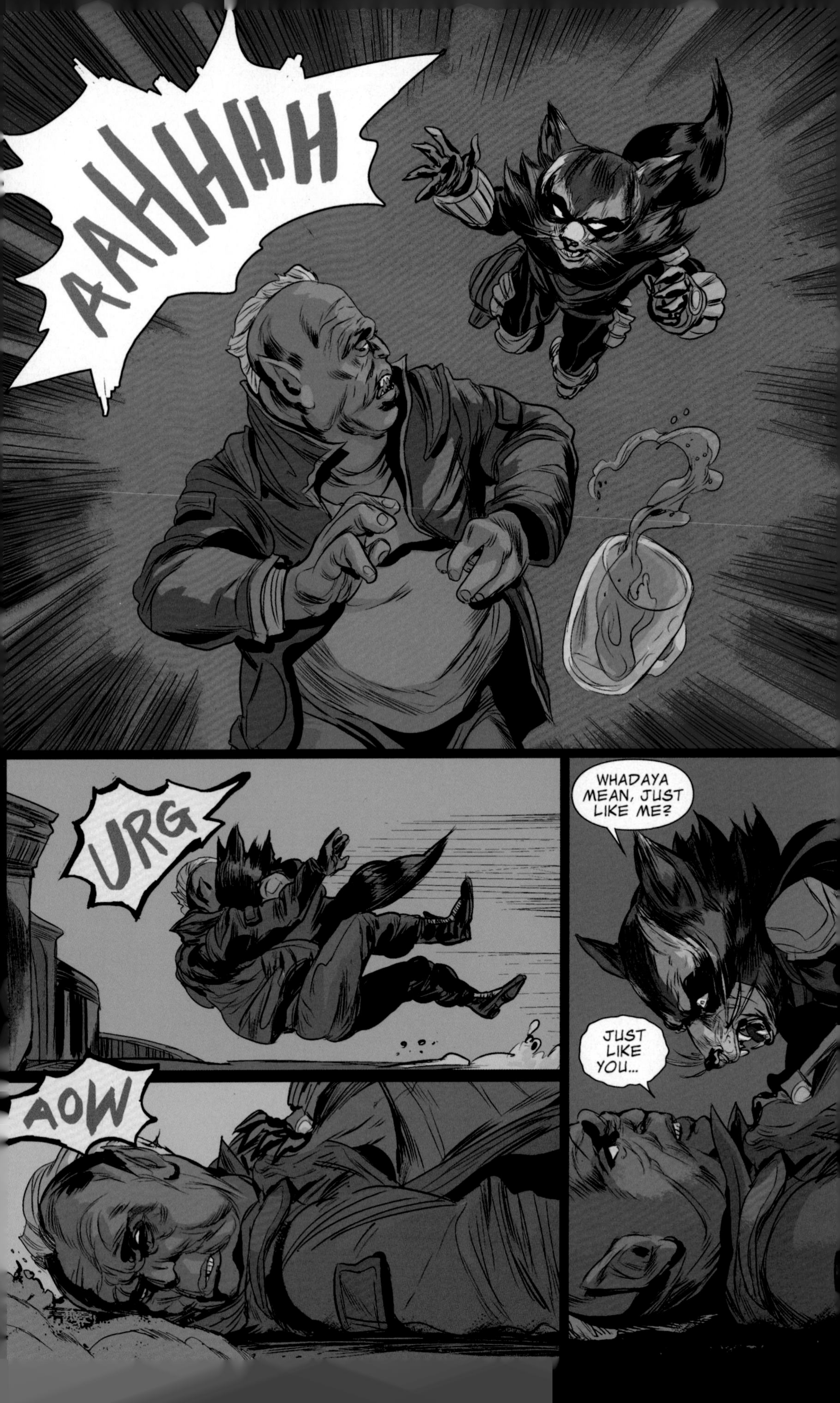
AAHHHH
URG
AOW
WHADAYA MEAN, JUST LIKE ME?
JUST LIKE YOU...

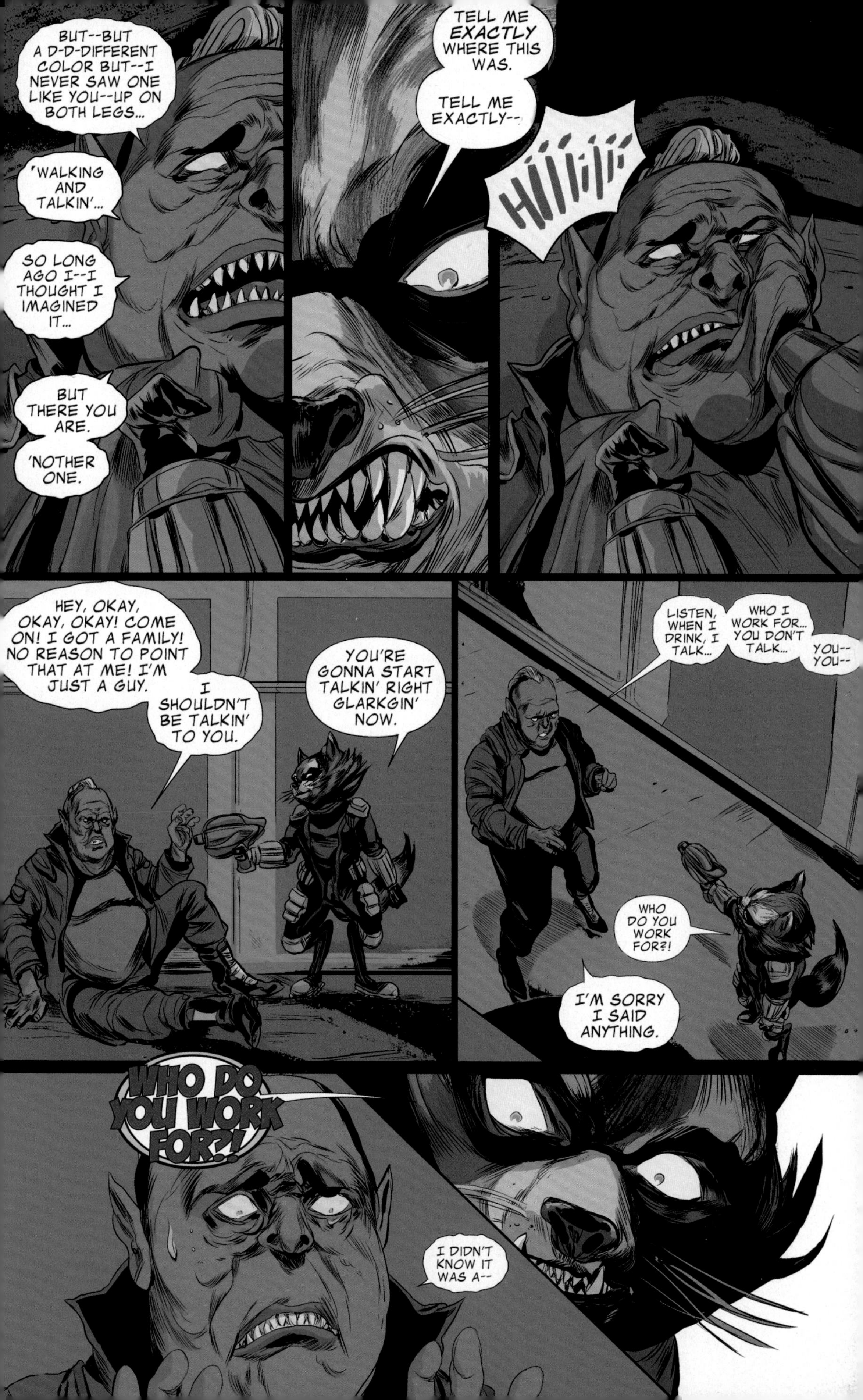
BUT--BUT A D-D-DIFFERENT COLOR BUT--I NEVER SAW ONE LIKE YOU--UP ON BOTH LEGS...
'WALKING AND TALKIN'...
SO LONG AGO I--I THOUGHT I IMAGINED IT...
BUT THERE YOU ARE.
'NOTHER ONE.
TELL ME EXACTLY WHERE THIS WAS.
TELL ME EXACTLY--
HIIIIII
HEY, OKAY, OKAY, OKAY! COME ON! I GOT A FAMILY! NO REASON TO POINT THAT AT ME! I'M JUST A GUY.
I SHOULDN'T BE TALKIN' TO YOU.
YOU'RE GONNA START TALKIN' RIGHT GLARKGIN' NOW.
LISTEN, WHEN I DRINK, I TALK...
WHO I WORK FOR... YOU DON'T TALK...
YOU-- YOU--
WHO DO YOU WORK FOR?!
I'M SORRY I SAID ANYTHING.
WHO DO YOU WORK FOR?!
I DIDN'T KNOW IT WAS A--

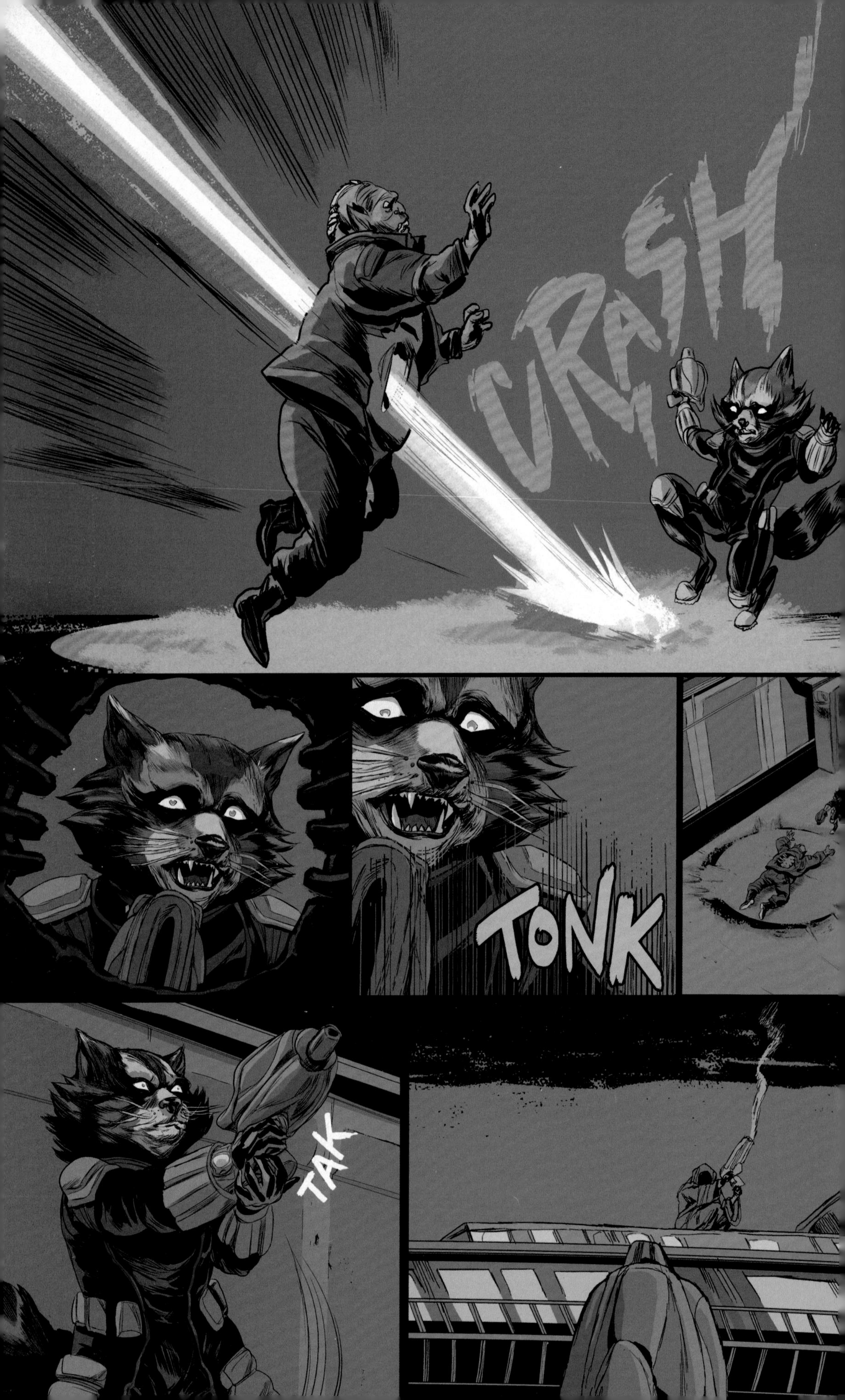
CRASH
TONK
TAK

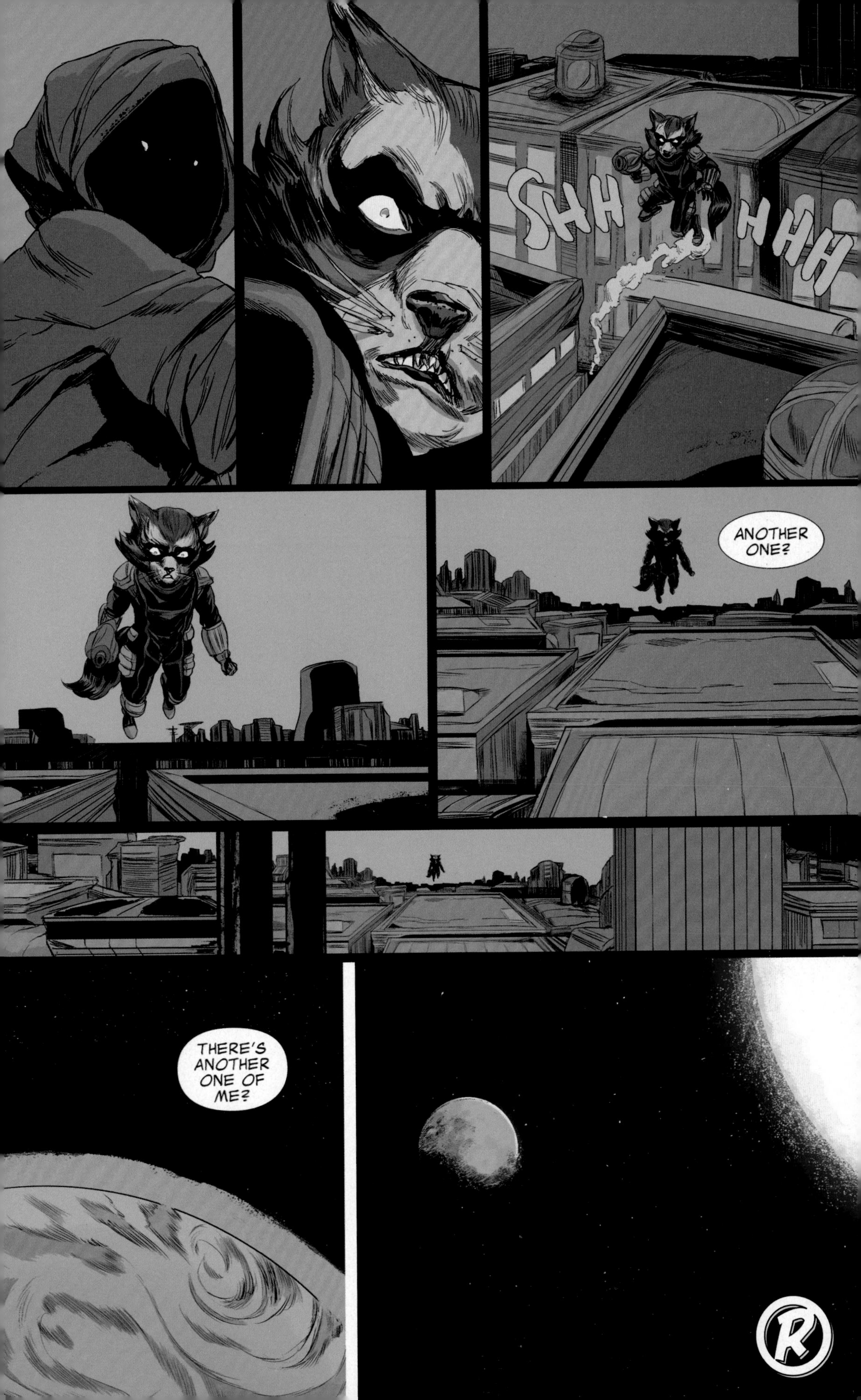
SHHHHHH
ANOTHER ONE?
THERE'S ANOTHER ONE OF ME?

TERRAN.

THE SIXTH MOON OF THE
GAS-GIANT PLANET MARMAN.

SEVENTH FROM THE SUN IN A
SOLAR SYSTEM 80,000 LIGHT
YEARS FROM EARTH.

ITS HOST PLANET WAS A VICTIM OF
THE ALL-CONSUMING PHOENIX FORCE.

ALL LIFE WAS WIPED
FROM THE PLANET.

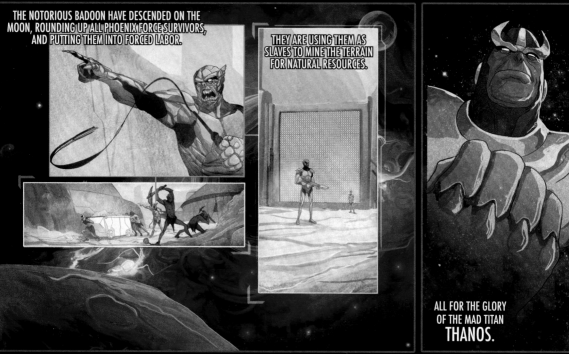

THE NOTORIOUS BADOON HAVE DESCENDED ON THE
MOON, ROUNDING UP ALL PHOENIX FORCE SURVIVORS,
AND PUTTING THEM INTO FORCED LABOR.

THEY ARE USING THEM AS
SLAVES TO MINE THE TERRAIN
FOR NATURAL RESOURCES.

ALL FOR THE GLORY
OF THE MAD TITAN
THANOS.

BUT THANOS HAS A DAUGHTER.

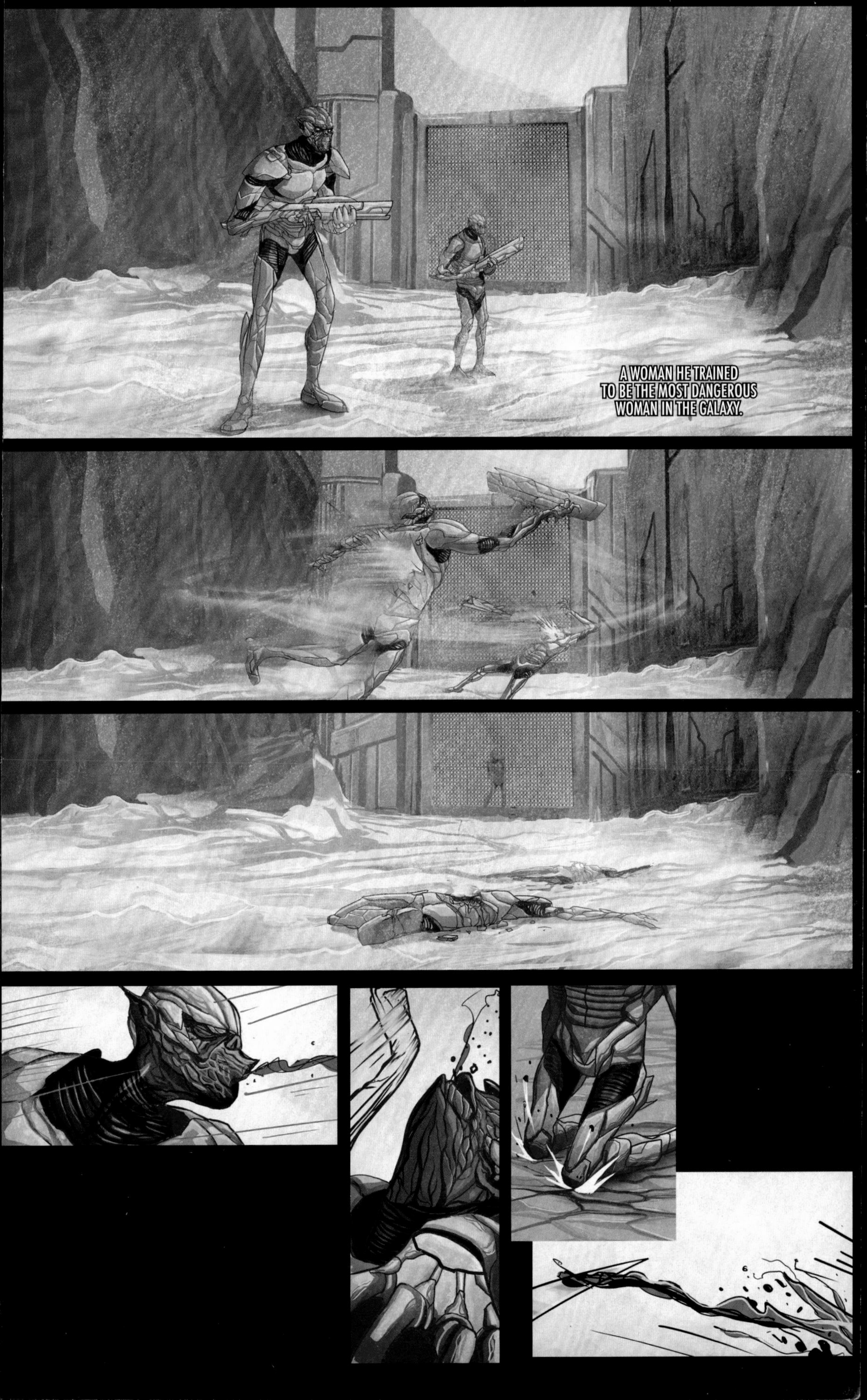
A WOMAN HE TRAINED
TO BE THE MOST DANGEROUS
WOMAN IN THE GALAXY.

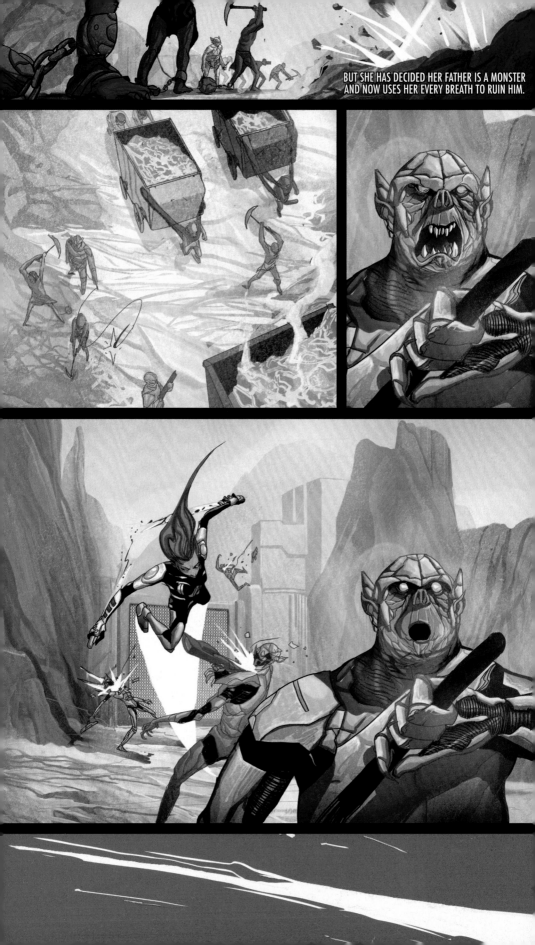

BUT SHE HAS DECIDED HER FATHER IS A MONSTER AND NOW USES HER EVERY BREATH TO RUIN HIM.

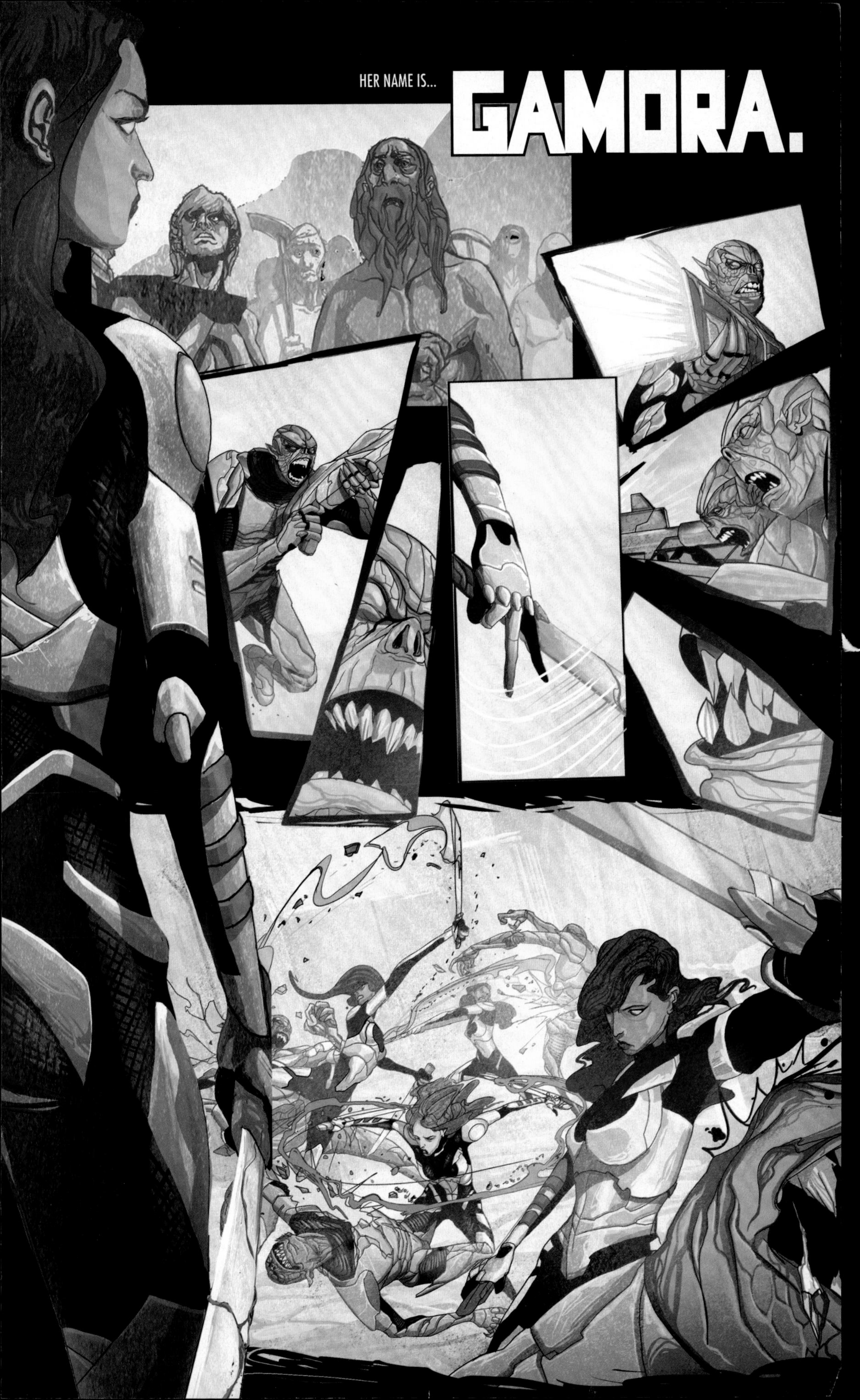
HER NAME IS...
GAMORA.

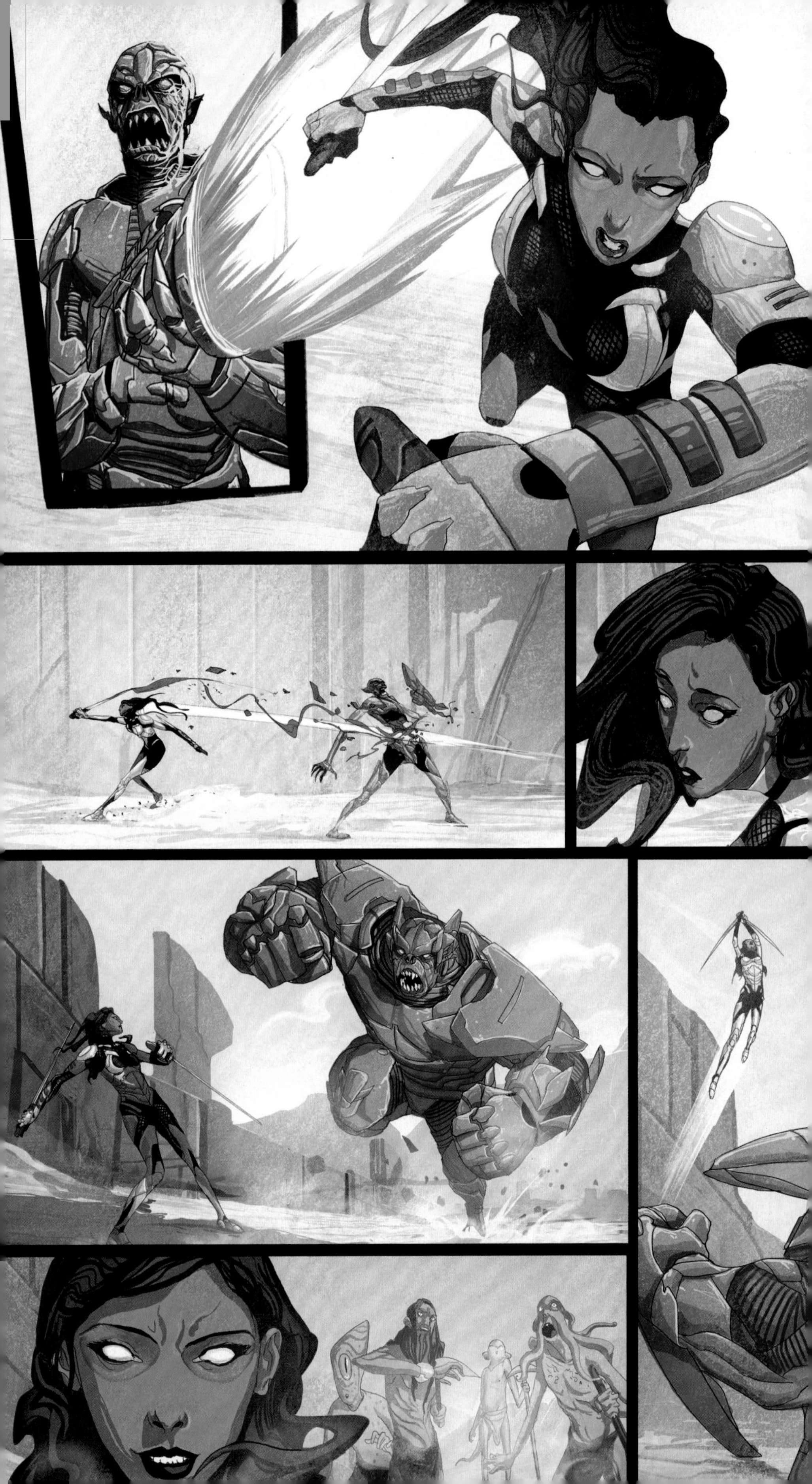

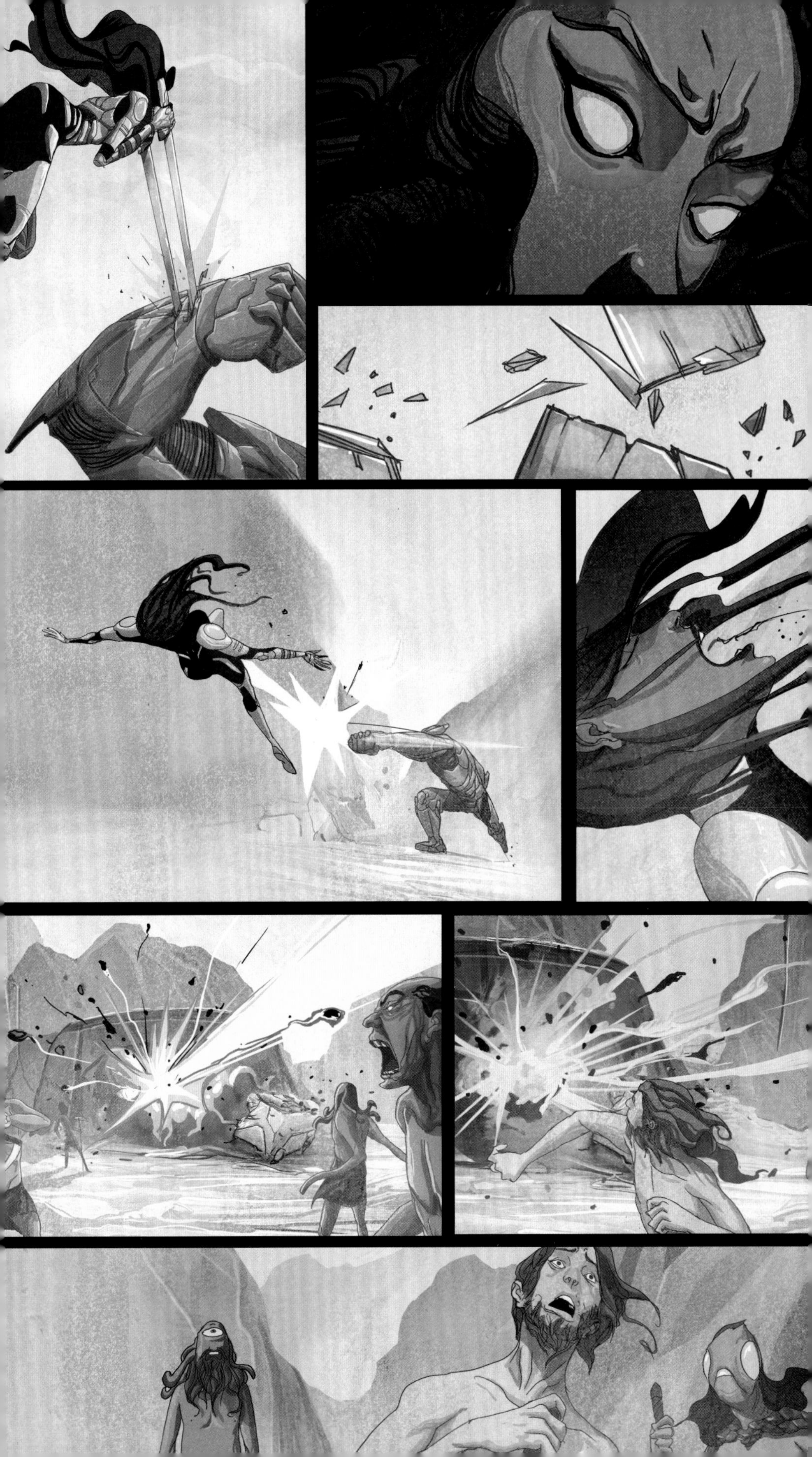

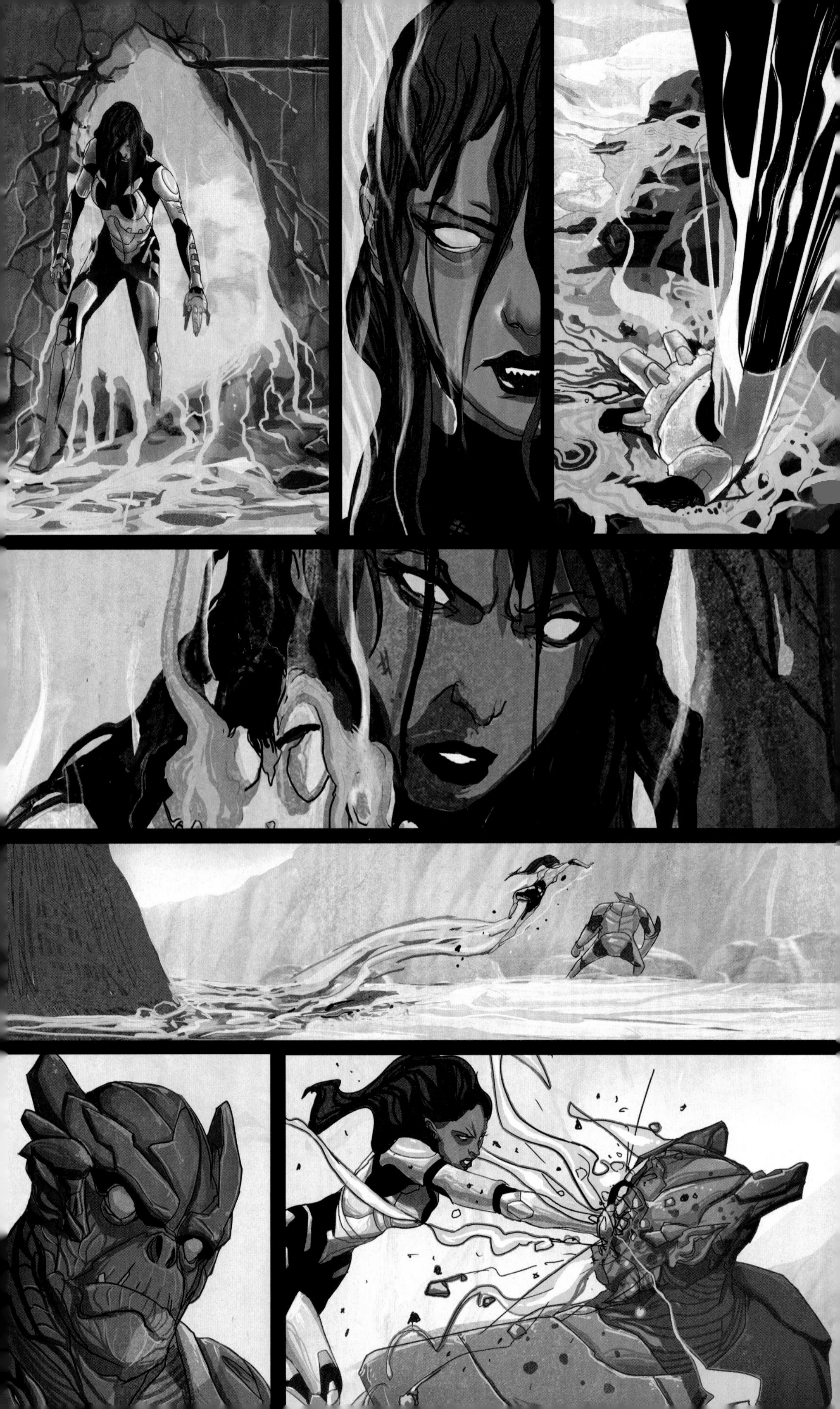

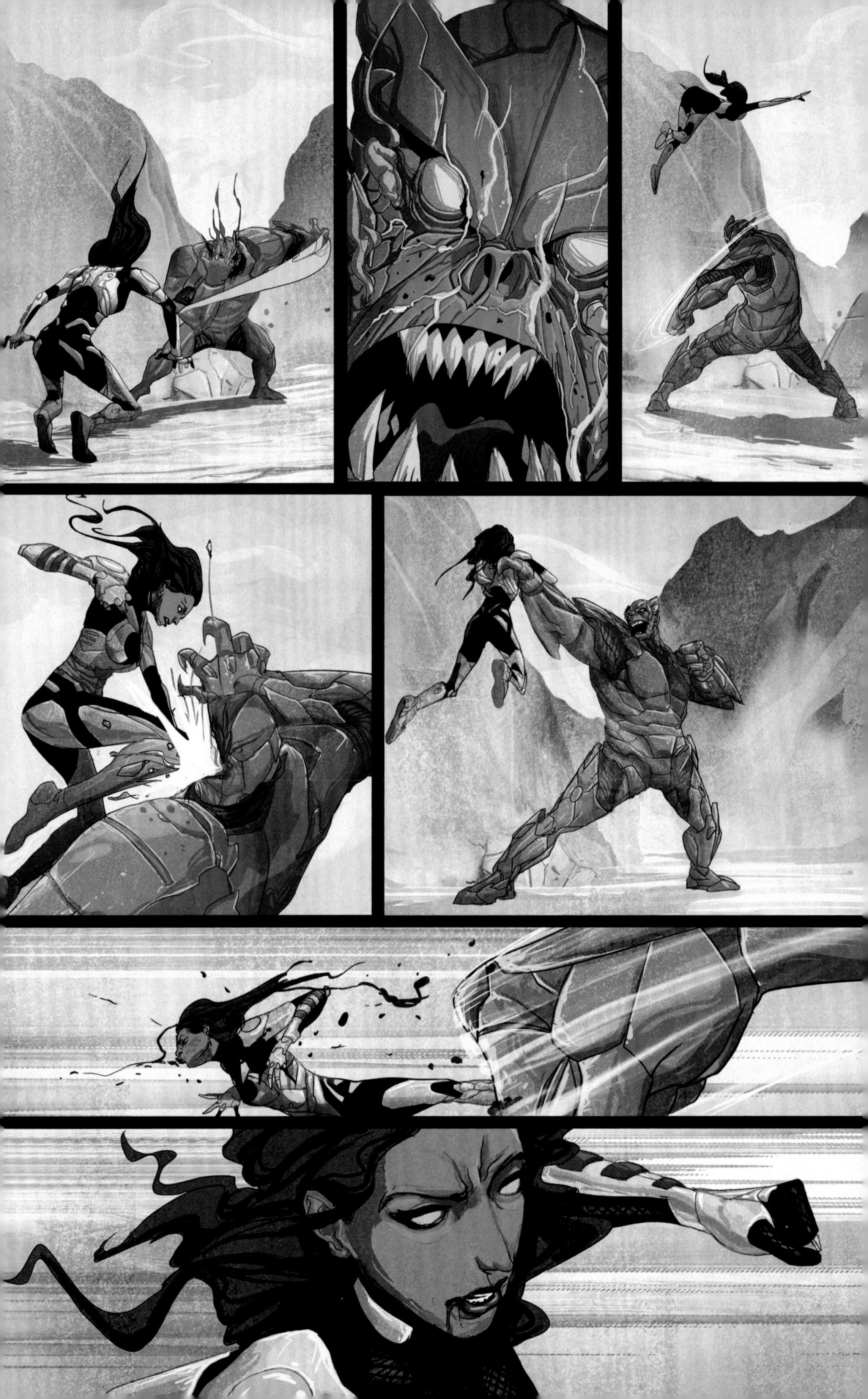

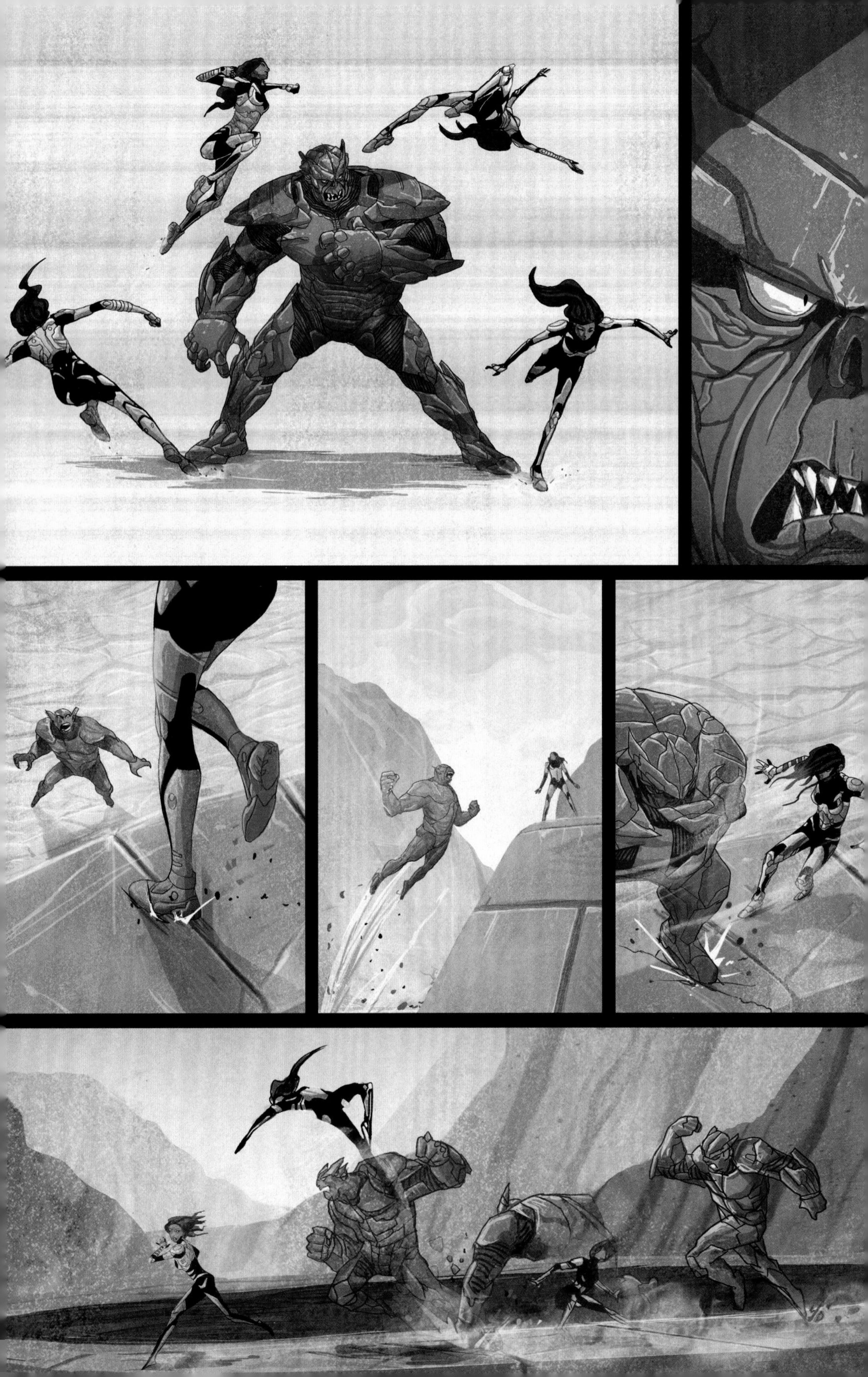

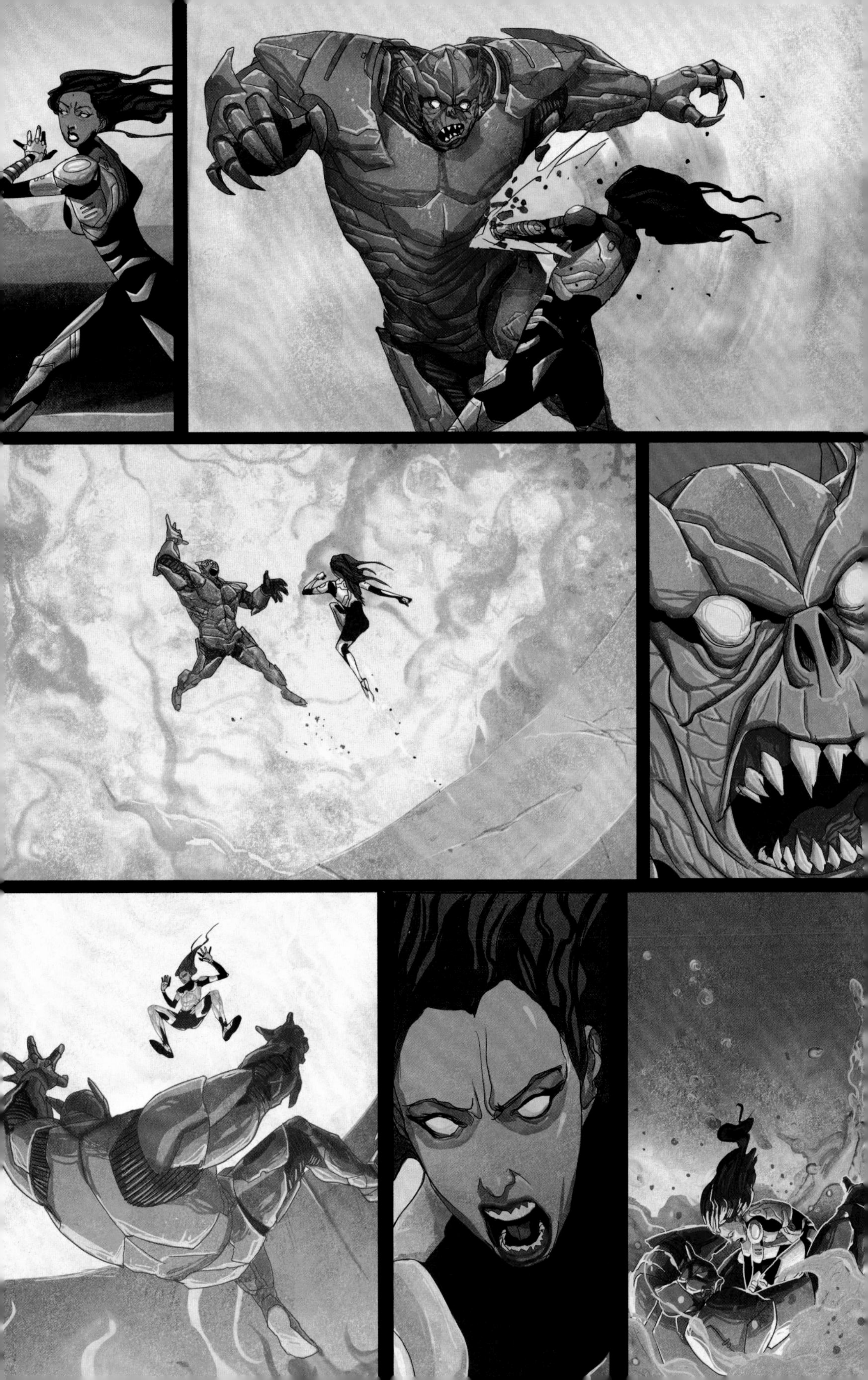

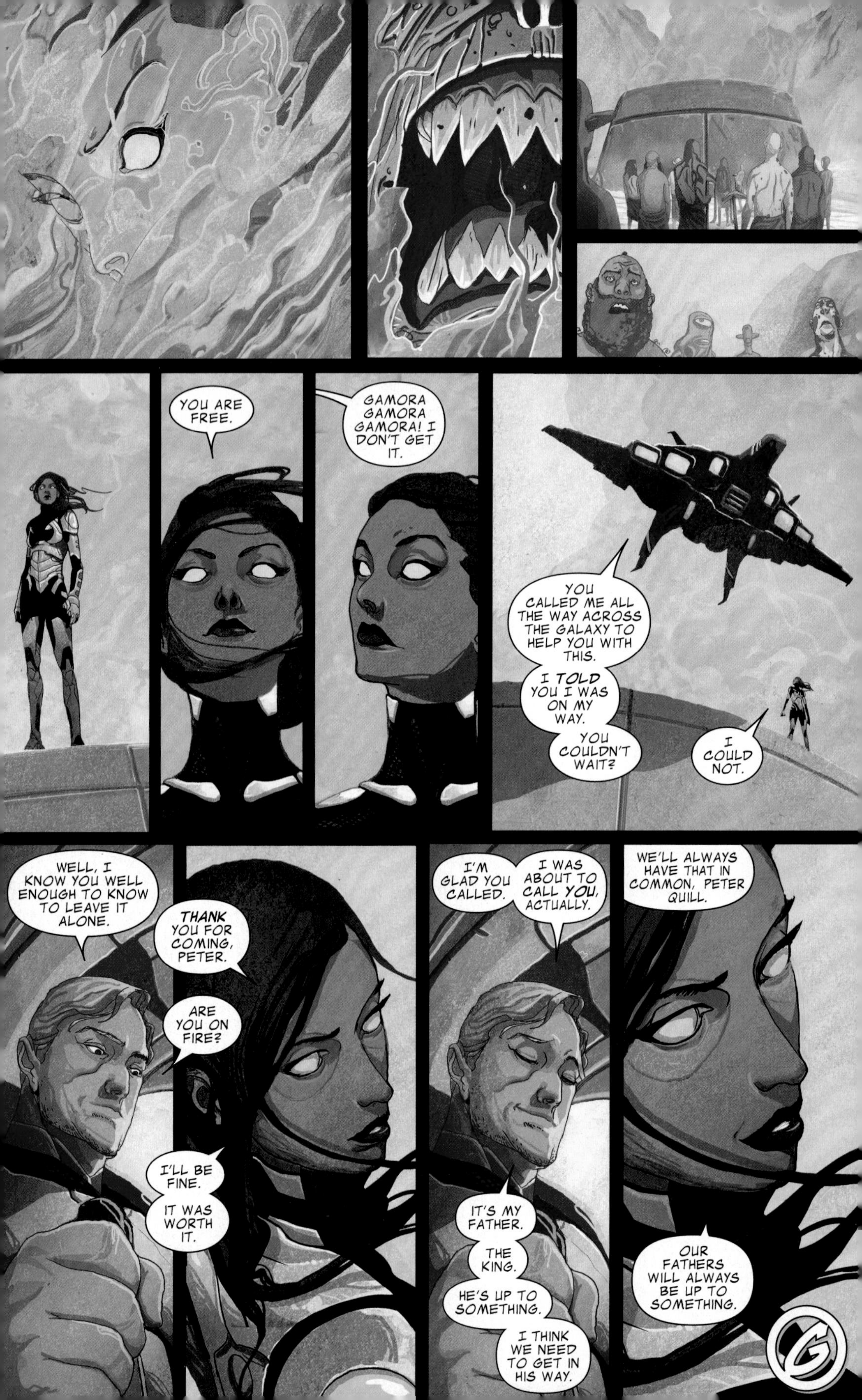
YOU ARE FREE.
GAMORA GAMORA GAMORA! I DON'T GET IT.
YOU CALLED ME ALL THE WAY ACROSS THE GALAXY TO HELP YOU WITH THIS.
I TOLD YOU I WAS ON MY WAY.
YOU COULDN'T WAIT?
I COULD NOT.
WELL, I KNOW YOU WELL ENOUGH TO KNOW TO LEAVE IT ALONE.
THANK YOU FOR COMING, PETER.
ARE YOU ON FIRE?
I'LL BE FINE.
IT WAS WORTH IT.
I'M GLAD YOU CALLED.
I WAS ABOUT TO CALL YOU, ACTUALLY.
IT'S MY FATHER.
THE KING.
HE'S UP TO SOMETHING.
I THINK WE NEED TO GET IN HIS WAY.
WE'LL ALWAYS HAVE THAT IN COMMON, PETER QUILL.
OUR FATHERS WILL ALWAYS BE UP TO SOMETHING.

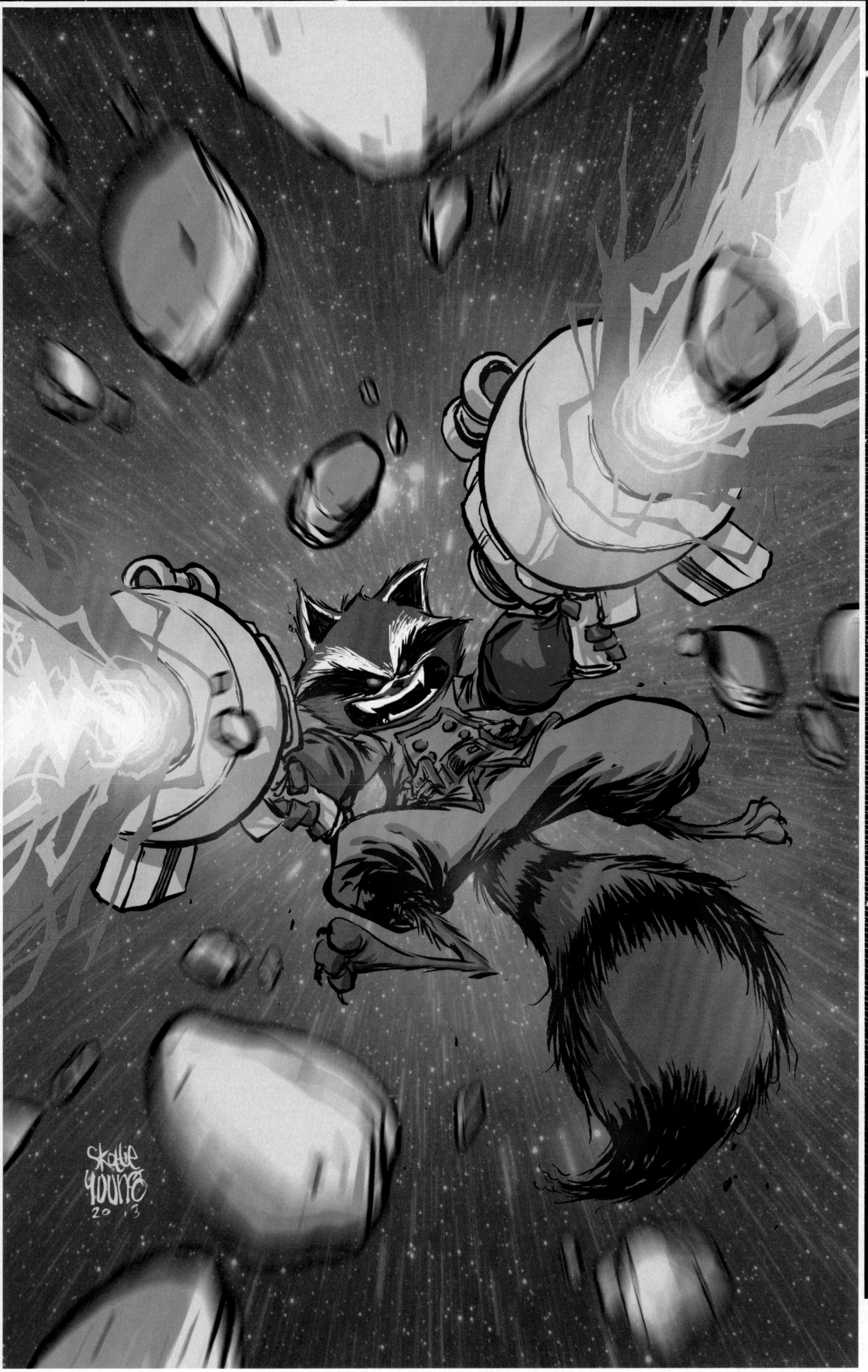

FREE COMIC BOOK DAY (ROCKET RACCOON) #1

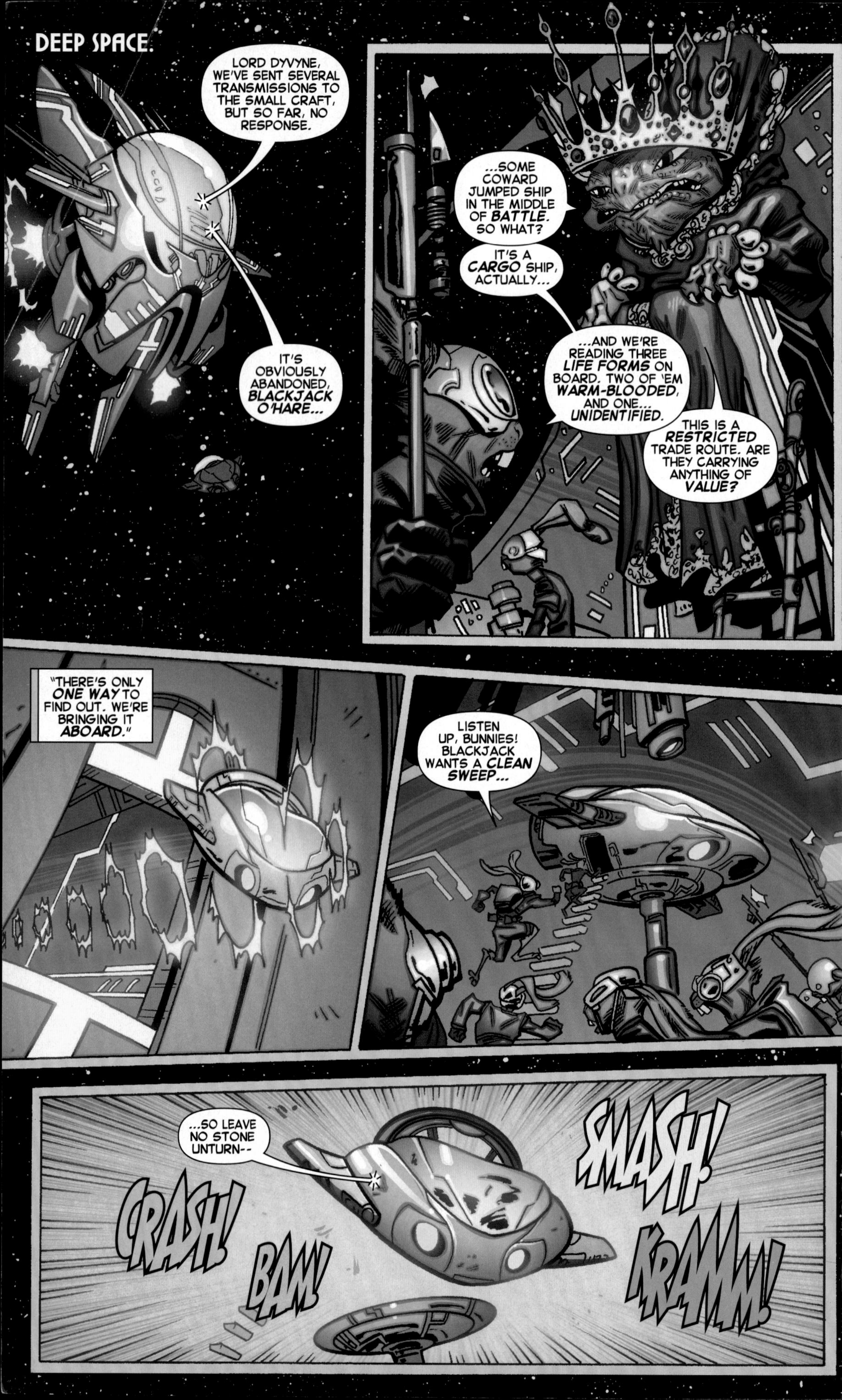
DEEP SPACE.
LORD DYVYNE, WE'VE SENT SEVERAL TRANSMISSIONS TO THE SMALL CRAFT, BUT SO FAR, NO RESPONSE.
IT'S OBVIOUSLY ABANDONED, BLACKJACK O'HARE...
...SOME COWARD JUMPED SHIP IN THE MIDDLE OF BATTLE. SO WHAT?
IT'S A CARGO SHIP, ACTUALLY...
...AND WE'RE READING THREE LIFE FORMS ON BOARD. TWO OF 'EM WARM-BLOODED, AND ONE... UNIDENTIFIED.
THIS IS A RESTRICTED TRADE ROUTE. ARE THEY CARRYING ANYTHING OF VALUE?
"THERE'S ONLY ONE WAY TO FIND OUT. WE'RE BRINGING IT ABOARD."
LISTEN UP, BUNNIES! BLACKJACK WANTS A CLEAN SWEEP...
...SO LEAVE NO STONE UNTURN--
CRASH!
BAM!
SMASH!
KRAMM!

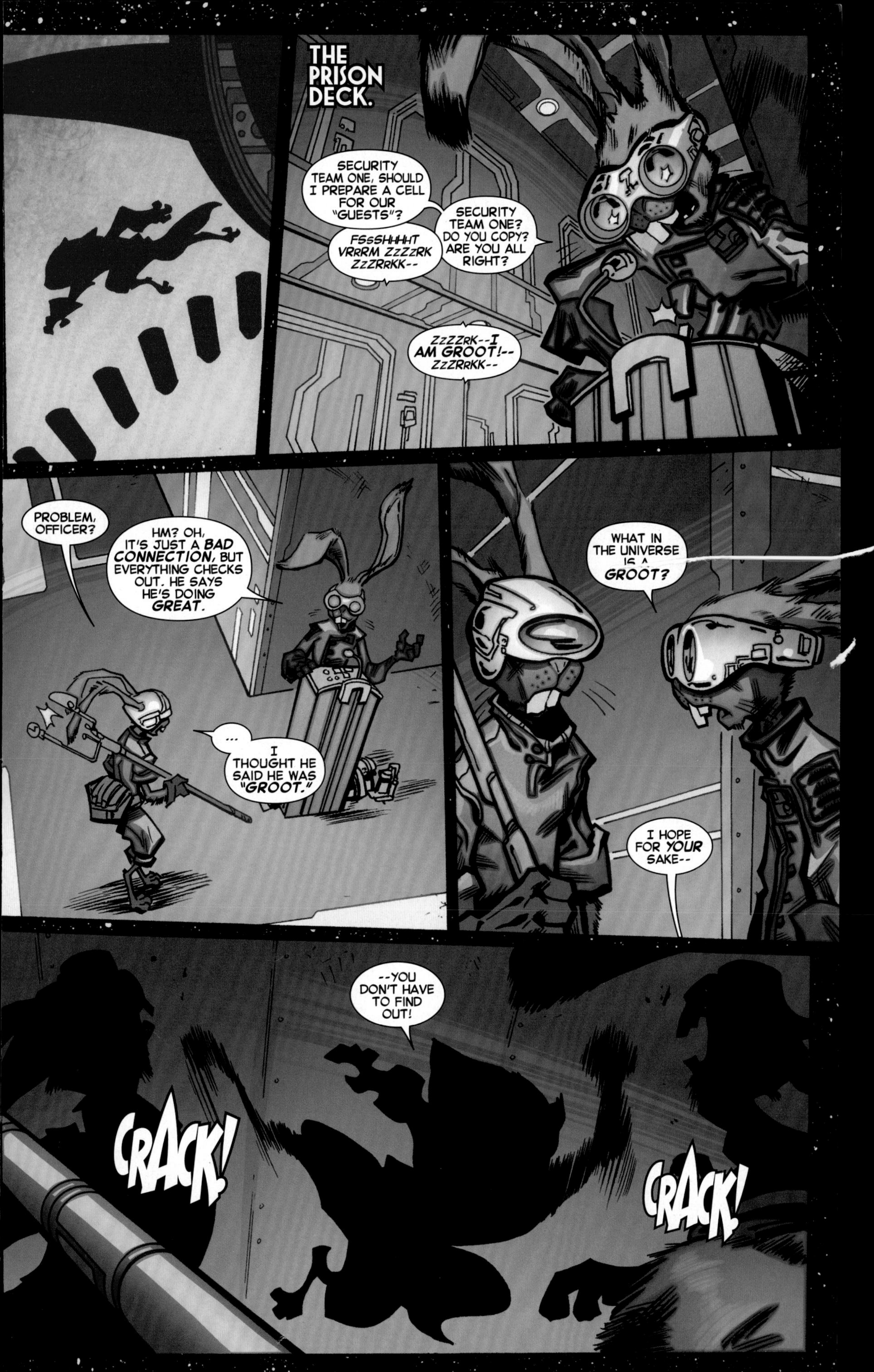
THE PRISON DECK.
SECURITY TEAM ONE, SHOULD I PREPARE A CELL FOR OUR "GUESTS"?
FSSSHHHHT VRRRM ZZZZRK ZZZRRKK--
SECURITY TEAM ONE? DO YOU COPY? ARE YOU ALL RIGHT?
ZZZZRK--I AM GROOT!--ZZZRRKK--
PROBLEM, OFFICER?
HM? OH, IT'S JUST A BAD CONNECTION, BUT EVERYTHING CHECKS OUT. HE SAYS HE'S DOING GREAT.
... I THOUGHT HE SAID HE WAS "GROOT."
WHAT IN THE UNIVERSE IS A GROOT?
I HOPE FOR YOUR SAKE--
--YOU DON'T HAVE TO FIND OUT!
CRACK!
CRACK!

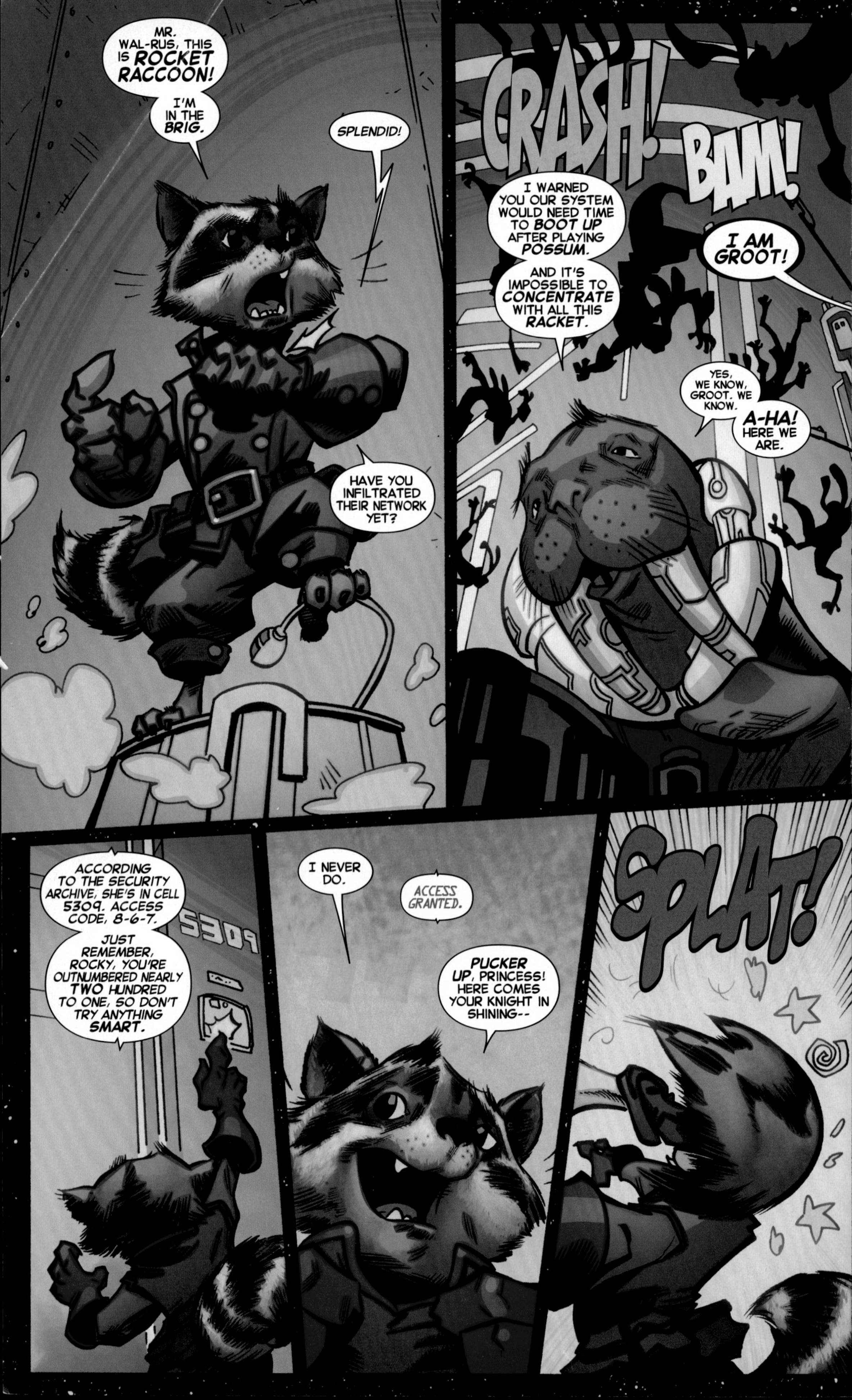
MR. WAL-RUS, THIS IS ROCKET RACCOON!
I'M IN THE BRIG.
SPLENDID!
HAVE YOU INFILTRATED THEIR NETWORK YET?
CRASH!
BAM!
I WARNED YOU OUR SYSTEM WOULD NEED TIME TO BOOT UP AFTER PLAYING POSSUM.
AND IT'S IMPOSSIBLE TO CONCENTRATE WITH ALL THIS RACKET.
I AM GROOT!
YES, WE KNOW, GROOT. WE KNOW.
A-HA! HERE WE ARE.
ACCORDING TO THE SECURITY ARCHIVE, SHE'S IN CELL 5309. ACCESS CODE, 8-6-7.
JUST REMEMBER, ROCKY, YOU'RE OUTNUMBERED NEARLY TWO HUNDRED TO ONE, SO DON'T TRY ANYTHING SMART.
5309
I NEVER DO.
ACCESS GRANTED.
PUCKER UP, PRINCESS! HERE COMES YOUR KNIGHT IN SHINING--
SPLAT!

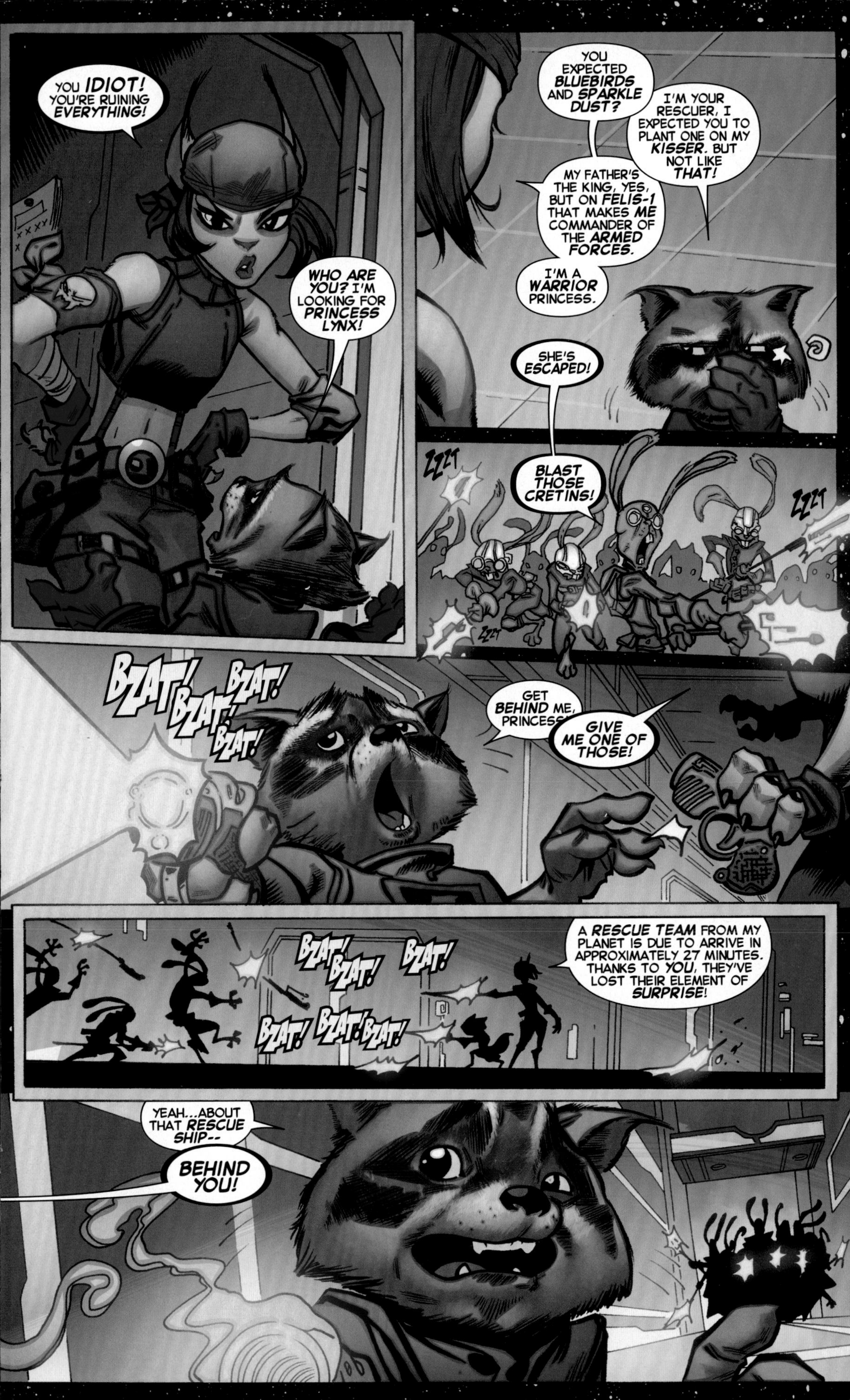
YOU IDIOT! YOU'RE RUINING EVERYTHING!
WHO ARE YOU? I'M LOOKING FOR PRINCESS LYNX!
YOU EXPECTED BLUEBIRDS AND SPARKLE DUST?
I'M YOUR RESCUER, I EXPECTED YOU TO PLANT ONE ON MY KISSER. BUT NOT LIKE THAT!
MY FATHER'S THE KING, YES, BUT ON FELIS-1 THAT MAKES ME COMMANDER OF THE ARMED FORCES.
I'M A WARRIOR PRINCESS.
SHE'S ESCAPED!
BLAST THOSE CRETINS!
ZZZT
ZZZT
ZZZT
BZAT! BZAT! BZAT! BZAT!
GET BEHIND ME, PRINCESS!
GIVE ME ONE OF THOSE!
BZAT! BZAT! BZAT!
BZAT! BZAT! BZAT!
A RESCUE TEAM FROM MY PLANET IS DUE TO ARRIVE IN APPROXIMATELY 27 MINUTES. THANKS TO YOU, THEY'VE LOST THEIR ELEMENT OF SURPRISE!
YEAH...ABOUT THAT RESCUE SHIP--
BEHIND YOU!

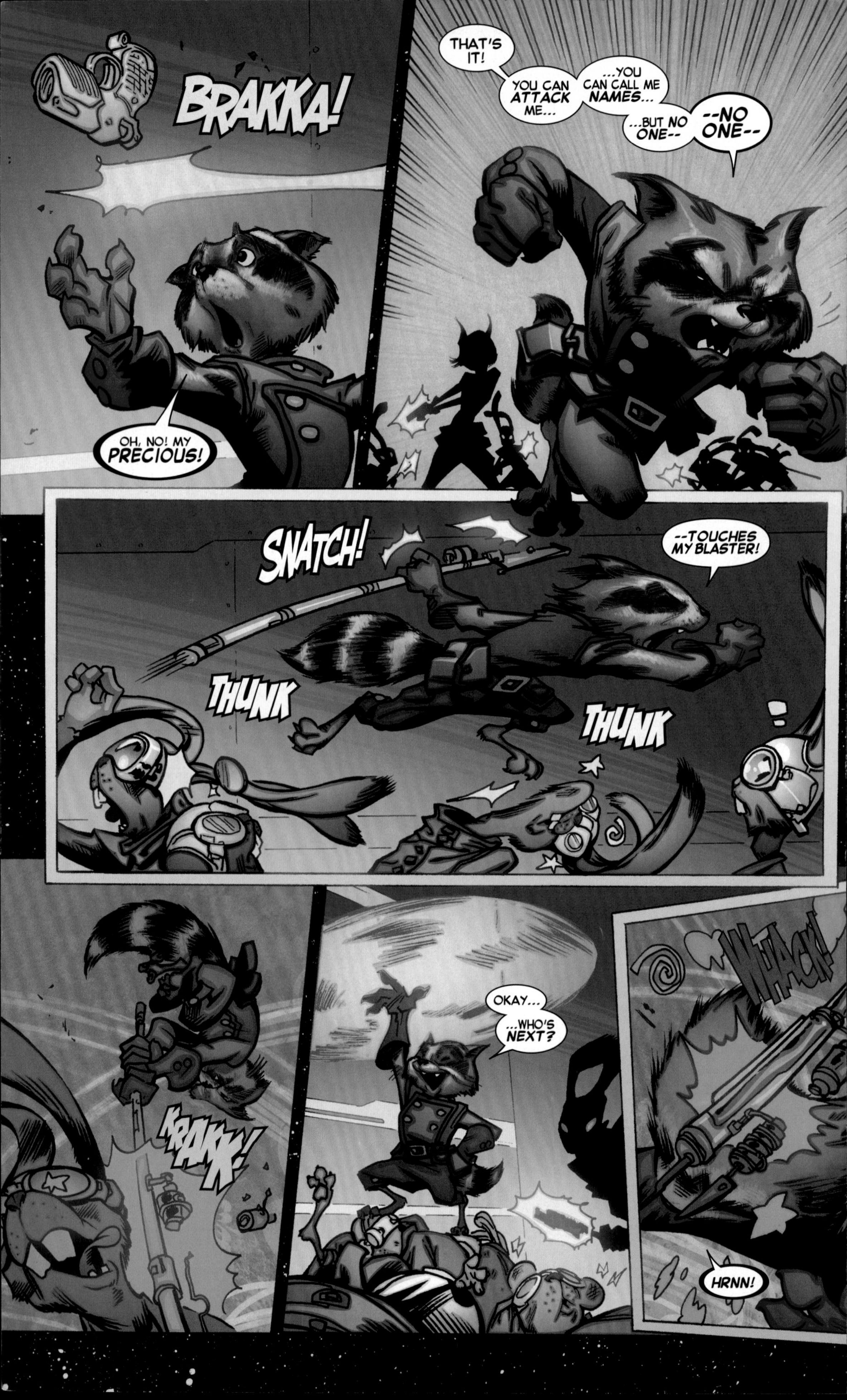
BRAKKA!
OH, NO! MY PRECIOUS!
THAT'S IT!
YOU CAN ATTACK ME...
...YOU CAN CALL ME NAMES...
...BUT NO ONE--
--NO ONE--
SNATCH!
--TOUCHES MY BLASTER!
THUNK
THUNK
KRAKK!
OKAY...
...WHO'S NEXT?
WHACK!
HRNN!

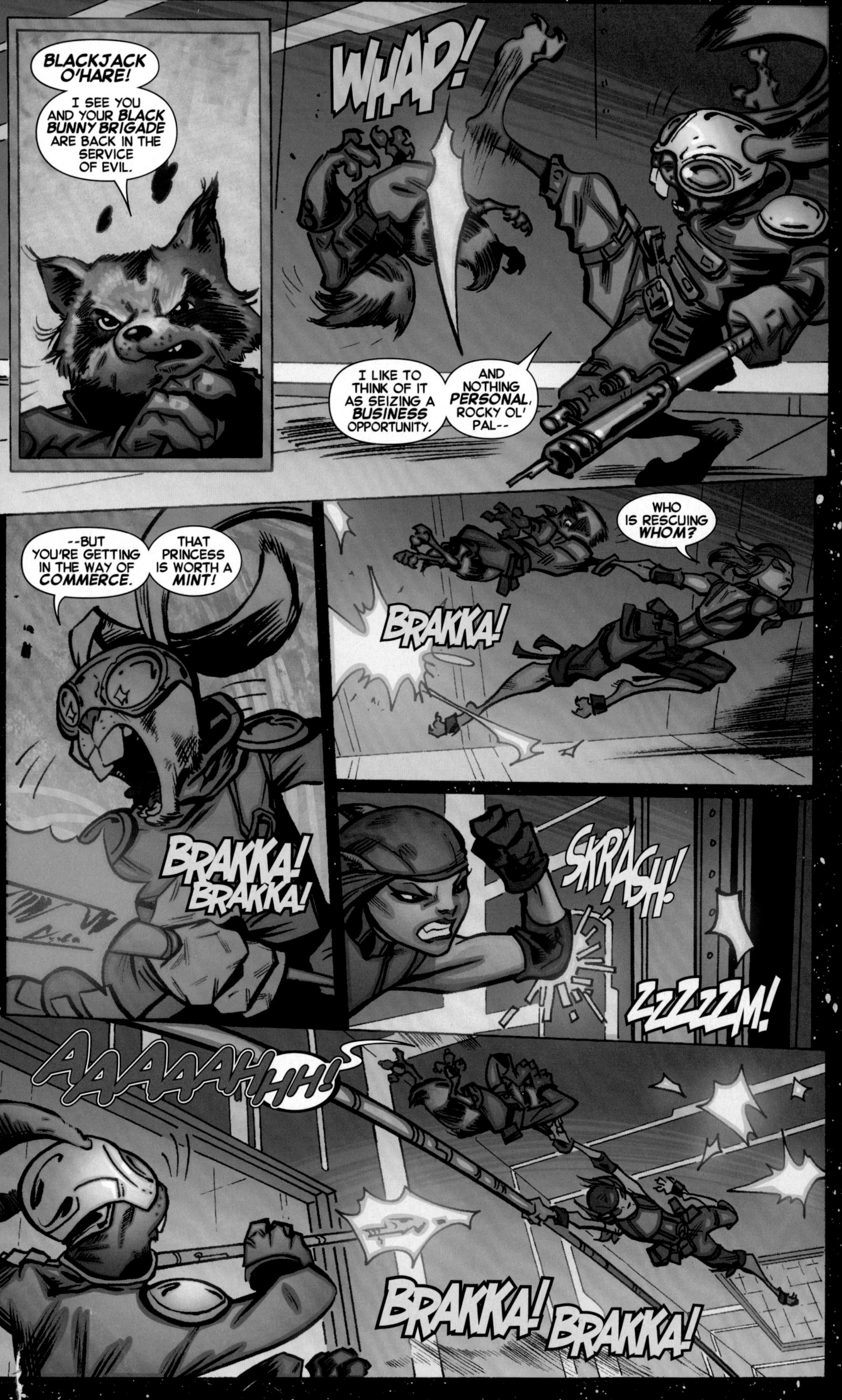
BLACKJACK O'HARE!
I SEE YOU AND YOUR BLACK BUNNY BRIGADE ARE BACK IN THE SERVICE OF EVIL.
WHAP!
I LIKE TO THINK OF IT AS SEIZING A BUSINESS OPPORTUNITY.
AND NOTHING PERSONAL, ROCKY OL' PAL--
--BUT YOU'RE GETTING IN THE WAY OF COMMERCE.
THAT PRINCESS IS WORTH A MINT!
BRAKKA! BRAKKA!
WHO IS RESCUING WHOM?
BRAKKA!
SKRASH!
ZZZZZM!
AAAAAHHH!
BRAKKA! BRAKKA!

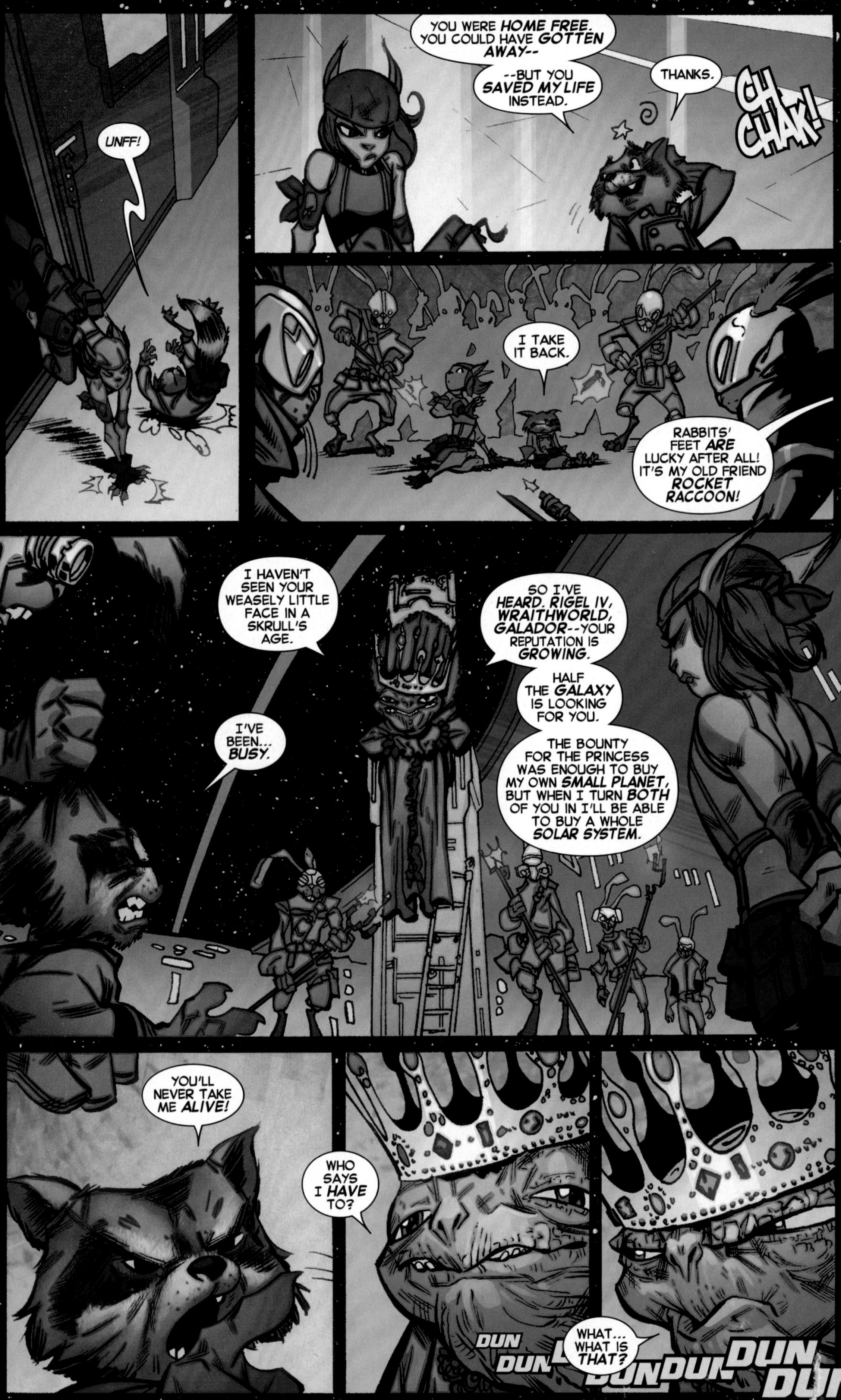
UNFF!
YOU WERE HOME FREE. YOU COULD HAVE GOTTEN AWAY--
--BUT YOU SAVED MY LIFE INSTEAD.
THANKS.
CH CHAK!
I TAKE IT BACK.
RABBITS' FEET ARE LUCKY AFTER ALL! IT'S MY OLD FRIEND ROCKET RACCOON!
I HAVEN'T SEEN YOUR WEASELY LITTLE FACE IN A SKRULL'S AGE.
I'VE BEEN... BUSY.
SO I'VE HEARD. RIGEL IV, WRAITHWORLD, GALADOR--YOUR REPUTATION IS GROWING.
HALF THE GALAXY IS LOOKING FOR YOU.
THE BOUNTY FOR THE PRINCESS WAS ENOUGH TO BUY MY OWN SMALL PLANET, BUT WHEN I TURN BOTH OF YOU IN I'LL BE ABLE TO BUY A WHOLE SOLAR SYSTEM.
YOU'LL NEVER TAKE ME ALIVE!
WHO SAYS I HAVE TO?
WHAT... WHAT IS THAT?
DUN DUN DUN DUN DUN DUN

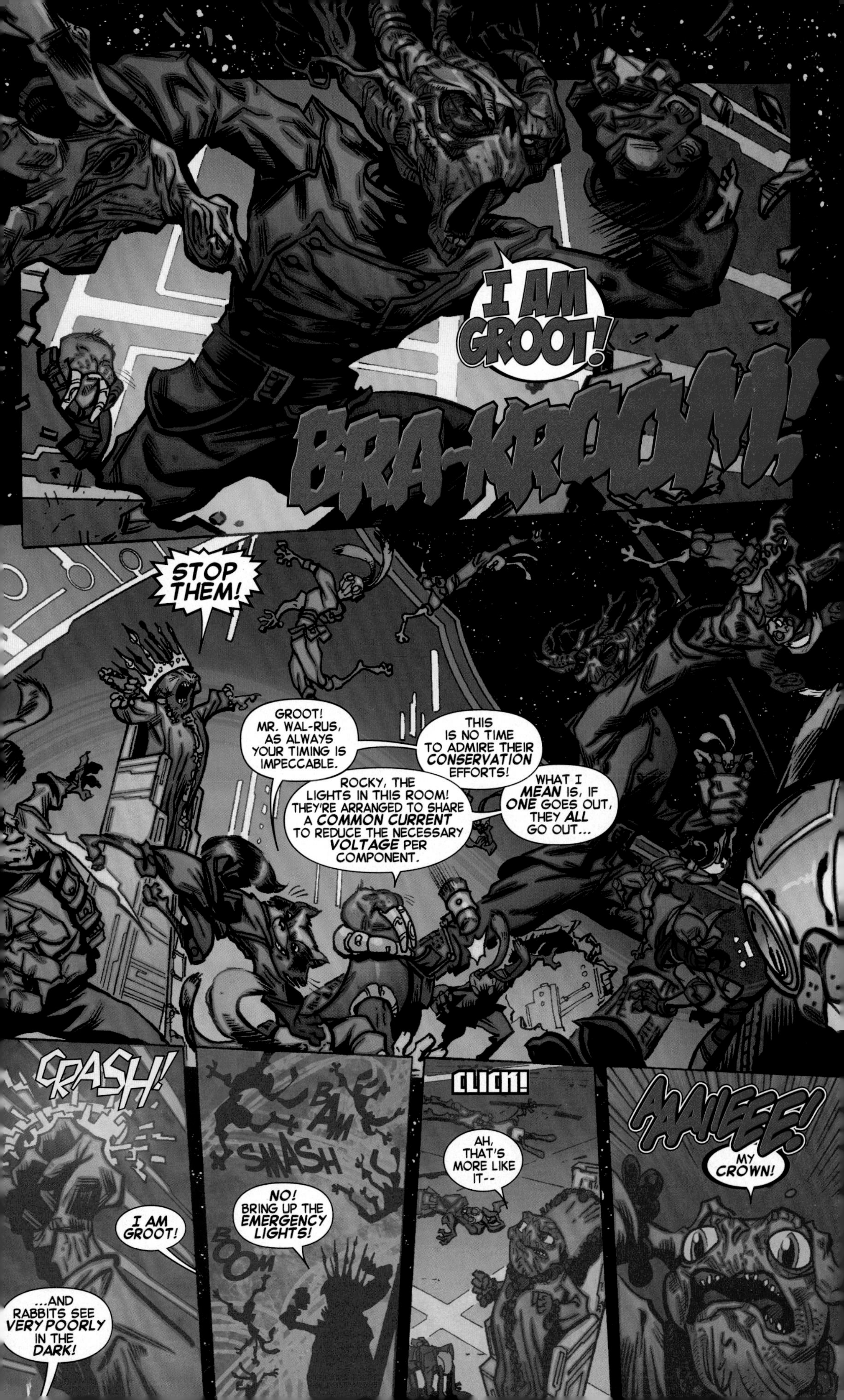
I AM GROOT!
BRA-KROOM!
STOP THEM!
GROOT! MR. WAL-RUS, AS ALWAYS YOUR TIMING IS IMPECCABLE.
THIS IS NO TIME TO ADMIRE THEIR CONSERVATION EFFORTS!
ROCKY, THE LIGHTS IN THIS ROOM! THEY'RE ARRANGED TO SHARE A COMMON CURRENT TO REDUCE THE NECESSARY VOLTAGE PER COMPONENT.
WHAT I MEAN IS, IF ONE GOES OUT, THEY ALL GO OUT...
CRASH!
I AM GROOT!
...AND RABBITS SEE VERY POORLY IN THE DARK!
BAM
SMASH
NO! BRING UP THE EMERGENCY LIGHTS!
BOOM
CLICK!
AH, THAT'S MORE LIKE IT--
AAAIIEEE!
MY CROWN!

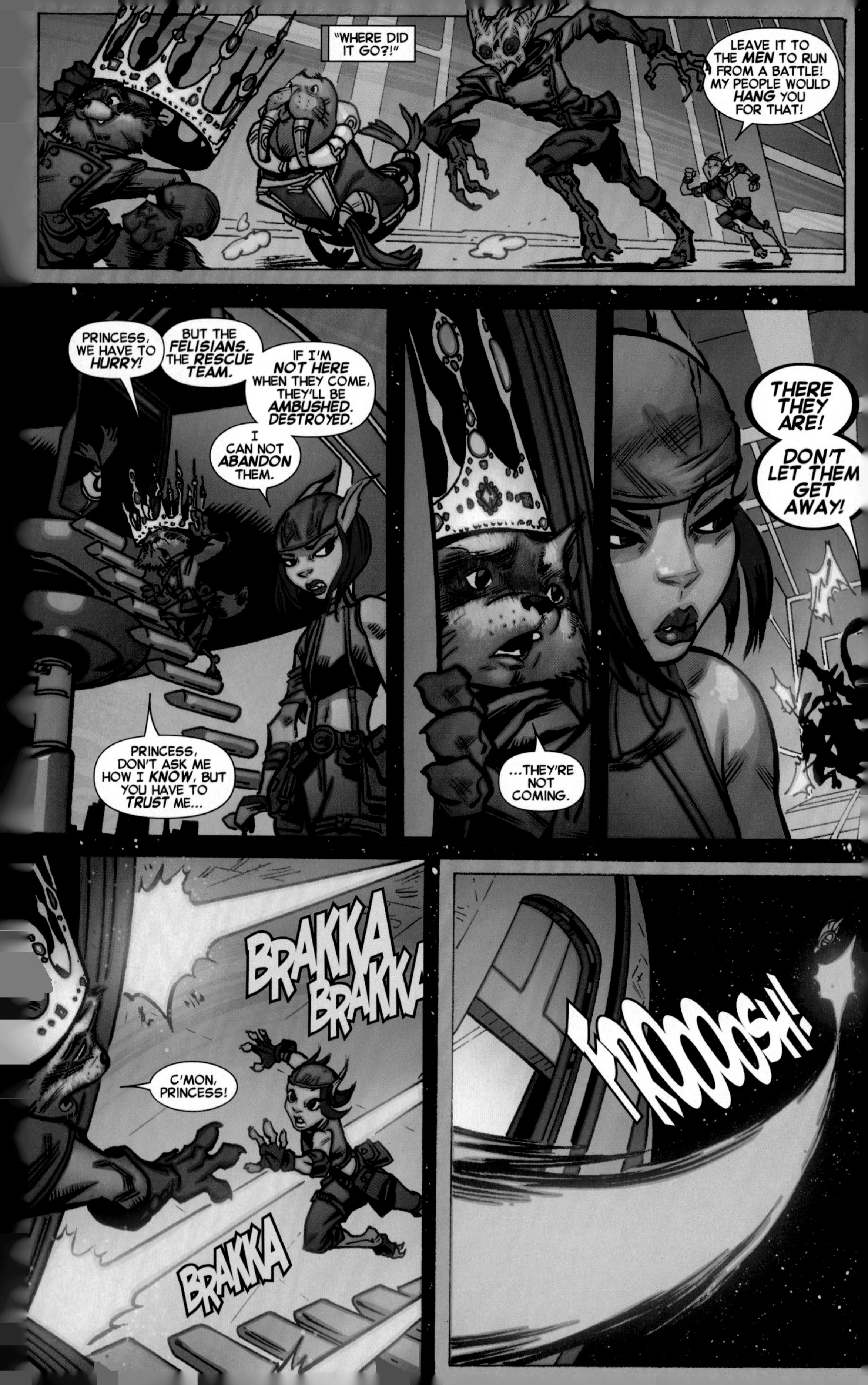
"WHERE DID IT GO?!"
LEAVE IT TO THE MEN TO RUN FROM A BATTLE! MY PEOPLE WOULD HANG YOU FOR THAT!
PRINCESS, WE HAVE TO HURRY!
BUT THE FELISIANS. THE RESCUE TEAM.
IF I'M NOT HERE WHEN THEY COME, THEY'LL BE AMBUSHED. DESTROYED.
I CAN NOT ABANDON THEM.
PRINCESS, DON'T ASK ME HOW I KNOW, BUT YOU HAVE TO TRUST ME...
...THEY'RE NOT COMING.
THERE THEY ARE!
DON'T LET THEM GET AWAY!
BRAKKA
BRAKKA
C'MON, PRINCESS!
BRAKKA
FROOOOSH!

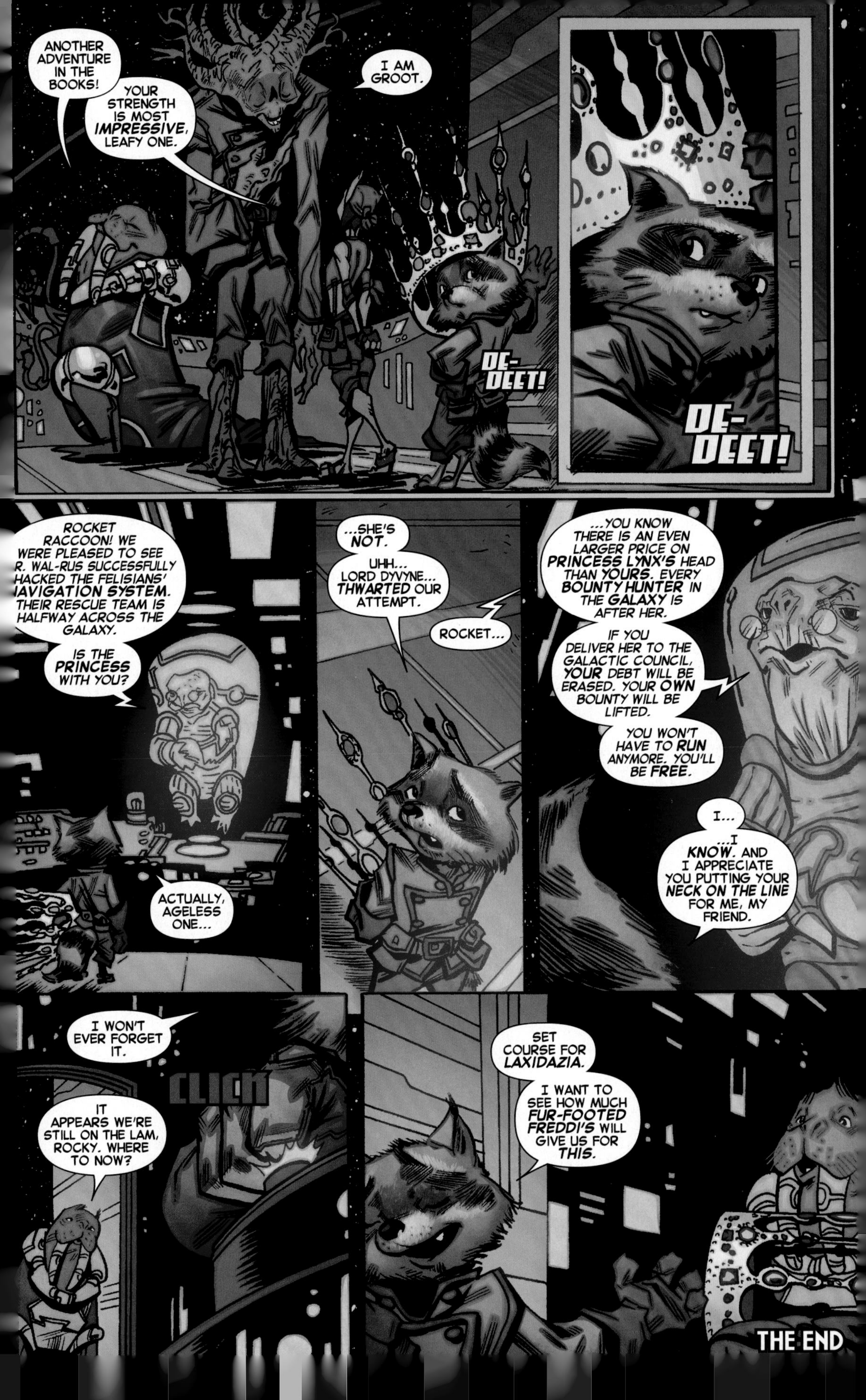

ANOTHER ADVENTURE IN THE BOOKS!
YOUR STRENGTH IS MOST IMPRESSIVE, LEAFY ONE.
I AM GROOT.
DE-DEET!
DE-DEET!
ROCKET RACCOON! WE WERE PLEASED TO SEE R. WAL-RUS SUCCESSFULLY HACKED THE FELISIANS' NAVIGATION SYSTEM. THEIR RESCUE TEAM IS HALFWAY ACROSS THE GALAXY.
IS THE PRINCESS WITH YOU?
ACTUALLY, AGELESS ONE...
...SHE'S NOT.
UHH... LORD DYVYNE... THWARTED OUR ATTEMPT.
ROCKET...
...YOU KNOW THERE IS AN EVEN LARGER PRICE ON PRINCESS LYNX'S HEAD THAN YOURS. EVERY BOUNTY HUNTER IN THE GALAXY IS AFTER HER.
IF YOU DELIVER HER TO THE GALACTIC COUNCIL, YOUR DEBT WILL BE ERASED. YOUR OWN BOUNTY WILL BE LIFTED.
YOU WON'T HAVE TO RUN ANYMORE. YOU'LL BE FREE.
I...
...I KNOW. AND I APPRECIATE YOU PUTTING YOUR NECK ON THE LINE FOR ME, MY FRIEND.
I WON'T EVER FORGET IT.
CLICK
IT APPEARS WE'RE STILL ON THE LAM, ROCKY. WHERE TO NOW?
SET COURSE FOR LAXIDAZIA.
I WANT TO SEE HOW MUCH FUR-FOOTED FREDDI'S WILL GIVE US FOR THIS.
THE END

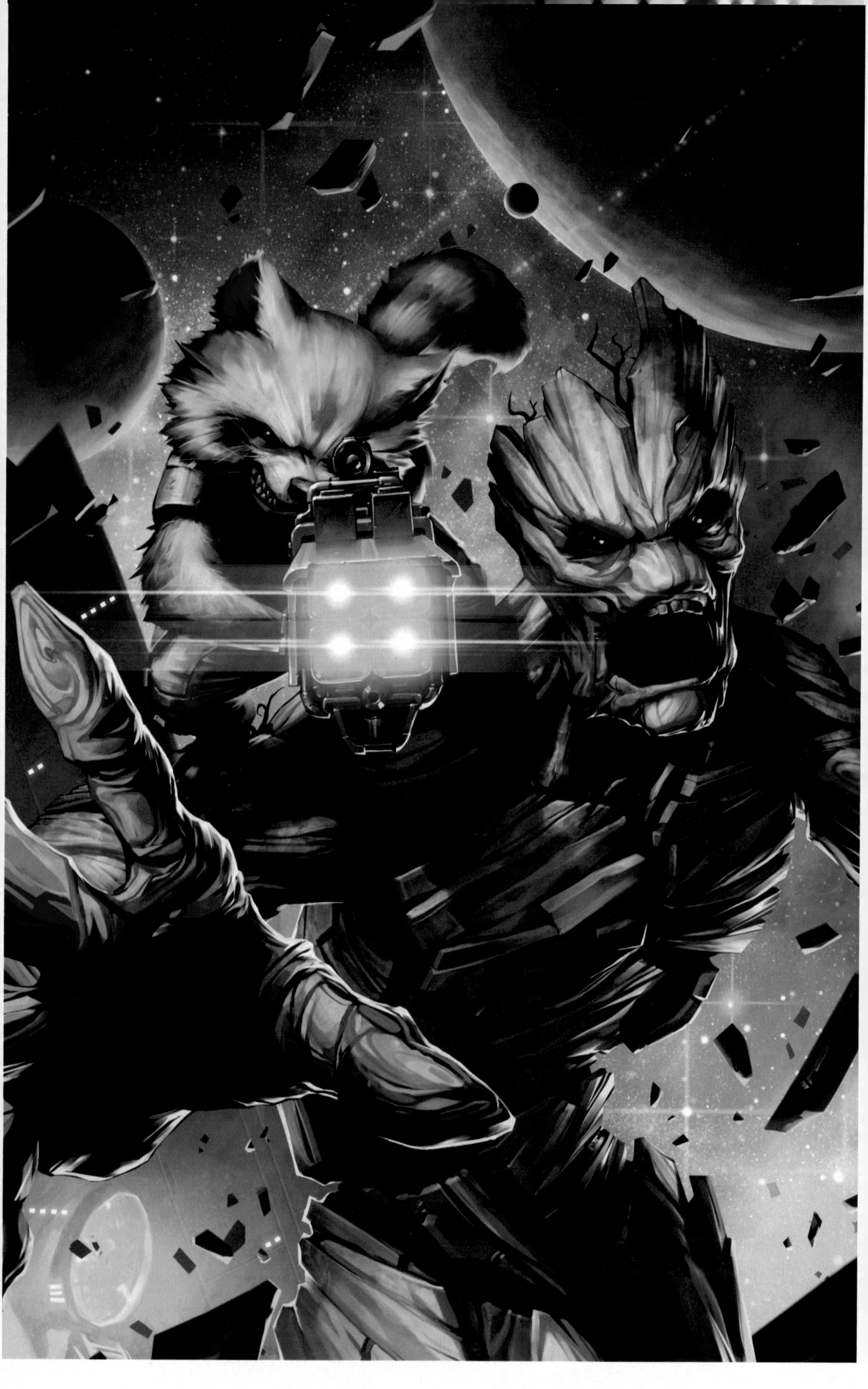

GUARDIANS OF THE GALAXY: GALAXY'S MOST WANTED #1

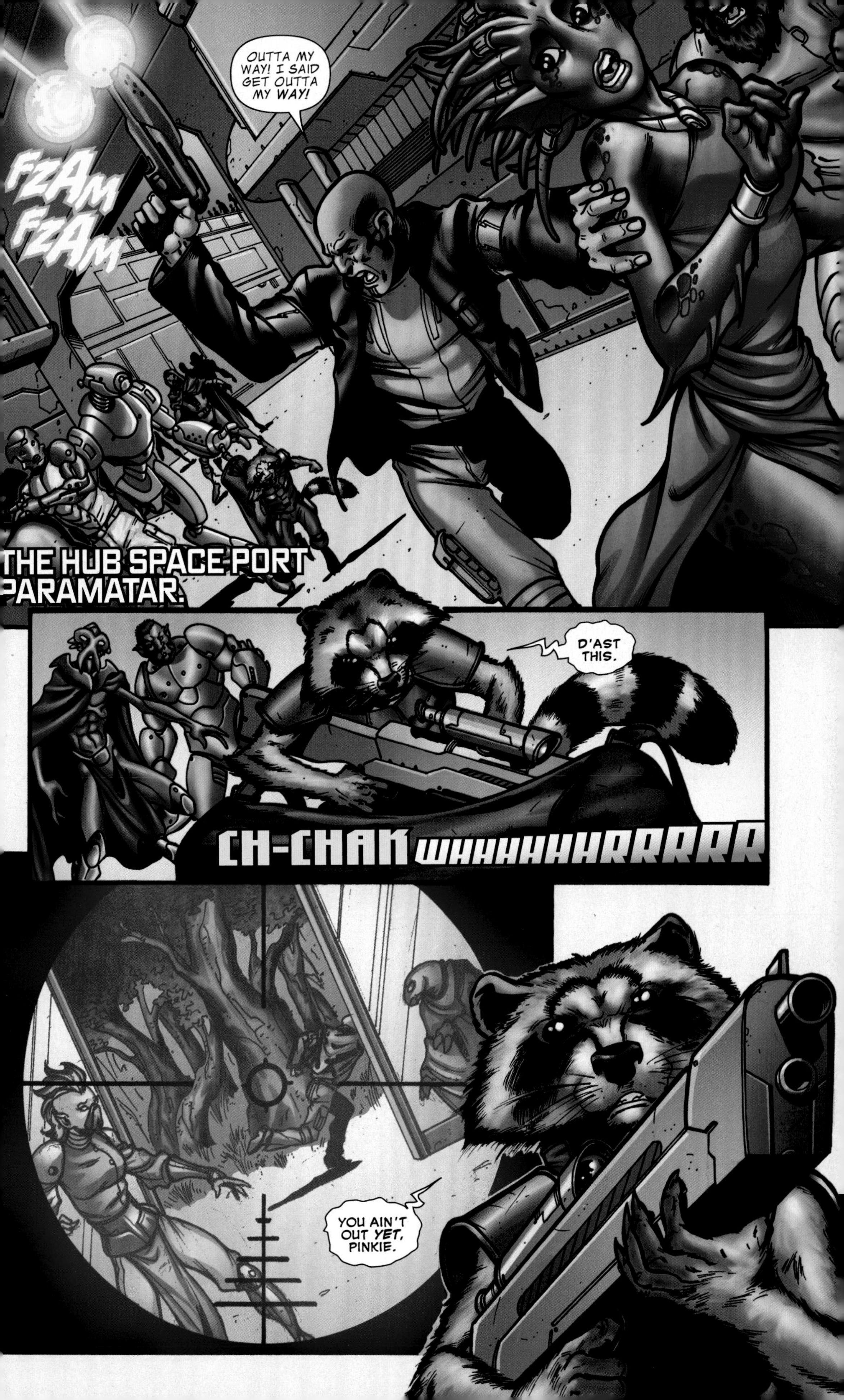
OUTTA MY WAY! I SAID GET OUTTA MY WAY!
FZAM FZAM
THE HUB SPACE PORT PARAMATAR.
D'AST THIS.
CH-CHAK WHHHHHHRRRRR
YOU AIN'T OUT YET, PINKIE.

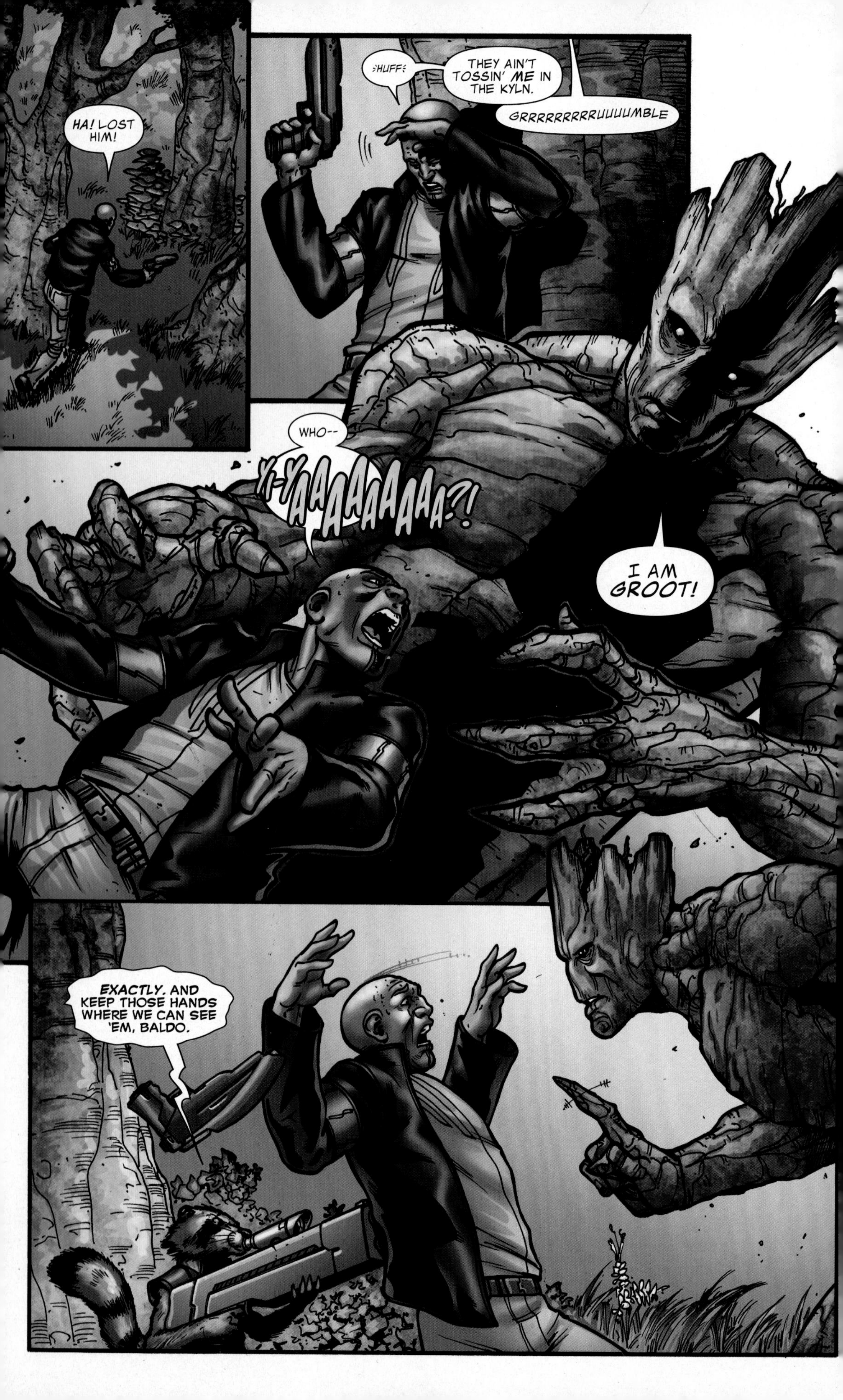
HA! LOST HIM!
:HUFF:
THEY AIN'T TOSSIN' ME IN THE KYLN.
GRRRRRRRRRUUUUMBLE
WHO--
Y-YAAAAAAAAA?!
I AM GROOT!
EXACTLY. AND KEEP THOSE HANDS WHERE WE CAN SEE 'EM, BALDO.

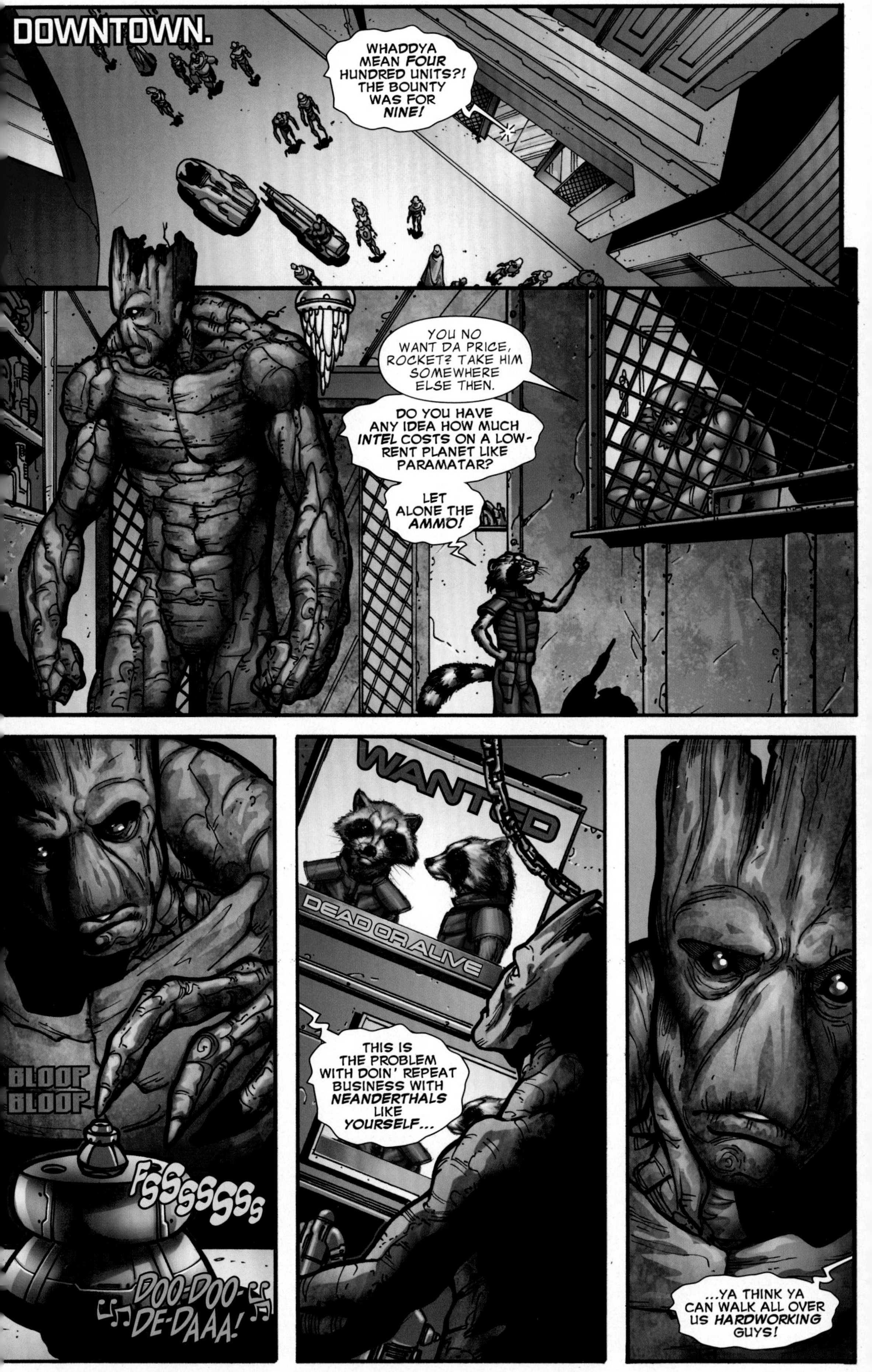
DOWNTOWN.
WHADDYA MEAN FOUR HUNDRED UNITS?! THE BOUNTY WAS FOR NINE!
YOU NO WANT DA PRICE, ROCKET? TAKE HIM SOMEWHERE ELSE THEN.
DO YOU HAVE ANY IDEA HOW MUCH INTEL COSTS ON A LOW-RENT PLANET LIKE PARAMATAR?
LET ALONE THE AMMO!
BLOOP BLOOP
FSSSSSSS
DOO-DOO-DE-DAAA!
WANTED
DEAD OR ALIVE
THIS IS THE PROBLEM WITH DOIN' REPEAT BUSINESS WITH NEANDERTHALS LIKE YOURSELF...
...YA THINK YA CAN WALK ALL OVER US HARDWORKING GUYS!

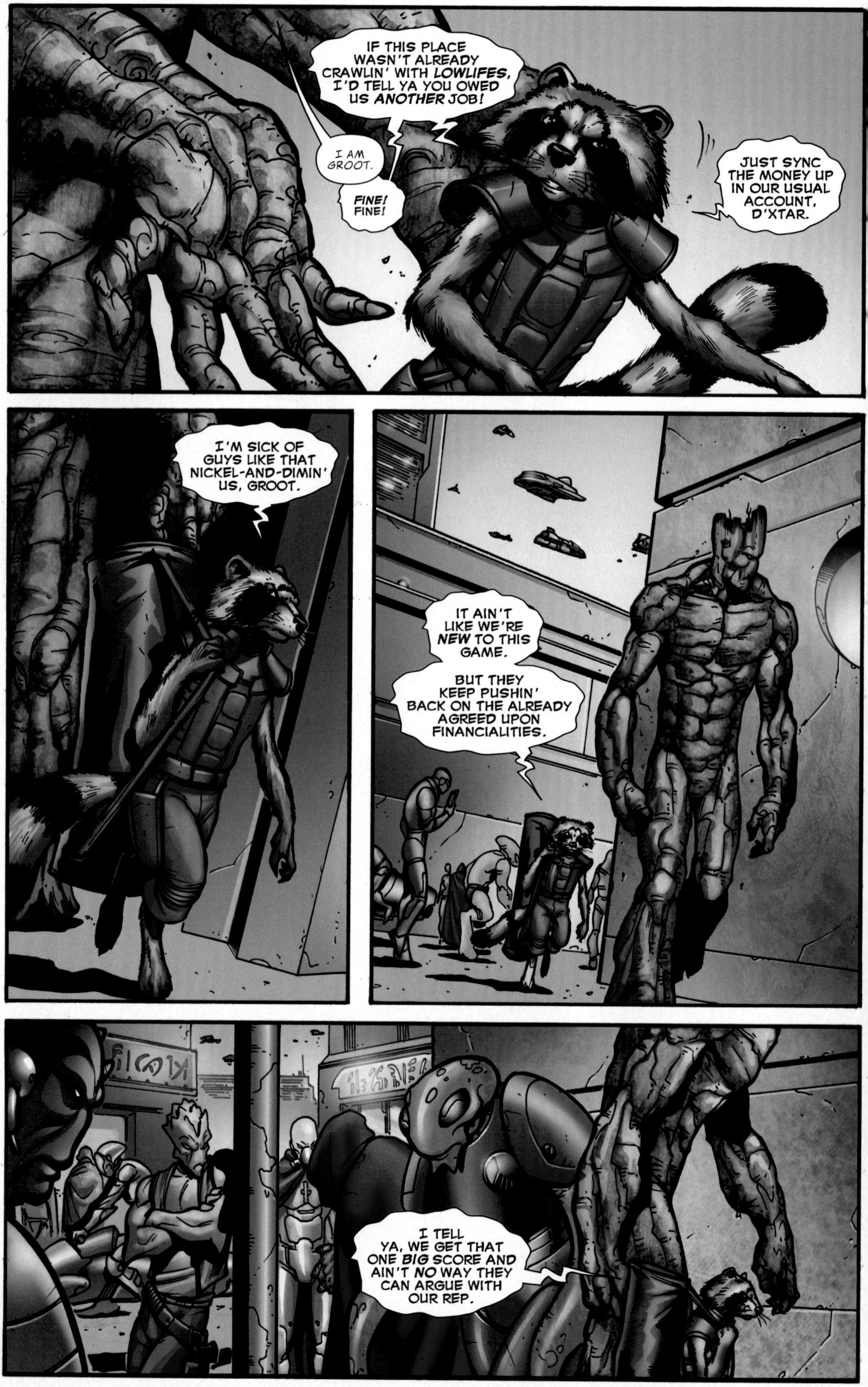
IF THIS PLACE WASN'T ALREADY CRAWLIN' WITH LOWLIFES, I'D TELL YA YOU OWED US ANOTHER JOB!
I AM GROOT.
FINE! FINE!
JUST SYNC THE MONEY UP IN OUR USUAL ACCOUNT, D'XTAR.
I'M SICK OF GUYS LIKE THAT NICKEL-AND-DIMIN' US, GROOT.
IT AIN'T LIKE WE'RE NEW TO THIS GAME.
BUT THEY KEEP PUSHIN' BACK ON THE ALREADY AGREED UPON FINANCIALITIES.
I TELL YA, WE GET THAT ONE BIG SCORE AND AIN'T NO WAY THEY CAN ARGUE WITH OUR REP.

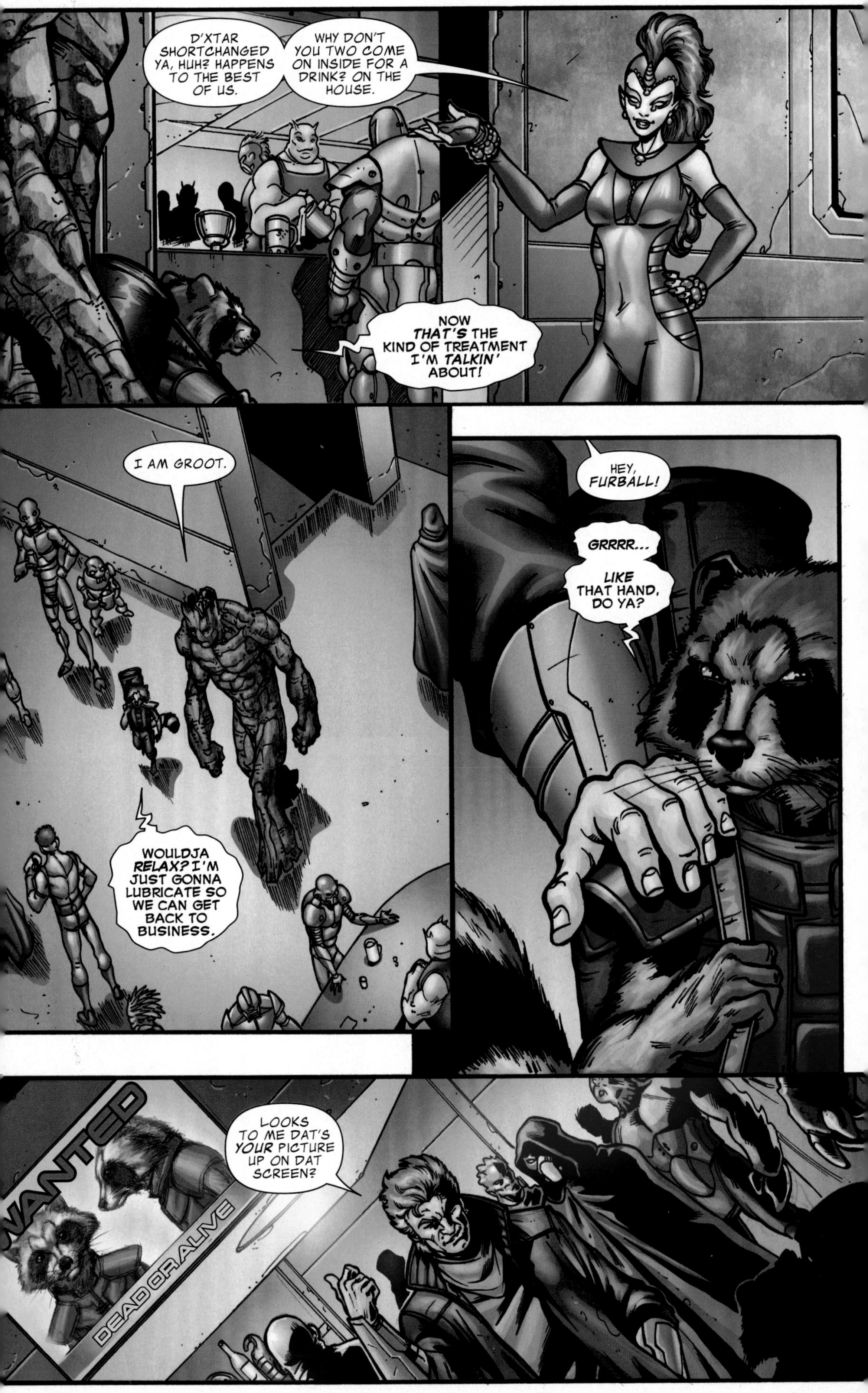

D'XTAR SHORTCHANGED YA, HUH? HAPPENS TO THE BEST OF US.
WHY DON'T YOU TWO COME ON INSIDE FOR A DRINK? ON THE HOUSE.
NOW THAT'S THE KIND OF TREATMENT I'M TALKIN' ABOUT!
I AM GROOT.
WOULDJA RELAX? I'M JUST GONNA LUBRICATE SO WE CAN GET BACK TO BUSINESS.
HEY, FURBALL!
GRRRR...
LIKE THAT HAND, DO YA?
WANTED
DEAD OR ALIVE
LOOKS TO ME DAT'S YOUR PICTURE UP ON DAT SCREEN?

HMMM...

CLICK-CLICK

CH-CHAK

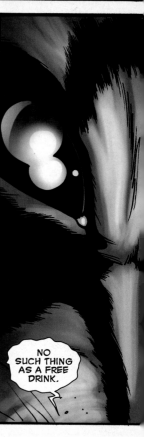

NO SUCH THING AS A FREE DRINK.

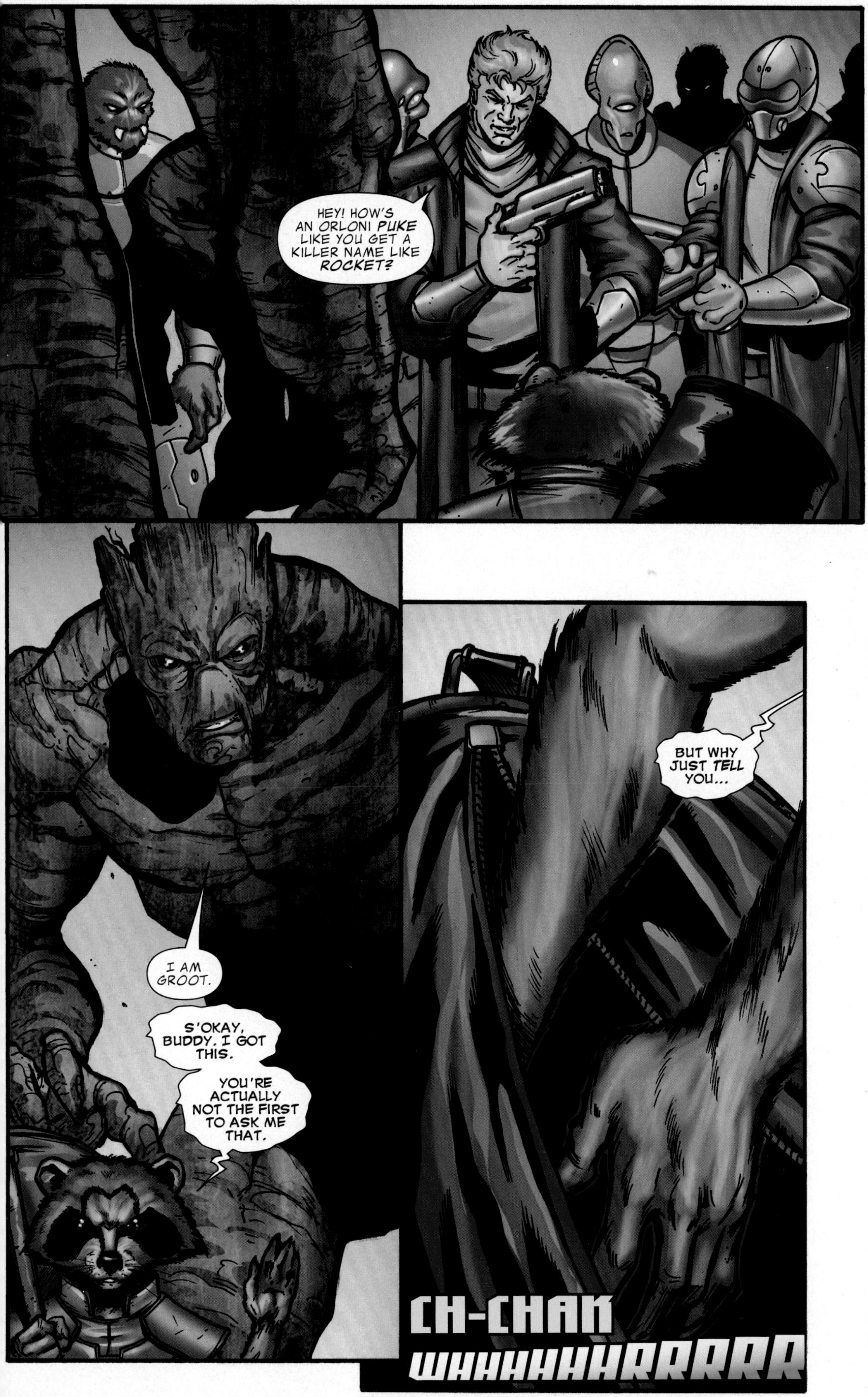
HEY! HOW'S AN ORLONI PUKE LIKE YOU GET A KILLER NAME LIKE ROCKET?
I AM GROOT.
S'OKAY, BUDDY. I GOT THIS.
YOU'RE ACTUALLY NOT THE FIRST TO ASK ME THAT.
BUT WHY JUST TELL YOU...
CH-CHAK
WHHHHHHRRRRR

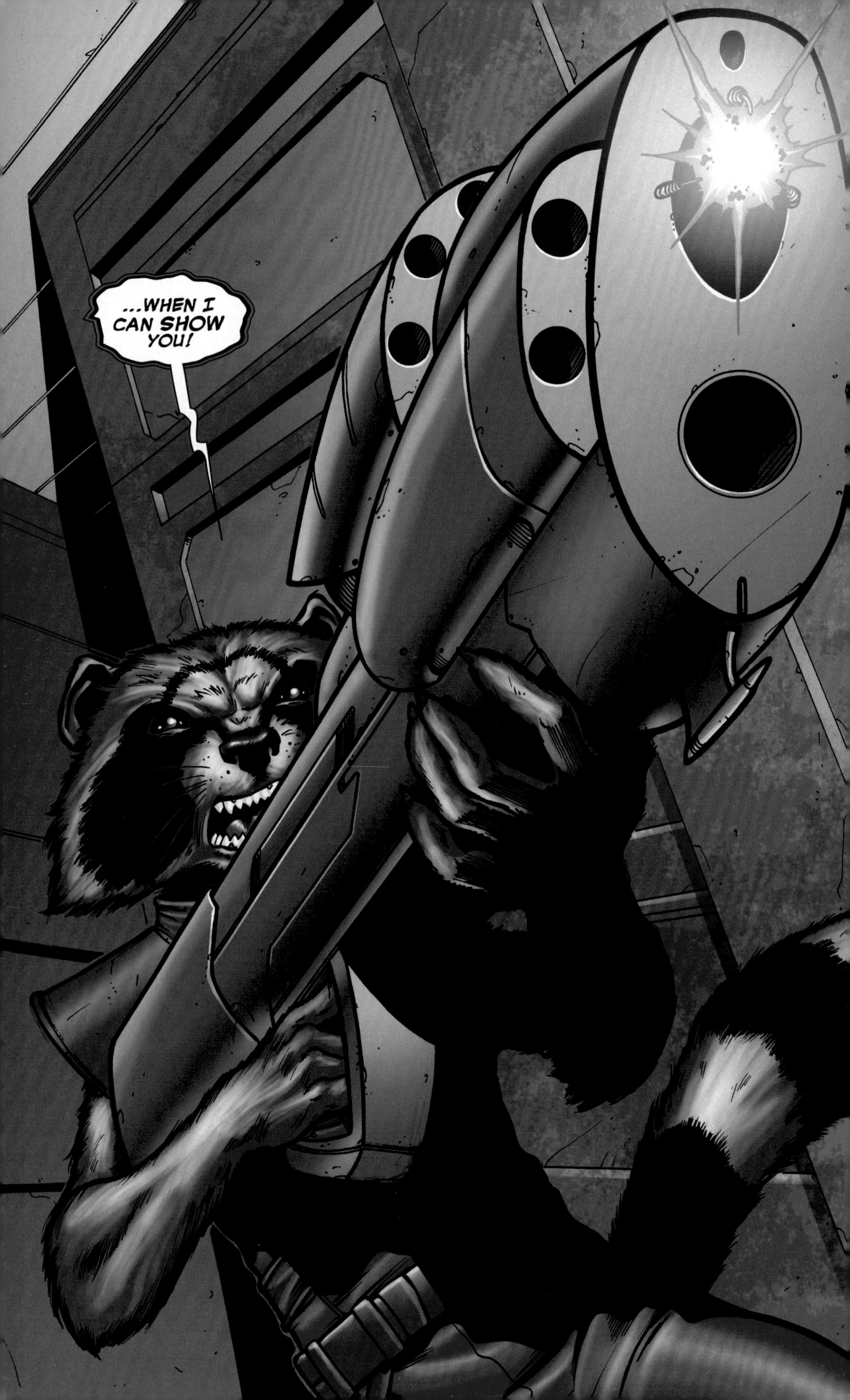
...WHEN I CAN SHOW YOU!

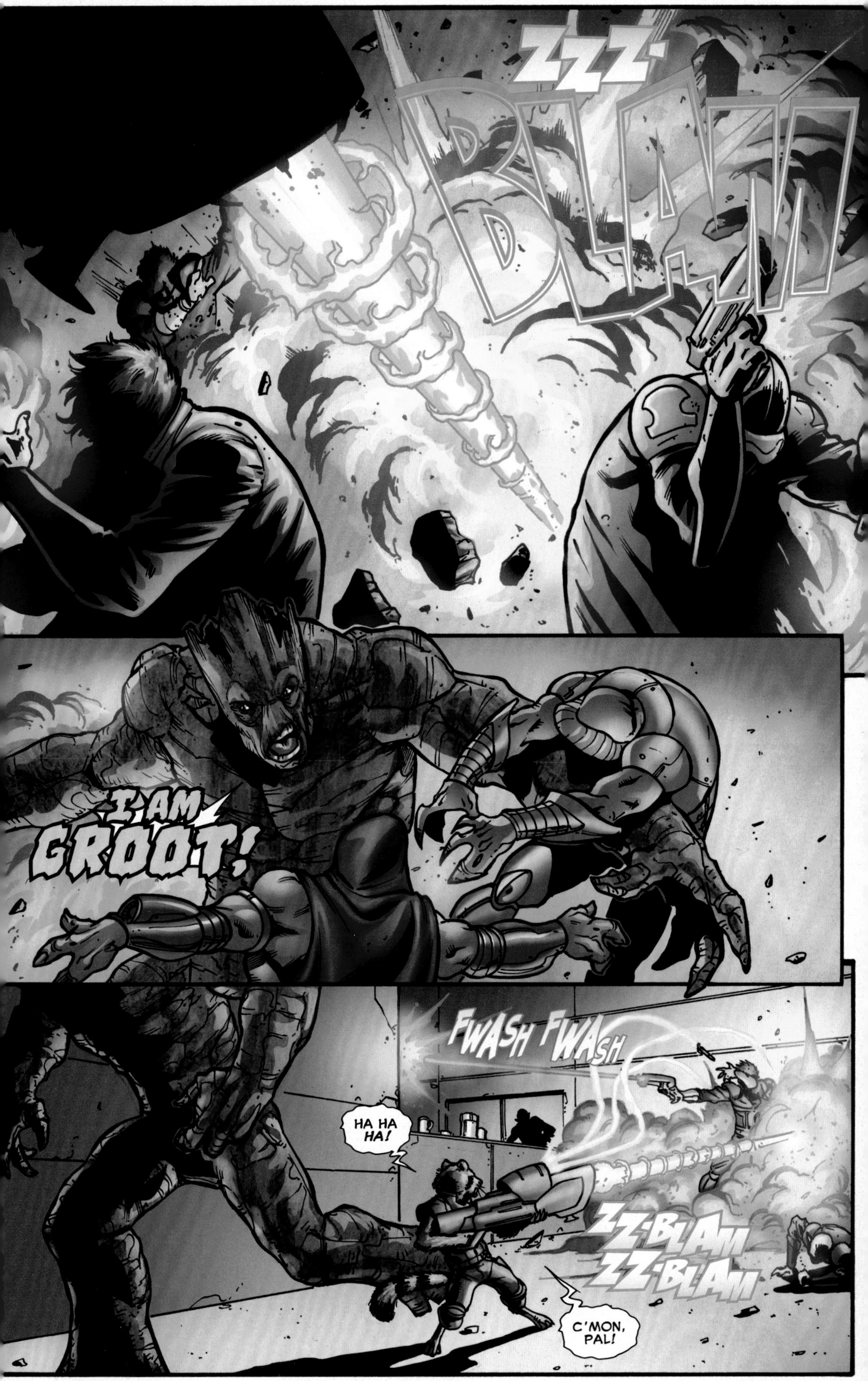
ZZZ-BLAM
I AM GROOT!
FWASH FWASH
HA HA HA!
ZZ-BLAM ZZ-BLAM
C'MON, PAL!

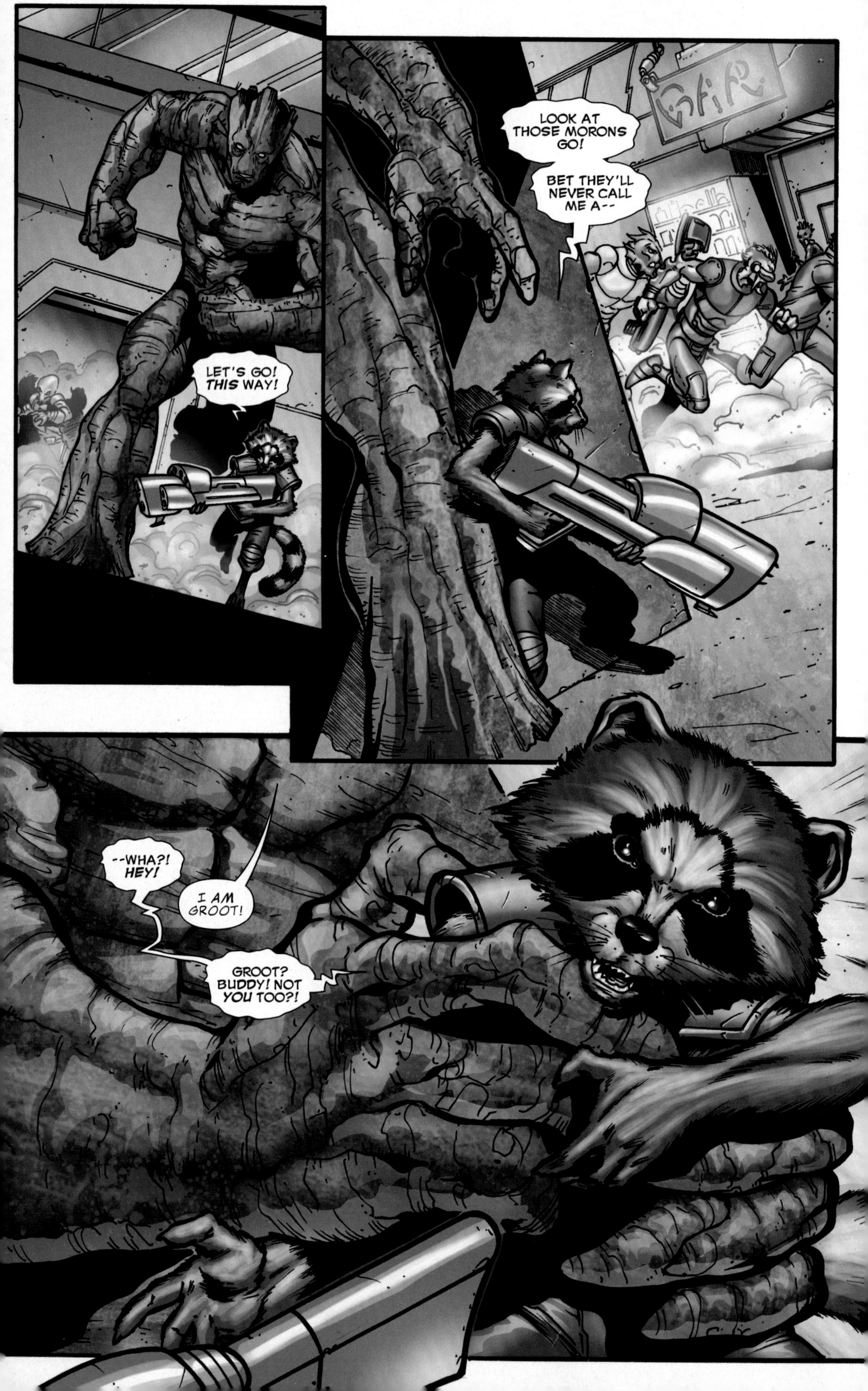
LET'S GO! THIS WAY!
LOOK AT THOSE MORONS GO!
BET THEY'LL NEVER CALL ME A--
--WHA?! HEY!
I AM GROOT!
GROOT? BUDDY! NOT YOU TOO?!

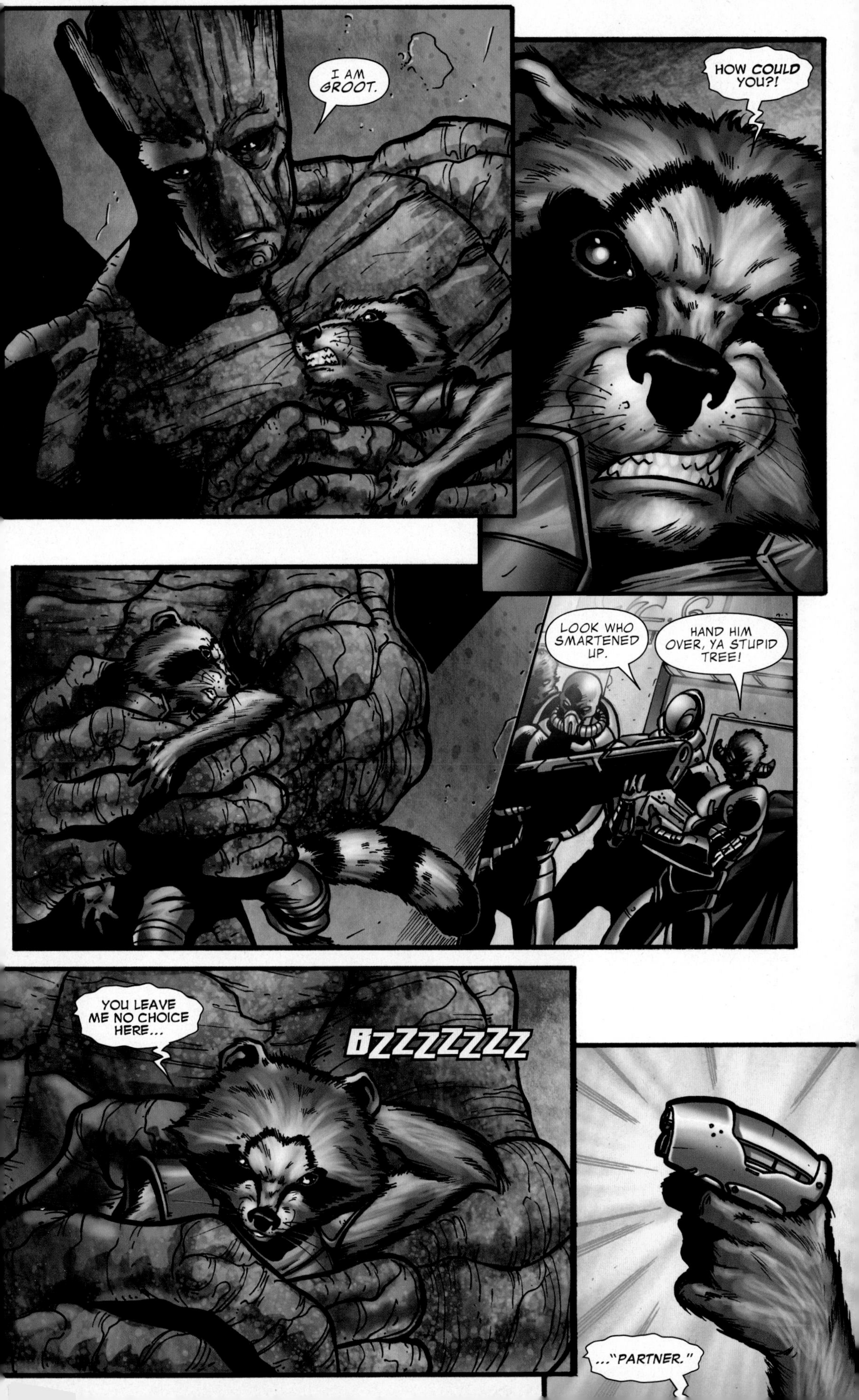
I AM GROOT.
HOW COULD YOU?!
LOOK WHO SMARTENED UP.
HAND HIM OVER, YA STUPID TREE!
YOU LEAVE ME NO CHOICE HERE...
BZZZZZZZ
..."PARTNER."

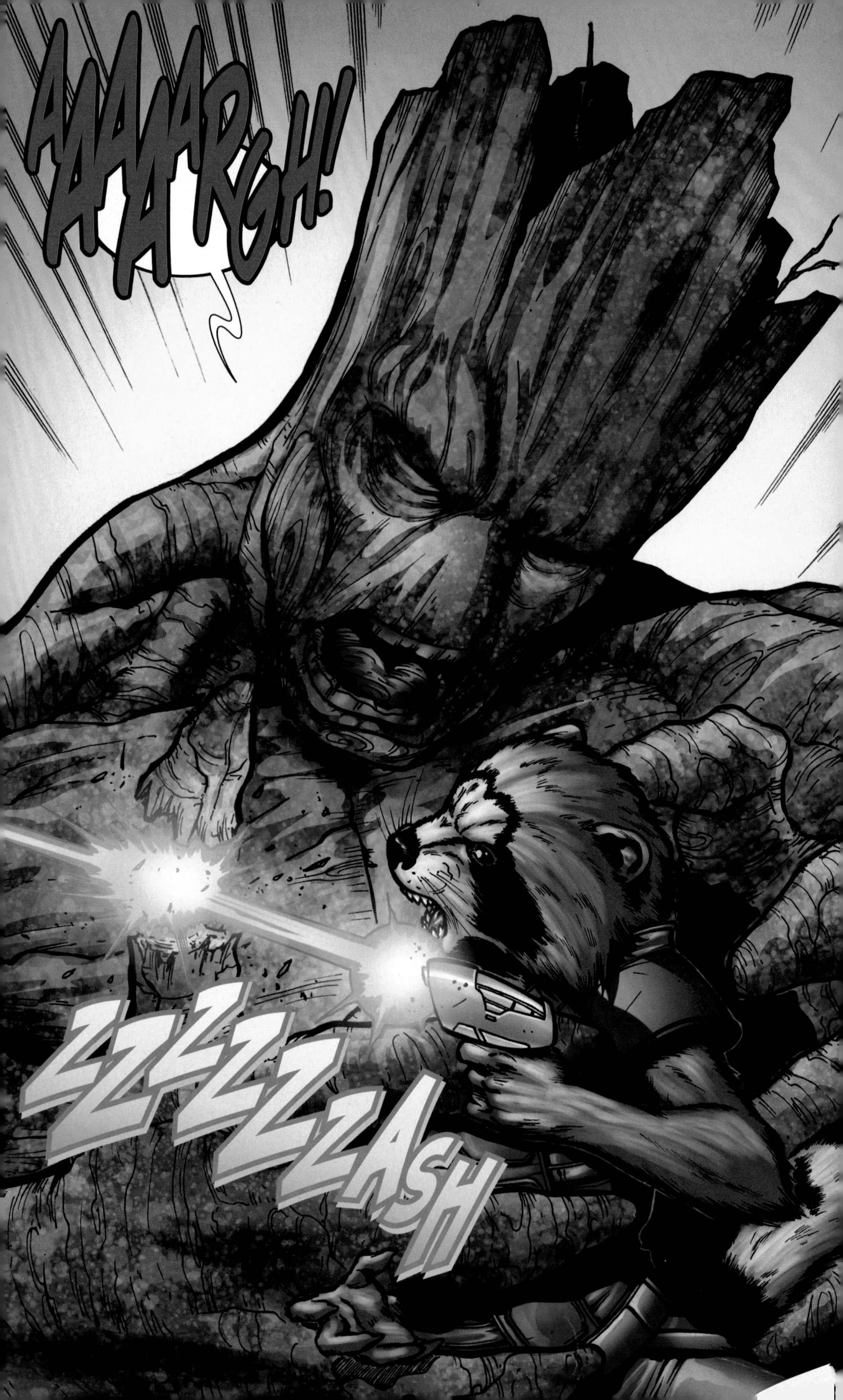
AAAAARGH!
ZZZZZZASH

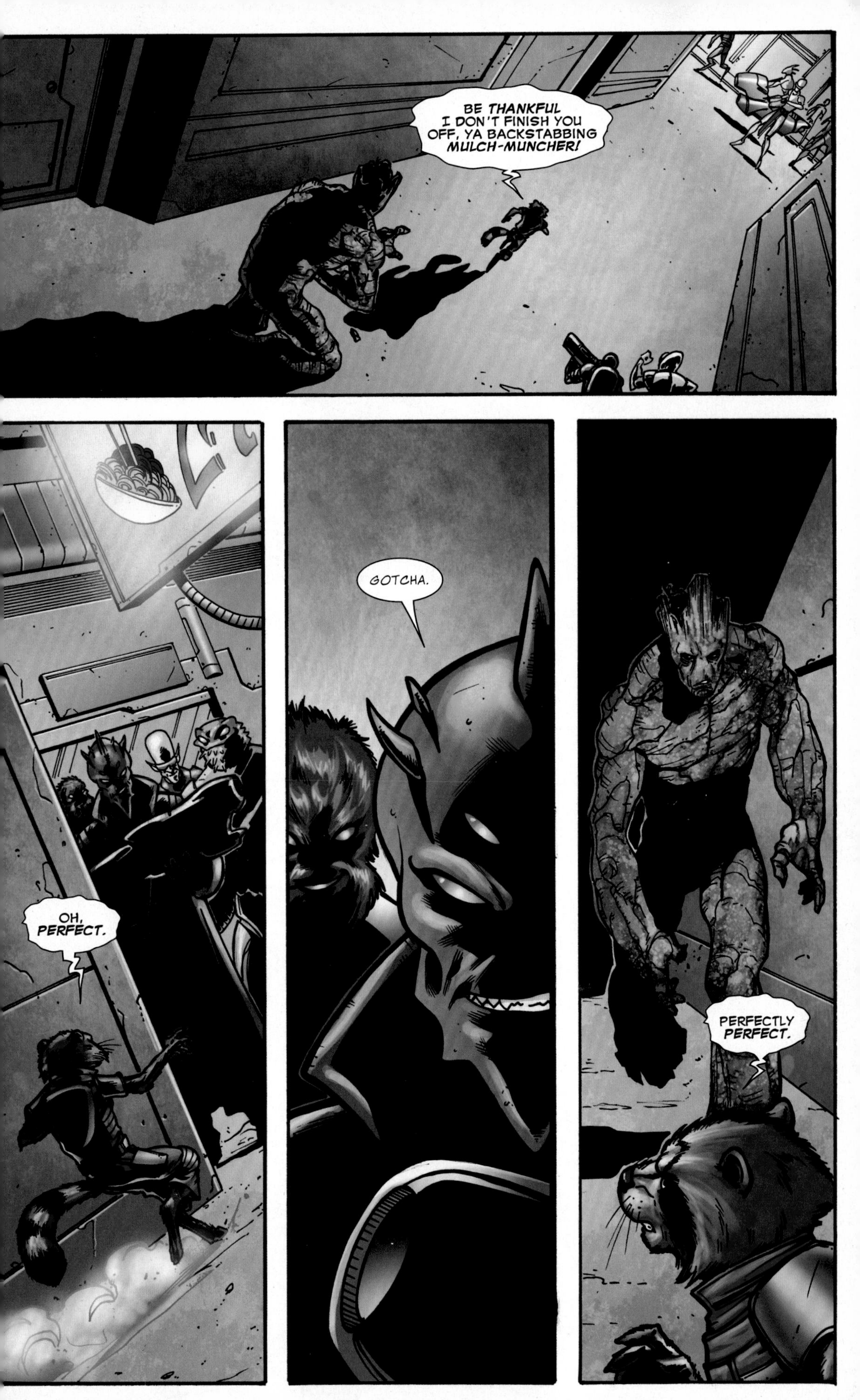
BE THANKFUL I DON'T FINISH YOU OFF, YA BACKSTABBING MULCH-MUNCHER!
OH, PERFECT.
GOTCHA.
PERFECTLY PERFECT.

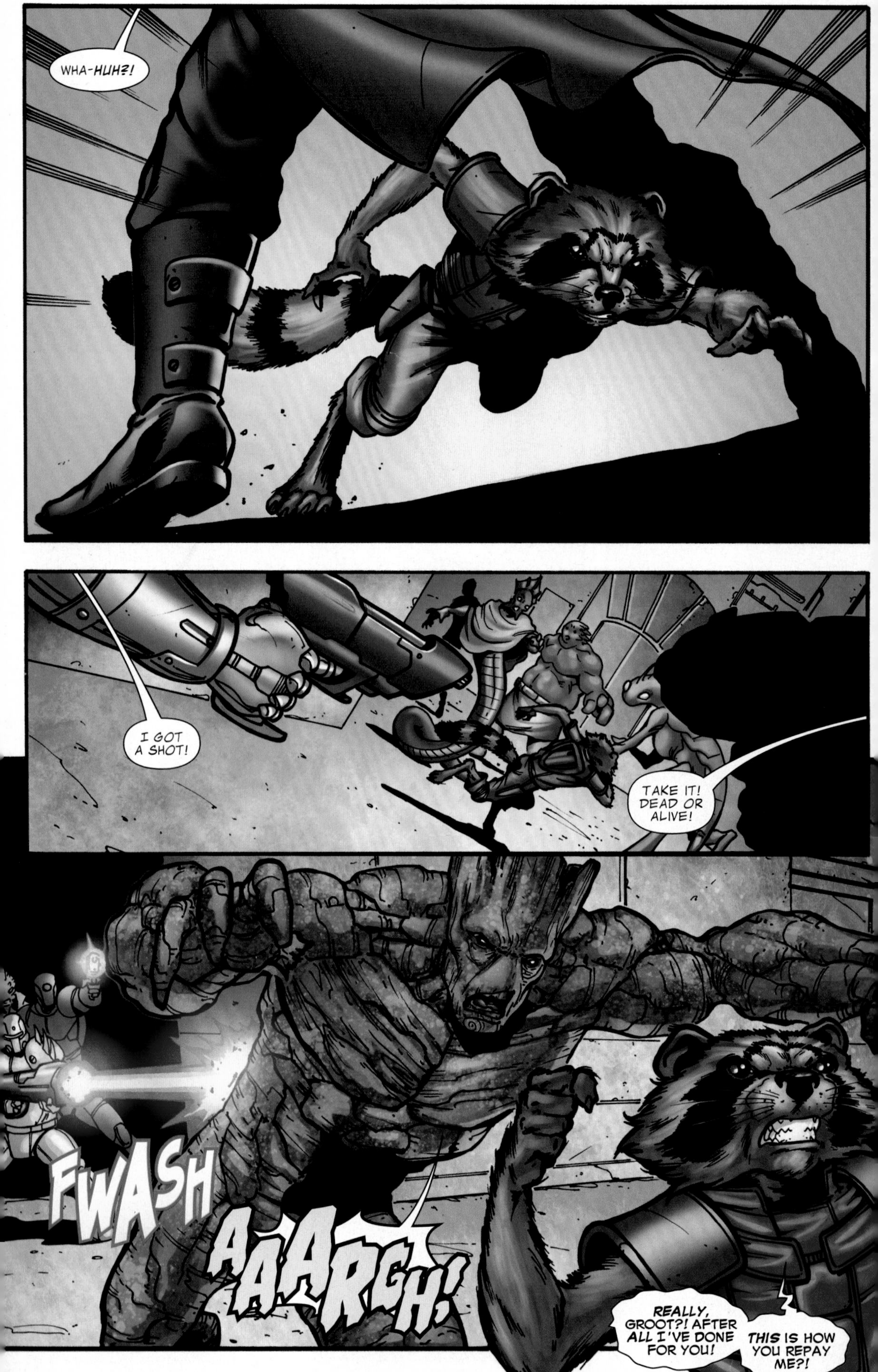

WHA-HUH?!
I GOT A SHOT!
TAKE IT! DEAD OR ALIVE!
FWASH
AAARGH!
REALLY, GROOT?! AFTER ALL I'VE DONE FOR YOU!
THIS IS HOW YOU REPAY ME?!

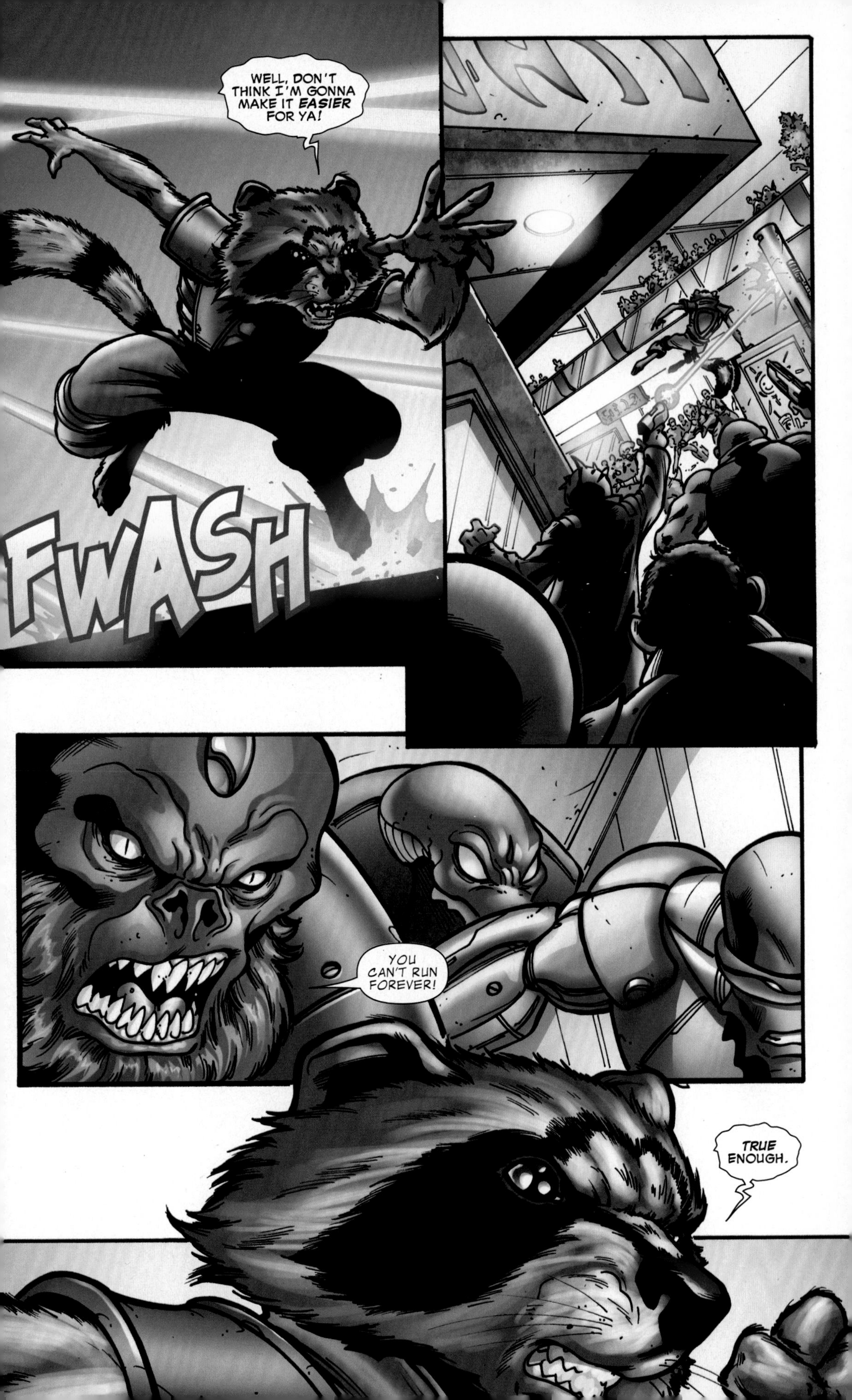
WELL, DON'T THINK I'M GONNA MAKE IT *EASIER* FOR YA!
FWASH
YOU CAN'T RUN FOREVER!
TRUE ENOUGH.

NOW WE'RE
TALKIN'!

FZZT

C'MON!

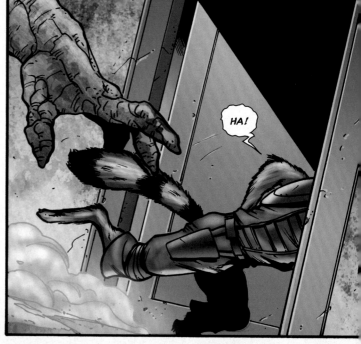

HA!

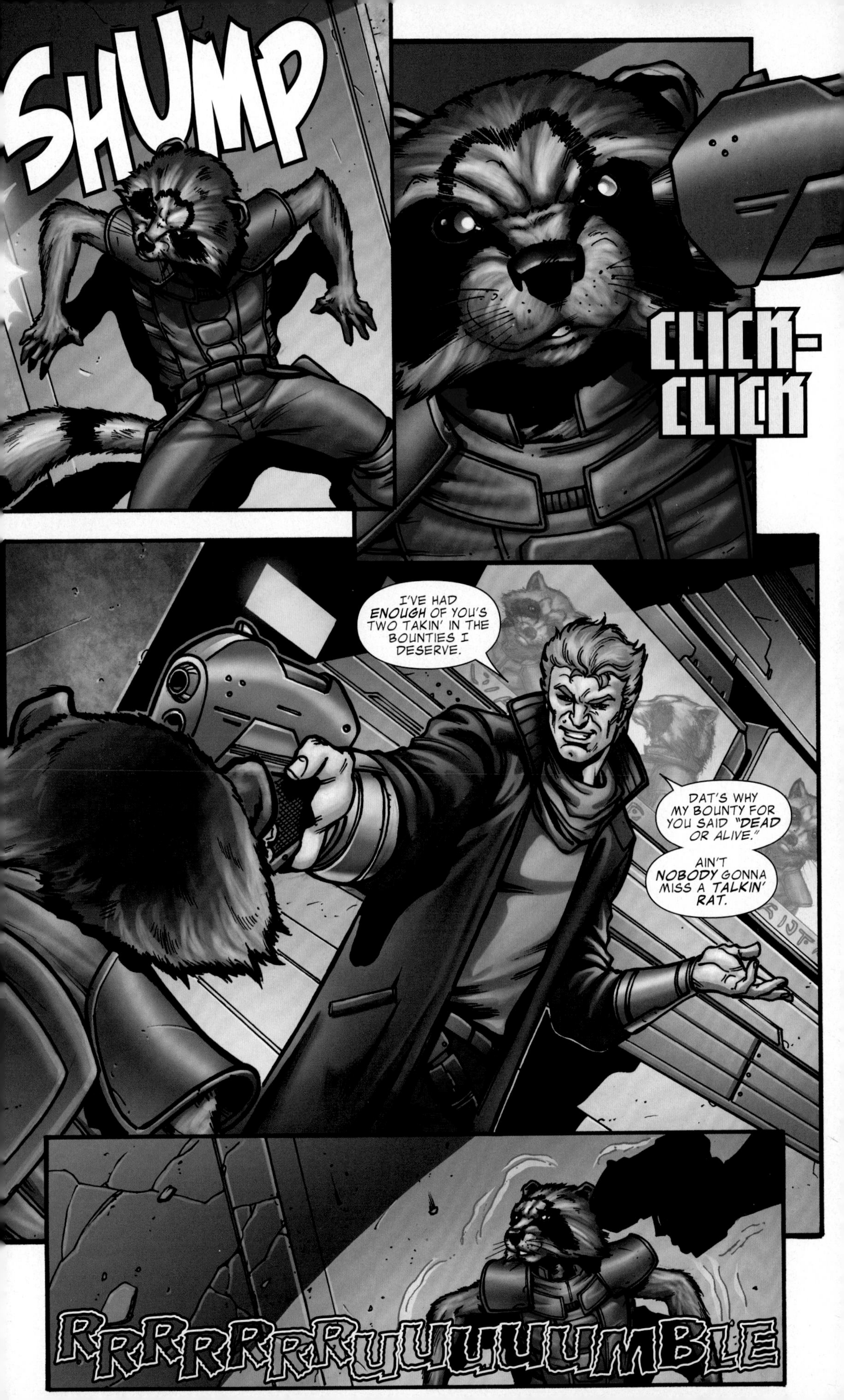
SHUMP
CLICK-CLICK
I'VE HAD ENOUGH OF YOU'S TWO TAKIN' IN THE BOUNTIES I DESERVE.
DAT'S WHY MY BOUNTY FOR YOU SAID "DEAD OR ALIVE."
AIN'T NOBODY GONNA MISS A TALKIN' RAT.
RRRRRRRRUUUUUUMBLE

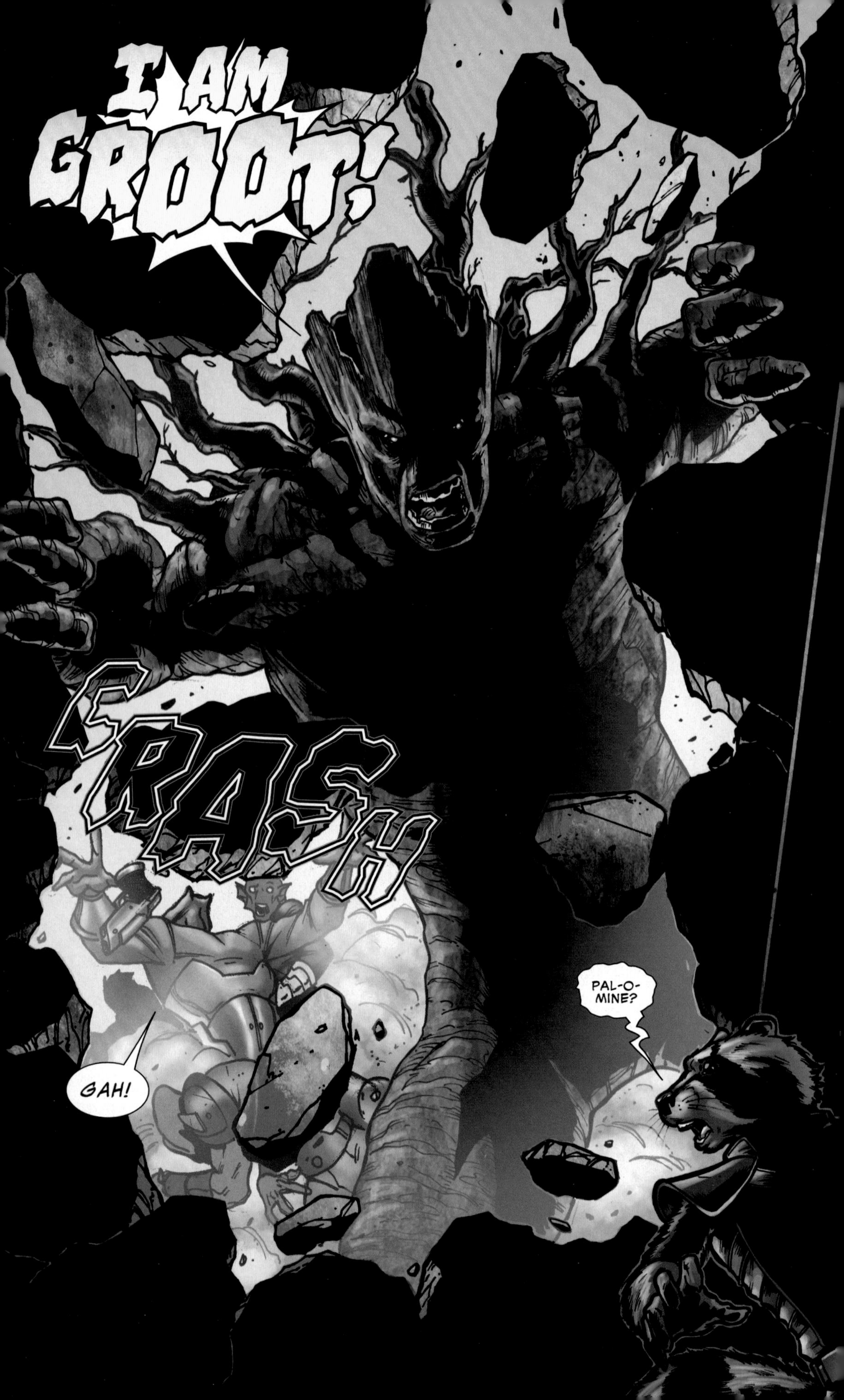
I AM GROOT!
CRASH
GAH!
PAL-O-MINE?

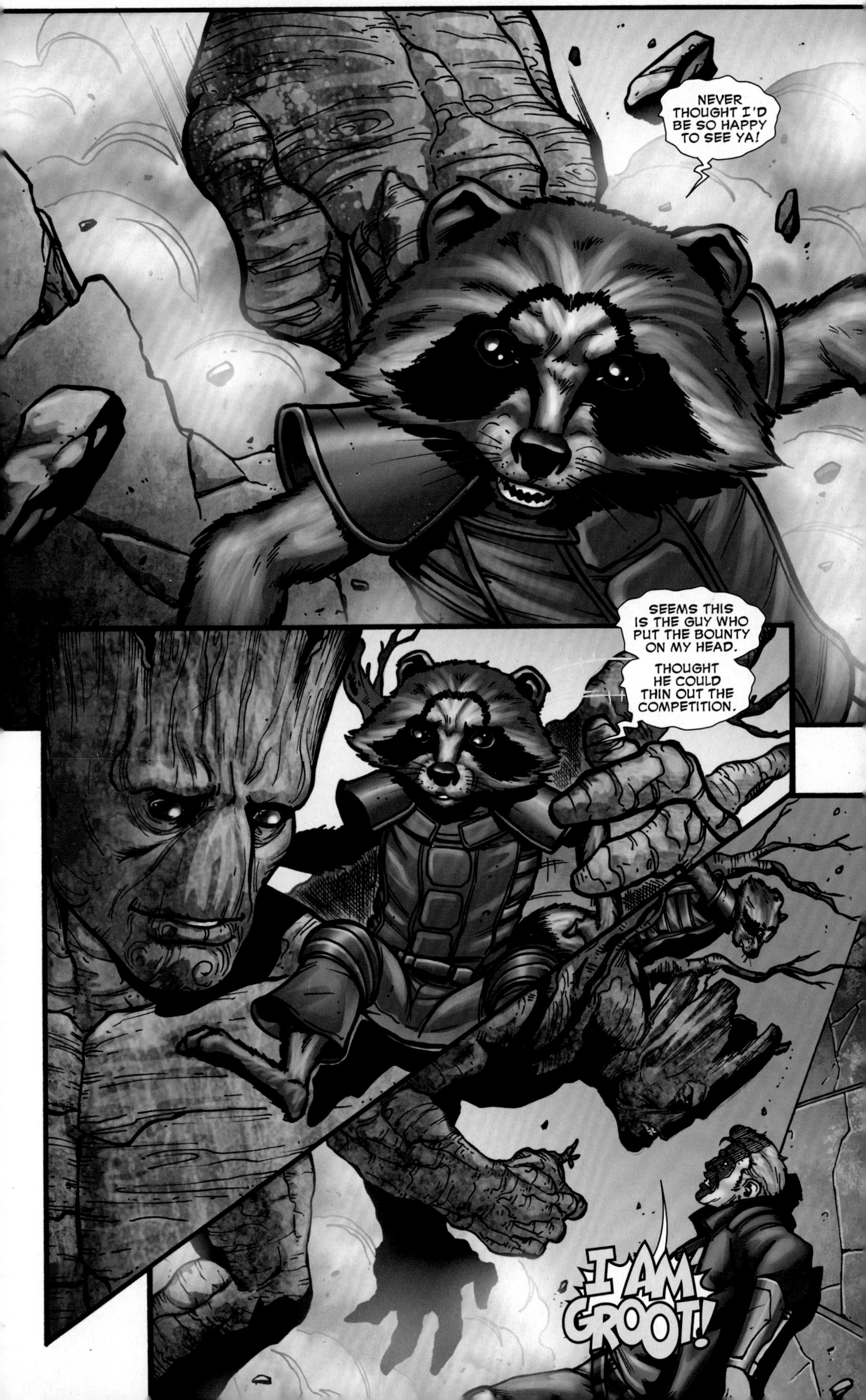
NEVER THOUGHT I'D BE SO HAPPY TO SEE YA!
SEEMS THIS IS THE GUY WHO PUT THE BOUNTY ON MY HEAD.
THOUGHT HE COULD THIN OUT THE COMPETITION.
I AM GROOT!

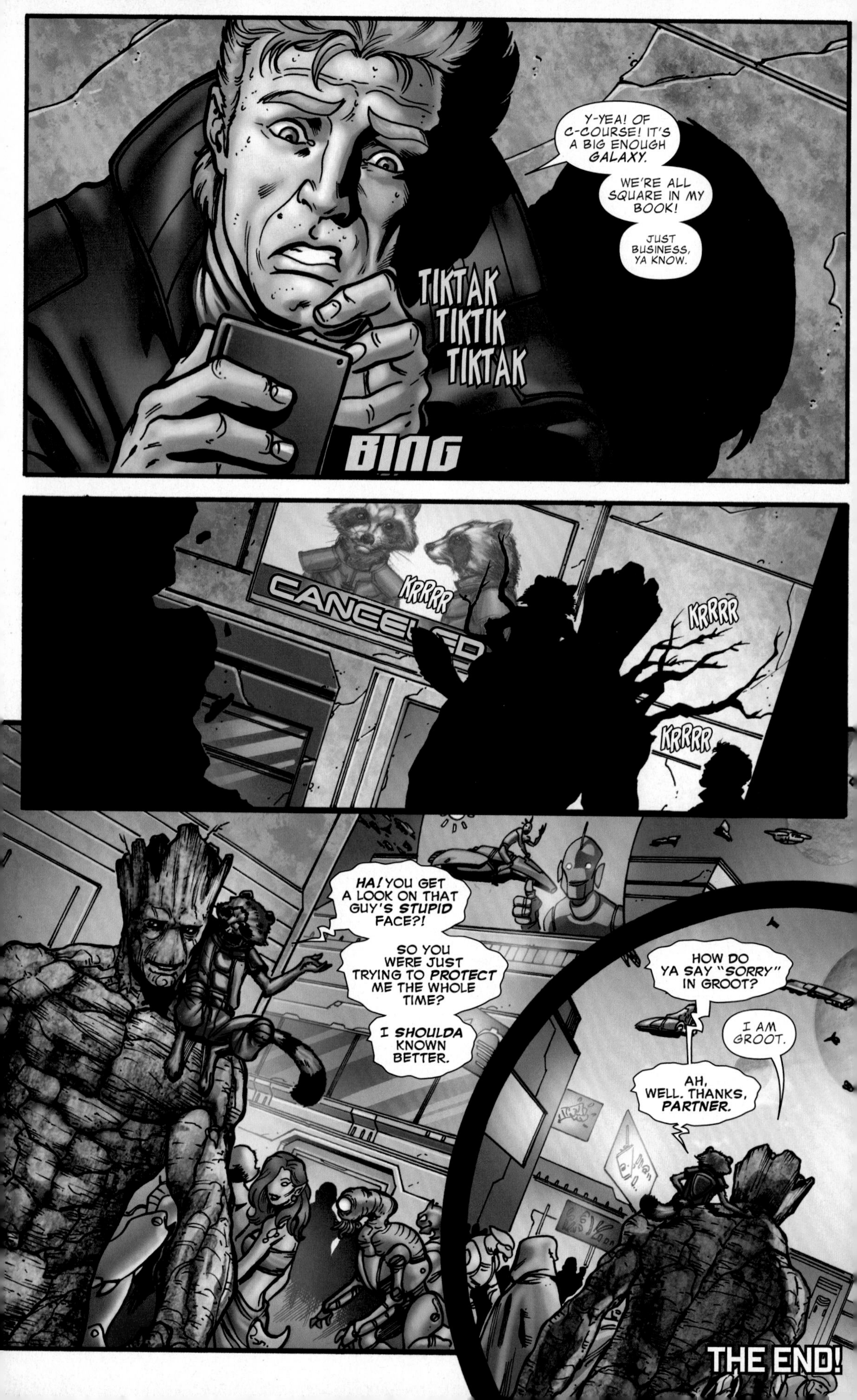
Y-YEA! OF C-COURSE! IT'S A BIG ENOUGH GALAXY.
WE'RE ALL SQUARE IN MY BOOK!
JUST BUSINESS, YA KNOW.
TIKTAK TIKTIK TIKTAK
BING
CANCELED
KRRRR
KRRRR
KRRRR
HA! YOU GET A LOOK ON THAT GUY'S STUPID FACE?!
SO YOU WERE JUST TRYING TO PROTECT ME THE WHOLE TIME?
I SHOULDA KNOWN BETTER.
HOW DO YA SAY "SORRY" IN GROOT?
I AM GROOT.
AH, WELL. THANKS, PARTNER.
THE END!

MARVEL® COMICS GROUP
50¢
314
DEC
02450
BEGINNING SEPT. 12th ON NBC
SPIDER-MAN
AND HIS AMAZING FRIENDS!
APPROVED BY THE COMICS CODE AUTHORITY
THE MIGHTY THOR™
©1981 MARVEL COMICS GROUP
I BEG YOU, THUNDER GOD, DESTROY ME--BEFORE IT'S TOO LATE!!
pollard
DEATH DAY OF DRAX THE DESTROYER!
(ALSO FEATURING THE MYSTERIOUS WOMAN CALLED MOON DRAGON!)

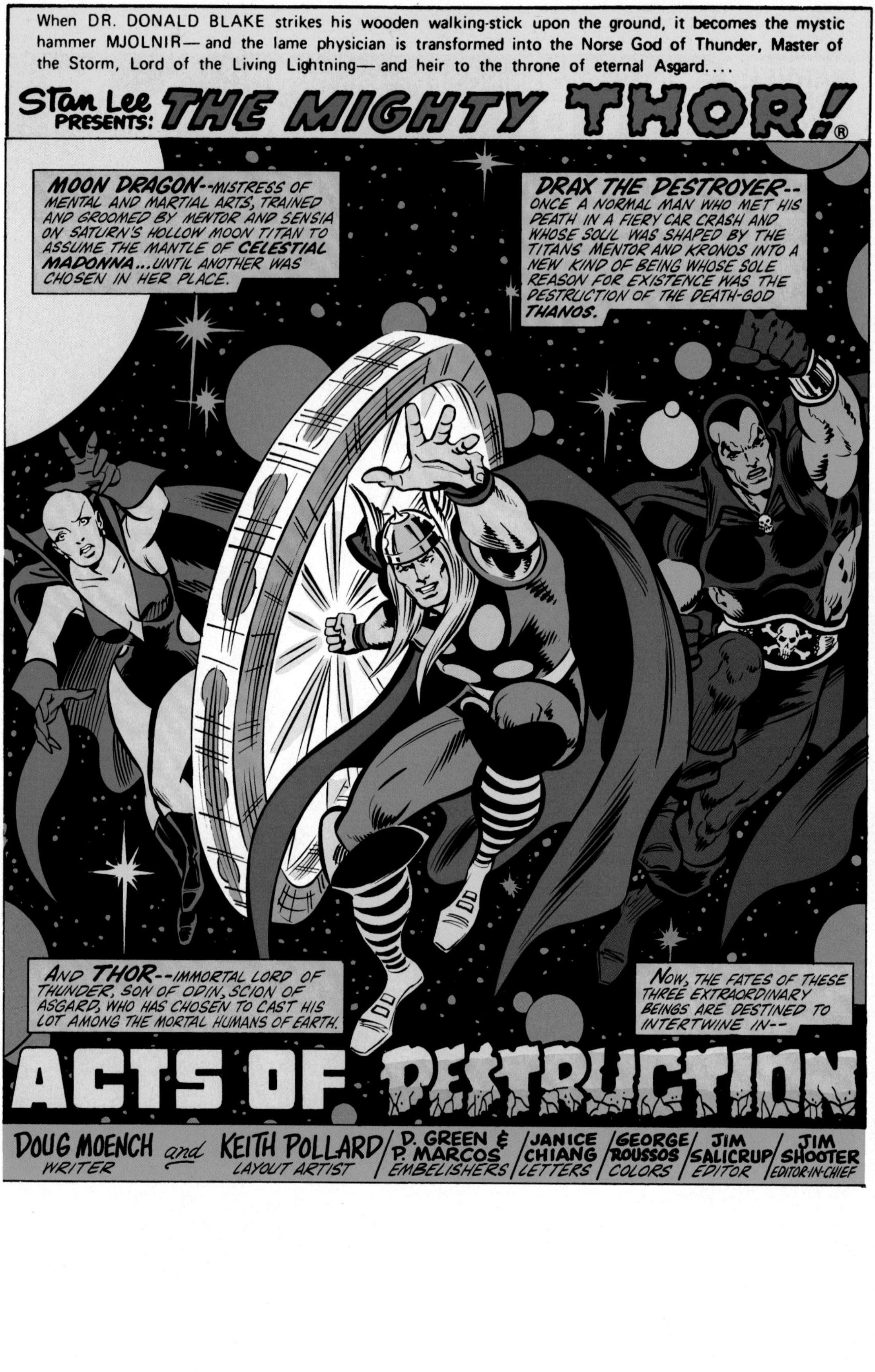
When DR. DONALD BLAKE strikes his wooden walking-stick upon the ground, it becomes the mystic hammer MJOLNIR— and the lame physician is transformed into the Norse God of Thunder, Master of the Storm, Lord of the Living Lightning— and heir to the throne of eternal Asgard....
STAN LEE PRESENTS: THE MIGHTY THOR!®
MOON DRAGON--MISTRESS OF MENTAL AND MARTIAL ARTS, TRAINED AND GROOMED BY MENTOR AND SENSIA ON SATURN'S HOLLOW MOON TITAN TO ASSUME THE MANTLE OF CELESTIAL MADONNA...UNTIL ANOTHER WAS CHOSEN IN HER PLACE.
DRAX THE DESTROYER--ONCE A NORMAL MAN WHO MET HIS DEATH IN A FIERY CAR CRASH AND WHOSE SOUL WAS SHAPED BY THE TITANS MENTOR AND KRONOS INTO A NEW KIND OF BEING WHOSE SOLE REASON FOR EXISTENCE WAS THE DESTRUCTION OF THE DEATH-GOD THANOS.
AND THOR--IMMORTAL LORD OF THUNDER, SON OF ODIN, SCION OF ASGARD, WHO HAS CHOSEN TO CAST HIS LOT AMONG THE MORTAL HUMANS OF EARTH.
NOW, THE FATES OF THESE THREE EXTRAORDINARY BEINGS ARE DESTINED TO INTERTWINE IN--
ACTS OF DESTRUCTION
DOUG MOENCH WRITER and KEITH POLLARD LAYOUT ARTIST / D. GREEN & P. MARCOS EMBELISHERS / JANICE CHIANG LETTERS / GEORGE ROUSSOS COLORS / JIM SALICRUP EDITOR / JIM SHOOTER EDITOR-IN-CHIEF

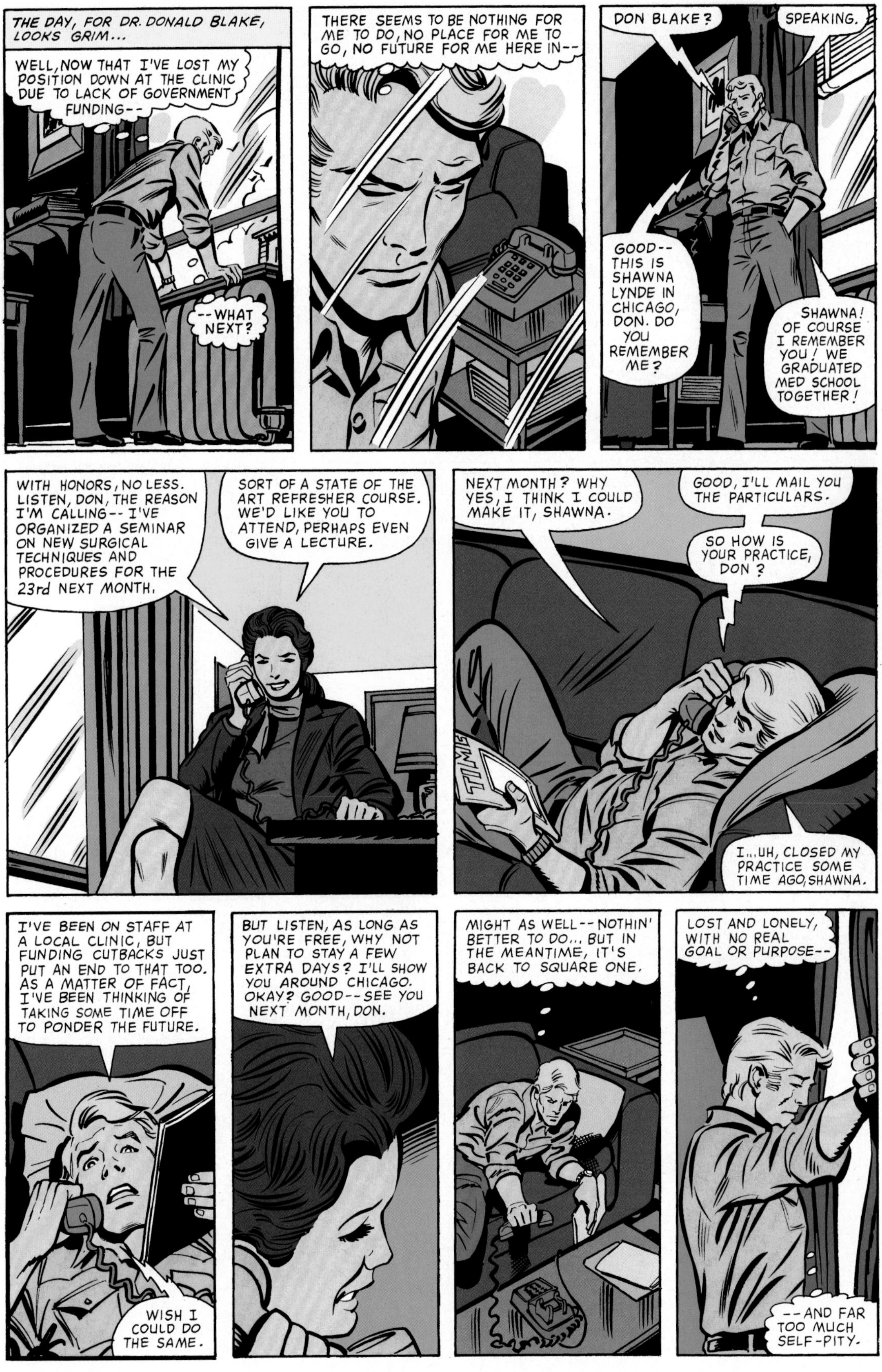
THE DAY, FOR DR. DONALD BLAKE, LOOKS GRIM...
WELL, NOW THAT I'VE LOST MY POSITION DOWN AT THE CLINIC DUE TO LACK OF GOVERNMENT FUNDING--
--WHAT NEXT?
THERE SEEMS TO BE NOTHING FOR ME TO DO, NO PLACE FOR ME TO GO, NO FUTURE FOR ME HERE IN--
DON BLAKE?
SPEAKING.
GOOD-- THIS IS SHAWNA LYNDE IN CHICAGO, DON. DO YOU REMEMBER ME?
SHAWNA! OF COURSE I REMEMBER YOU! WE GRADUATED MED SCHOOL TOGETHER!
WITH HONORS, NO LESS. LISTEN, DON, THE REASON I'M CALLING-- I'VE ORGANIZED A SEMINAR ON NEW SURGICAL TECHNIQUES AND PROCEDURES FOR THE 23rd NEXT MONTH.
SORT OF A STATE OF THE ART REFRESHER COURSE. WE'D LIKE YOU TO ATTEND, PERHAPS EVEN GIVE A LECTURE.
NEXT MONTH? WHY YES, I THINK I COULD MAKE IT, SHAWNA.
GOOD, I'LL MAIL YOU THE PARTICULARS.
SO HOW IS YOUR PRACTICE, DON?
TIME
I...UH, CLOSED MY PRACTICE SOME TIME AGO, SHAWNA.
I'VE BEEN ON STAFF AT A LOCAL CLINIC, BUT FUNDING CUTBACKS JUST PUT AN END TO THAT TOO. AS A MATTER OF FACT, I'VE BEEN THINKING OF TAKING SOME TIME OFF TO PONDER THE FUTURE.
WISH I COULD DO THE SAME.
BUT LISTEN, AS LONG AS YOU'RE FREE, WHY NOT PLAN TO STAY A FEW EXTRA DAYS? I'LL SHOW YOU AROUND CHICAGO. OKAY? GOOD-- SEE YOU NEXT MONTH, DON.
MIGHT AS WELL-- NOTHIN' BETTER TO DO... BUT IN THE MEANTIME, IT'S BACK TO SQUARE ONE.
LOST AND LONELY, WITH NO REAL GOAL OR PURPOSE--
--AND FAR TOO MUCH SELF-PITY.

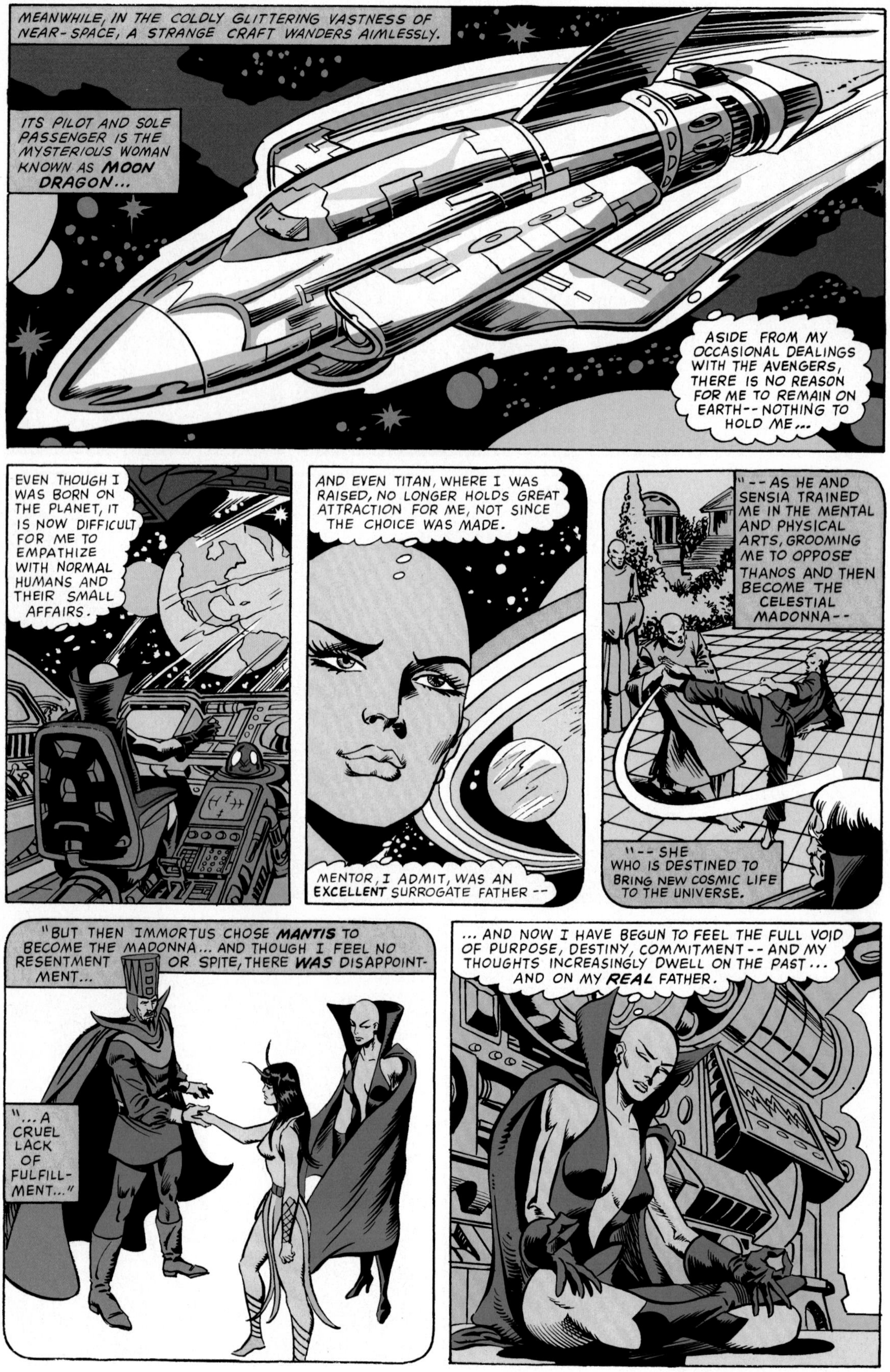
MEANWHILE, IN THE COLDLY GLITTERING VASTNESS OF NEAR-SPACE, A STRANGE CRAFT WANDERS AIMLESSLY.
ITS PILOT AND SOLE PASSENGER IS THE MYSTERIOUS WOMAN KNOWN AS MOON DRAGON...
ASIDE FROM MY OCCASIONAL DEALINGS WITH THE AVENGERS, THERE IS NO REASON FOR ME TO REMAIN ON EARTH--NOTHING TO HOLD ME...
EVEN THOUGH I WAS BORN ON THE PLANET, IT IS NOW DIFFICULT FOR ME TO EMPATHIZE WITH NORMAL HUMANS AND THEIR SMALL AFFAIRS.
AND EVEN TITAN, WHERE I WAS RAISED, NO LONGER HOLDS GREAT ATTRACTION FOR ME, NOT SINCE THE CHOICE WAS MADE.
MENTOR, I ADMIT, WAS AN EXCELLENT SURROGATE FATHER--
"--AS HE AND SENSIA TRAINED ME IN THE MENTAL AND PHYSICAL ARTS, GROOMING ME TO OPPOSE THANOS AND THEN BECOME THE CELESTIAL MADONNA--
"--SHE WHO IS DESTINED TO BRING NEW COSMIC LIFE TO THE UNIVERSE.
"BUT THEN IMMORTUS CHOSE MANTIS TO BECOME THE MADONNA... AND THOUGH I FEEL NO RESENTMENT OR SPITE, THERE WAS DISAPPOINT-MENT...
"...A CRUEL LACK OF FULFILL-MENT..."
...AND NOW I HAVE BEGUN TO FEEL THE FULL VOID OF PURPOSE, DESTINY, COMMITMENT--AND MY THOUGHTS INCREASINGLY DWELL ON THE PAST... AND ON MY REAL FATHER.

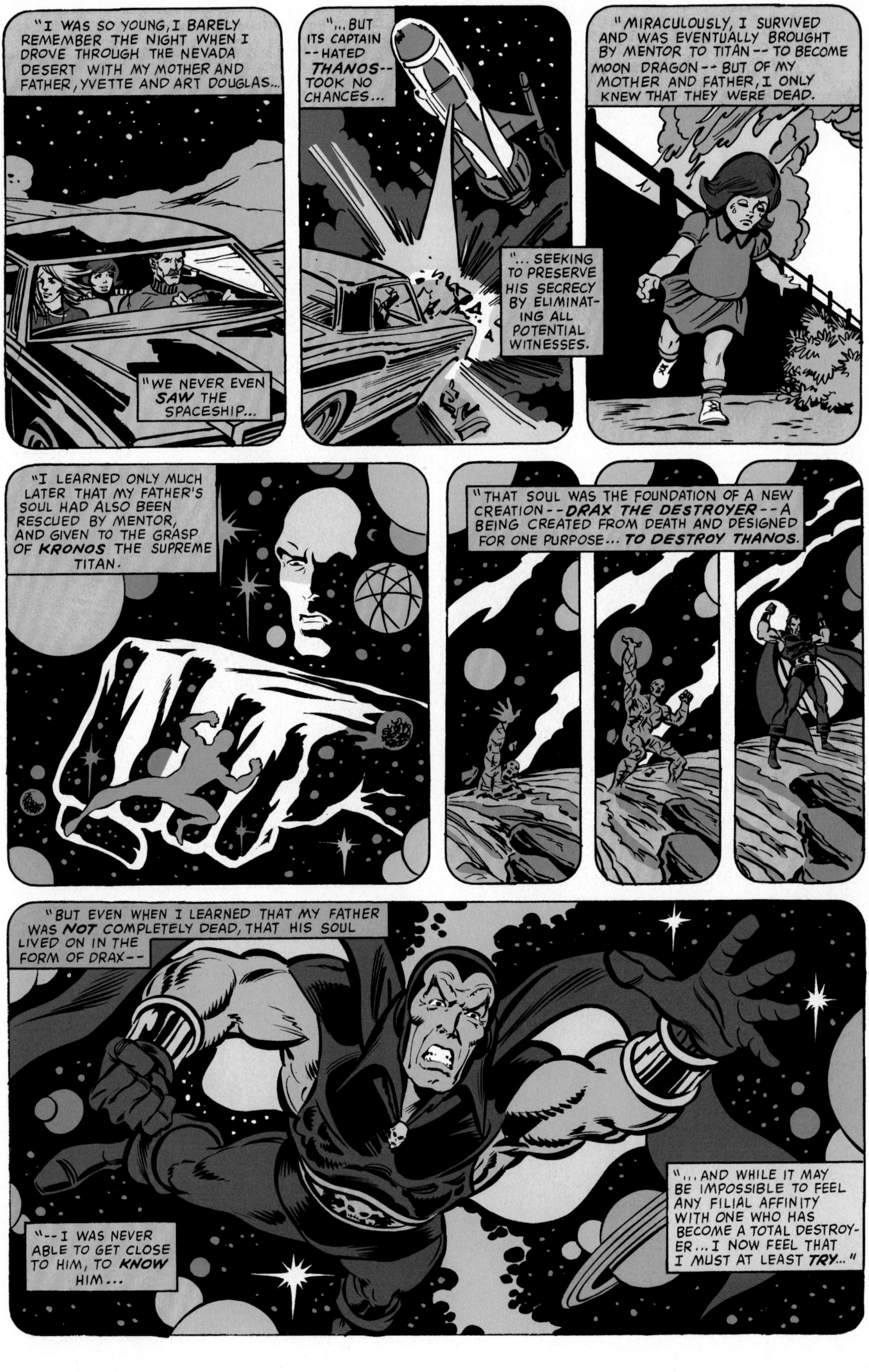
"I WAS SO YOUNG, I BARELY REMEMBER THE NIGHT WHEN I DROVE THROUGH THE NEVADA DESERT WITH MY MOTHER AND FATHER, YVETTE AND ART DOUGLAS...
"WE NEVER EVEN SAW THE SPACESHIP...
"...BUT ITS CAPTAIN --HATED THANOS-- TOOK NO CHANCES...
"... SEEKING TO PRESERVE HIS SECRECY BY ELIMINATING ALL POTENTIAL WITNESSES.
"MIRACULOUSLY, I SURVIVED AND WAS EVENTUALLY BROUGHT BY MENTOR TO TITAN -- TO BECOME MOON DRAGON -- BUT OF MY MOTHER AND FATHER, I ONLY KNEW THAT THEY WERE DEAD.
"I LEARNED ONLY MUCH LATER THAT MY FATHER'S SOUL HAD ALSO BEEN RESCUED BY MENTOR, AND GIVEN TO THE GRASP OF KRONOS THE SUPREME TITAN.
"THAT SOUL WAS THE FOUNDATION OF A NEW CREATION -- DRAX THE DESTROYER -- A BEING CREATED FROM DEATH AND DESIGNED FOR ONE PURPOSE... TO DESTROY THANOS.
"BUT EVEN WHEN I LEARNED THAT MY FATHER WAS NOT COMPLETELY DEAD, THAT HIS SOUL LIVED ON IN THE FORM OF DRAX--
"-- I WAS NEVER ABLE TO GET CLOSE TO HIM, TO KNOW HIM...
"...AND WHILE IT MAY BE IMPOSSIBLE TO FEEL ANY FILIAL AFFINITY WITH ONE WHO HAS BECOME A TOTAL DESTROYER... I NOW FEEL THAT I MUST AT LEAST TRY..."

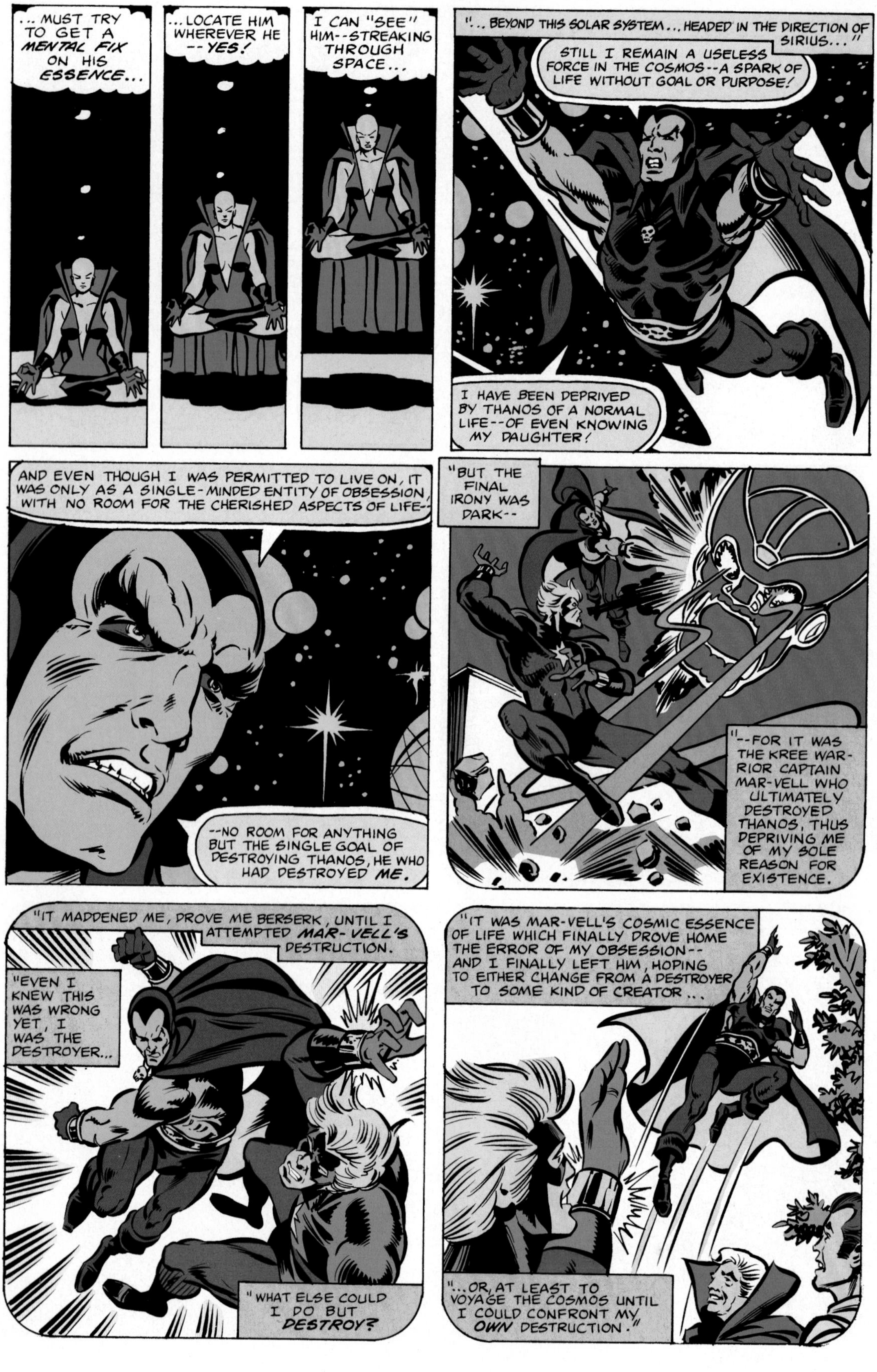
...MUST TRY TO GET A MENTAL FIX ON HIS ESSENCE...
...LOCATE HIM WHEREVER HE --YES!
I CAN "SEE" HIM--STREAKING THROUGH SPACE...
"...BEYOND THIS SOLAR SYSTEM... HEADED IN THE DIRECTION OF SIRIUS..."
STILL I REMAIN A USELESS FORCE IN THE COSMOS--A SPARK OF LIFE WITHOUT GOAL OR PURPOSE!
I HAVE BEEN DEPRIVED BY THANOS OF A NORMAL LIFE--OF EVEN KNOWING MY DAUGHTER!
AND EVEN THOUGH I WAS PERMITTED TO LIVE ON, IT WAS ONLY AS A SINGLE-MINDED ENTITY OF OBSESSION, WITH NO ROOM FOR THE CHERISHED ASPECTS OF LIFE--
--NO ROOM FOR ANYTHING BUT THE SINGLE GOAL OF DESTROYING THANOS, HE WHO HAD DESTROYED ME.
"BUT THE FINAL IRONY WAS DARK--
"--FOR IT WAS THE KREE WARRIOR CAPTAIN MAR-VELL WHO ULTIMATELY DESTROYED THANOS, THUS DEPRIVING ME OF MY SOLE REASON FOR EXISTENCE.
"IT MADDENED ME, DROVE ME BERSERK, UNTIL I ATTEMPTED MAR-VELL'S DESTRUCTION.
"EVEN I KNEW THIS WAS WRONG YET, I WAS THE DESTROYER...
"WHAT ELSE COULD I DO BUT DESTROY?
"IT WAS MAR-VELL'S COSMIC ESSENCE OF LIFE WHICH FINALLY DROVE HOME THE ERROR OF MY OBSESSION-- AND I FINALLY LEFT HIM, HOPING TO EITHER CHANGE FROM A DESTROYER TO SOME KIND OF CREATOR...
"...OR, AT LEAST TO VOYAGE THE COSMOS UNTIL I COULD CONFRONT MY OWN DESTRUCTION."

BUT MY FIRST HOPE WAS IN VAIN. OUT HERE, ALL BEYOND MAR-VELL'S INFLUENCE, I REALIZE THAT THE CONCEPT OF BECOMING A CREATOR IS--FOR ME--A JEST OF HUGE AND DARK PROPORTIONS.

THERE IS NOTHING LEFT FOR ME, THEN, BUT TO SEEK MY OWN DESTRUCTION AND--

--EH? THAT SHIMMERING GLOBE! WHAT MANNER OF--

HALT! COME NO CLOSER --ON PERIL OF YOUR LIFE!

IT...IT'S COMMUNICATING WITH SOME FORM OF TELEPATHY! IT'S... ALIVE!

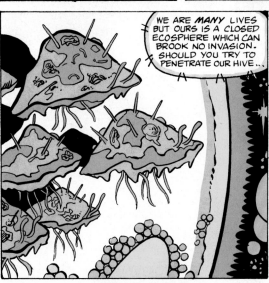

WE ARE MANY LIVES BUT OURS IS A CLOSED ECOSPHERE WHICH CAN BROOK NO INVASION. SHOULD YOU TRY TO PENETRATE OUR HIVE...

YOU WILL BE DESTROYED!

THE CHOICE HAS BEEN MADE.

NO! HALT!

DO NOT TRY TO PENETRATE US!

AND THOUGH THE MANY TELEPATHIC VOICES SCREAM IN UNISON...

--IT IS FAR TOO LATE FOR REASONING WITH THE MIND OF THE DESTROYER.

97

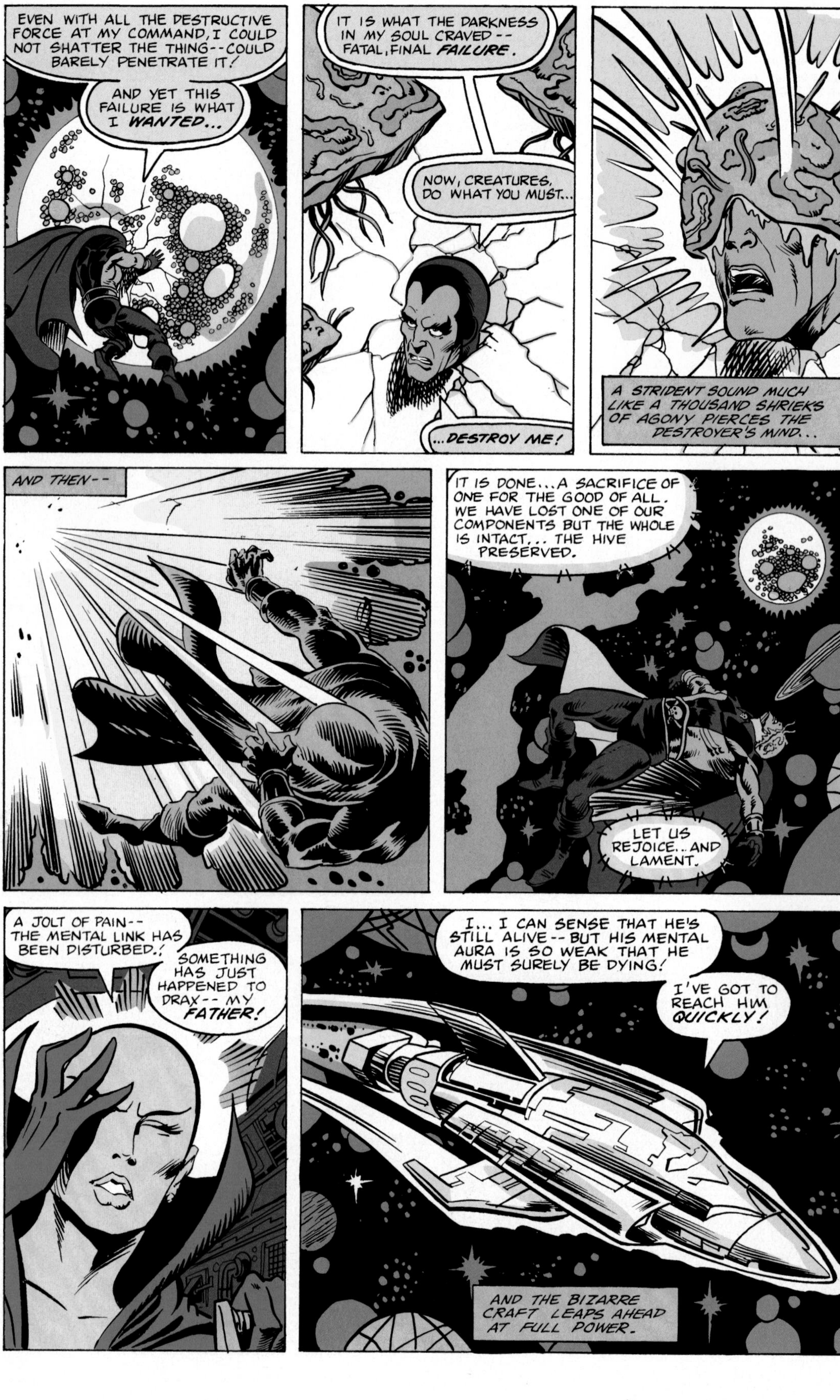
EVEN WITH ALL THE DESTRUCTIVE FORCE AT MY COMMAND, I COULD NOT SHATTER THE THING--COULD BARELY PENETRATE IT!
AND YET THIS FAILURE IS WHAT I WANTED...
IT IS WHAT THE DARKNESS IN MY SOUL CRAVED-- FATAL, FINAL FAILURE.
NOW, CREATURES, DO WHAT YOU MUST...
...DESTROY ME!
A STRIDENT SOUND MUCH LIKE A THOUSAND SHRIEKS OF AGONY PIERCES THE DESTROYER'S MIND...
AND THEN--
IT IS DONE... A SACRIFICE OF ONE FOR THE GOOD OF ALL. WE HAVE LOST ONE OF OUR COMPONENTS BUT THE WHOLE IS INTACT... THE HIVE PRESERVED.
LET US REJOICE... AND LAMENT.
A JOLT OF PAIN-- THE MENTAL LINK HAS BEEN DISTURBED.!
SOMETHING HAS JUST HAPPENED TO DRAX-- MY FATHER!
I... I CAN SENSE THAT HE'S STILL ALIVE-- BUT HIS MENTAL AURA IS SO WEAK THAT HE MUST SURELY BE DYING!
I'VE GOT TO REACH HIM QUICKLY!
AND THE BIZARRE CRAFT LEAPS AHEAD AT FULL POWER.

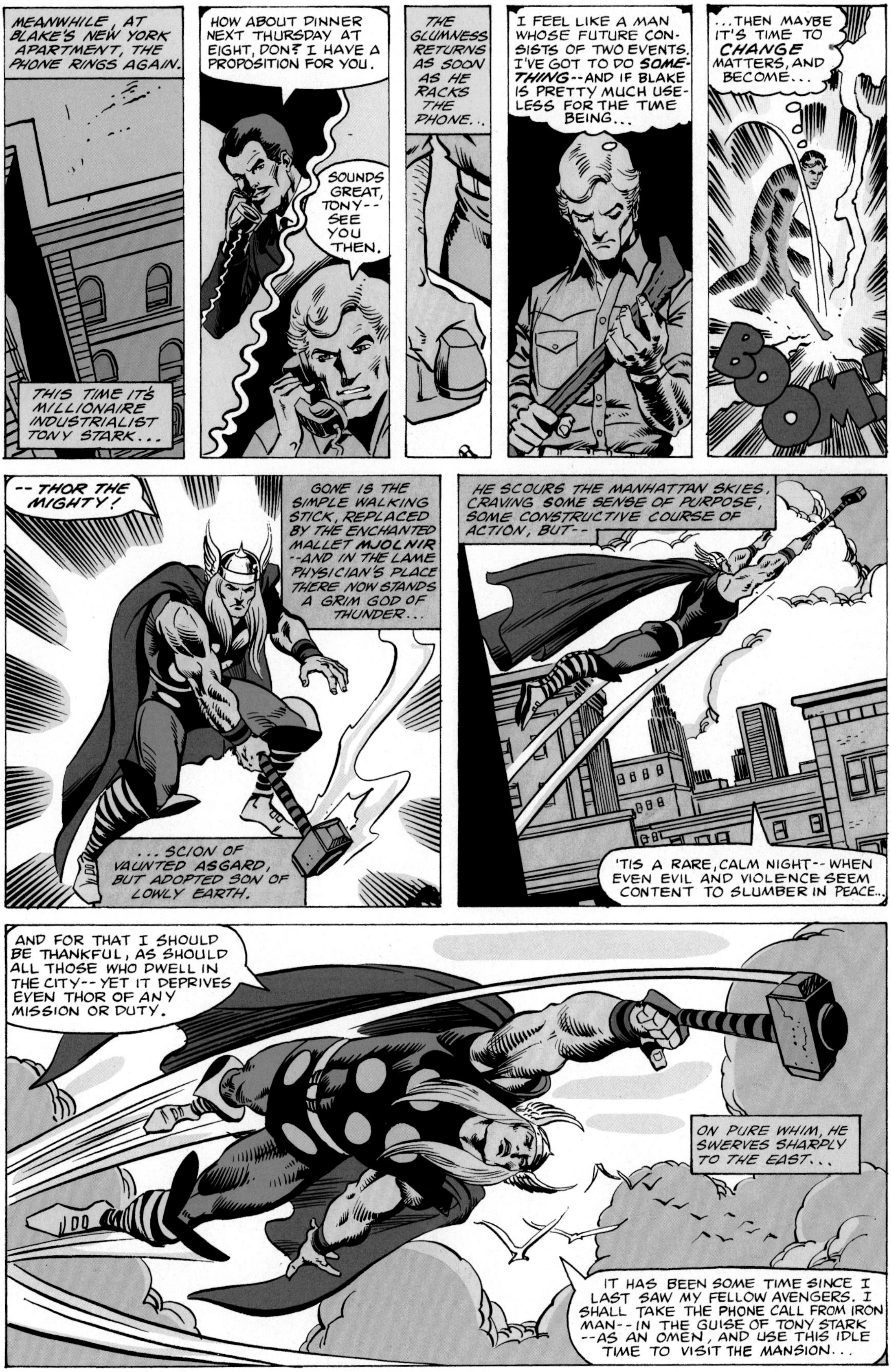
MEANWHILE, AT BLAKE'S NEW YORK APARTMENT, THE PHONE RINGS AGAIN.
THIS TIME IT'S MILLIONAIRE INDUSTRIALIST TONY STARK...
HOW ABOUT DINNER NEXT THURSDAY AT EIGHT, DON? I HAVE A PROPOSITION FOR YOU.
SOUNDS GREAT, TONY-- SEE YOU THEN.
THE GLUMNESS RETURNS AS SOON AS HE RACKS THE PHONE...
I FEEL LIKE A MAN WHOSE FUTURE CONSISTS OF TWO EVENTS. I'VE GOT TO DO SOMETHING--AND IF BLAKE IS PRETTY MUCH USELESS FOR THE TIME BEING...
...THEN MAYBE IT'S TIME TO CHANGE MATTERS, AND BECOME...
BOOM!
--THOR THE MIGHTY!
GONE IS THE SIMPLE WALKING STICK, REPLACED BY THE ENCHANTED MALLET MJOLNIR --AND IN THE LAME PHYSICIAN'S PLACE THERE NOW STANDS A GRIM GOD OF THUNDER...
...SCION OF VAUNTED ASGARD, BUT ADOPTED SON OF LOWLY EARTH.
HE SCOURS THE MANHATTAN SKIES, CRAVING SOME SENSE OF PURPOSE, SOME CONSTRUCTIVE COURSE OF ACTION, BUT--
'TIS A RARE, CALM NIGHT--WHEN EVEN EVIL AND VIOLENCE SEEM CONTENT TO SLUMBER IN PEACE...
AND FOR THAT I SHOULD BE THANKFUL, AS SHOULD ALL THOSE WHO DWELL IN THE CITY--YET IT DEPRIVES EVEN THOR OF ANY MISSION OR DUTY.
ON PURE WHIM, HE SWERVES SHARPLY TO THE EAST...
IT HAS BEEN SOME TIME SINCE I LAST SAW MY FELLOW AVENGERS. I SHALL TAKE THE PHONE CALL FROM IRON MAN--IN THE GUISE OF TONY STARK --AS AN OMEN, AND USE THIS IDLE TIME TO VISIT THE MANSION...

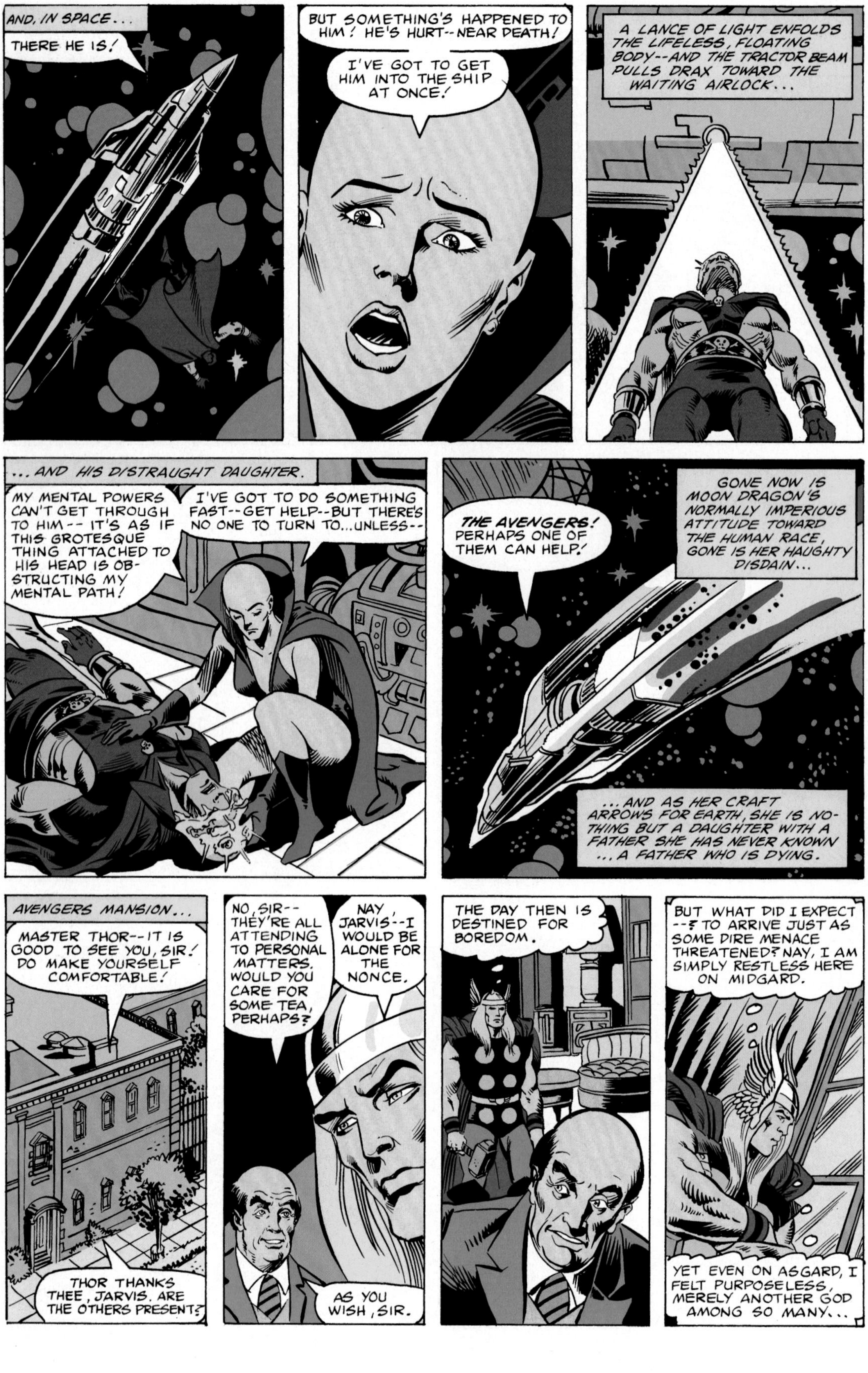
AND, IN SPACE...
THERE HE IS!
BUT SOMETHING'S HAPPENED TO HIM! HE'S HURT--NEAR DEATH!
I'VE GOT TO GET HIM INTO THE SHIP AT ONCE!
A LANCE OF LIGHT ENFOLDS THE LIFELESS, FLOATING BODY--AND THE TRACTOR BEAM PULLS DRAX TOWARD THE WAITING AIRLOCK...
...AND HIS DISTRAUGHT DAUGHTER.
MY MENTAL POWERS CAN'T GET THROUGH TO HIM-- IT'S AS IF THIS GROTESQUE THING ATTACHED TO HIS HEAD IS OBSTRUCTING MY MENTAL PATH!
I'VE GOT TO DO SOMETHING FAST--GET HELP--BUT THERE'S NO ONE TO TURN TO...UNLESS--
THE AVENGERS! PERHAPS ONE OF THEM CAN HELP!
GONE NOW IS MOON DRAGON'S NORMALLY IMPERIOUS ATTITUDE TOWARD THE HUMAN RACE, GONE IS HER HAUGHTY DISDAIN...
...AND AS HER CRAFT ARROWS FOR EARTH, SHE IS NOTHING BUT A DAUGHTER WITH A FATHER SHE HAS NEVER KNOWN ...A FATHER WHO IS DYING.
AVENGERS MANSION...
MASTER THOR--IT IS GOOD TO SEE YOU, SIR! DO MAKE YOURSELF COMFORTABLE!
THOR THANKS THEE, JARVIS. ARE THE OTHERS PRESENT?
NO, SIR--THEY'RE ALL ATTENDING TO PERSONAL MATTERS. WOULD YOU CARE FOR SOME TEA, PERHAPS?
NAY, JARVIS--I WOULD BE ALONE FOR THE NONCE.
AS YOU WISH, SIR.
THE DAY THEN IS DESTINED FOR BOREDOM.
BUT WHAT DID I EXPECT--? TO ARRIVE JUST AS SOME DIRE MENACE THREATENED? NAY, I AM SIMPLY RESTLESS HERE ON MIDGARD.
YET EVEN ON ASGARD, I FELT PURPOSELESS, MERELY ANOTHER GOD AMONG SO MANY...

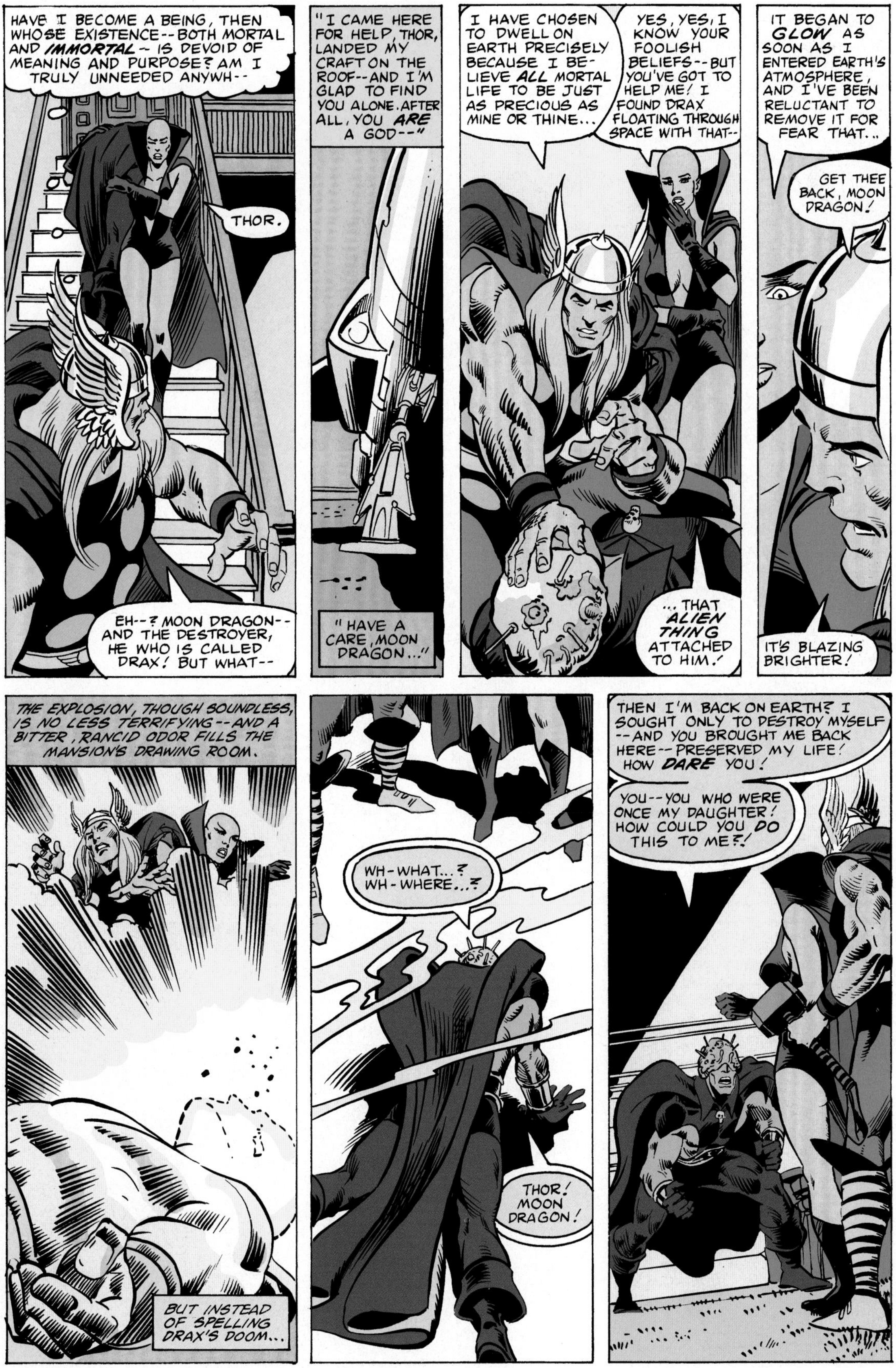
HAVE I BECOME A BEING, THEN WHOSE EXISTENCE--BOTH MORTAL AND IMMORTAL--IS DEVOID OF MEANING AND PURPOSE? AM I TRULY UNNEEDED ANYWH--
THOR.
EH--? MOON DRAGON--AND THE DESTROYER, HE WHO IS CALLED DRAX! BUT WHAT--
"I CAME HERE FOR HELP, THOR, LANDED MY CRAFT ON THE ROOF--AND I'M GLAD TO FIND YOU ALONE. AFTER ALL, YOU ARE A GOD--"
"HAVE A CARE, MOON DRAGON..."
I HAVE CHOSEN TO DWELL ON EARTH PRECISELY BECAUSE I BELIEVE ALL MORTAL LIFE TO BE JUST AS PRECIOUS AS MINE OR THINE...
YES, YES, I KNOW YOUR FOOLISH BELIEFS--BUT YOU'VE GOT TO HELP ME! I FOUND DRAX FLOATING THROUGH SPACE WITH THAT--
...THAT ALIEN THING ATTACHED TO HIM!
IT BEGAN TO GLOW AS SOON AS I ENTERED EARTH'S ATMOSPHERE, AND I'VE BEEN RELUCTANT TO REMOVE IT FOR FEAR THAT...
GET THEE BACK, MOON DRAGON!
IT'S BLAZING BRIGHTER!
THE EXPLOSION, THOUGH SOUNDLESS, IS NO LESS TERRIFYING--AND A BITTER, RANCID ODOR FILLS THE MANSION'S DRAWING ROOM.
BUT INSTEAD OF SPELLING DRAX'S DOOM...
WH-WHAT...? WH-WHERE...?
THOR! MOON DRAGON!
THEN I'M BACK ON EARTH? I SOUGHT ONLY TO DESTROY MYSELF--AND YOU BROUGHT ME BACK HERE--PRESERVED MY LIFE! HOW DARE YOU!
YOU--YOU WHO WERE ONCE MY DAUGHTER! HOW COULD YOU DO THIS TO ME?!

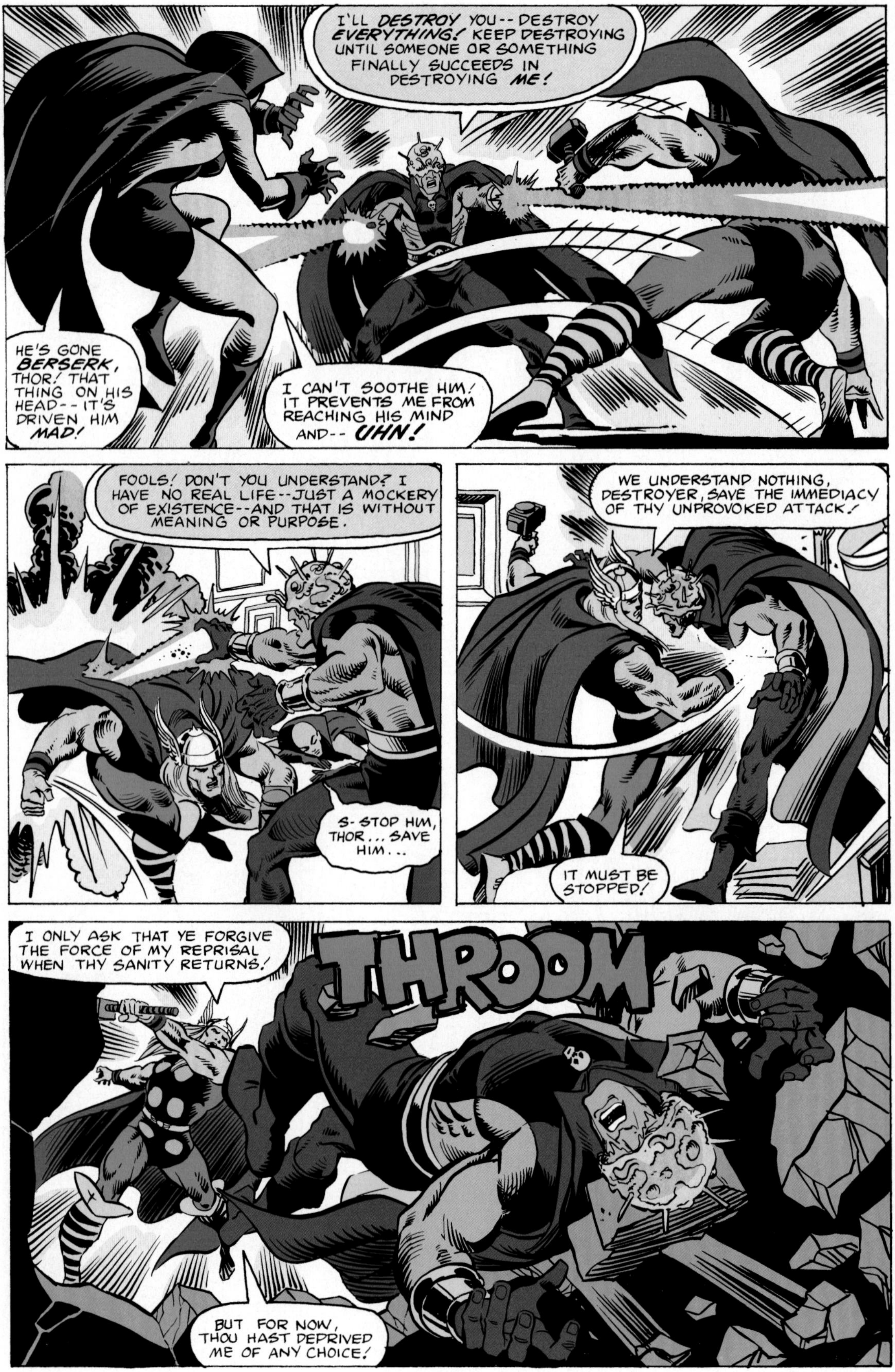
I'LL DESTROY YOU--DESTROY EVERYTHING! KEEP DESTROYING UNTIL SOMEONE OR SOMETHING FINALLY SUCCEEDS IN DESTROYING ME!
HE'S GONE BERSERK, THOR! THAT THING ON HIS HEAD--IT'S DRIVEN HIM MAD!
I CAN'T SOOTHE HIM! IT PREVENTS ME FROM REACHING HIS MIND AND-- UHN!
FOOLS! DON'T YOU UNDERSTAND? I HAVE NO REAL LIFE--JUST A MOCKERY OF EXISTENCE--AND THAT IS WITHOUT MEANING OR PURPOSE.
S-STOP HIM, THOR... SAVE HIM...
WE UNDERSTAND NOTHING, DESTROYER, SAVE THE IMMEDIACY OF THY UNPROVOKED ATTACK!
IT MUST BE STOPPED!
I ONLY ASK THAT YE FORGIVE THE FORCE OF MY REPRISAL WHEN THY SANITY RETURNS!
THROOM
BUT FOR NOW, THOU HAST DEPRIVED ME OF ANY CHOICE!

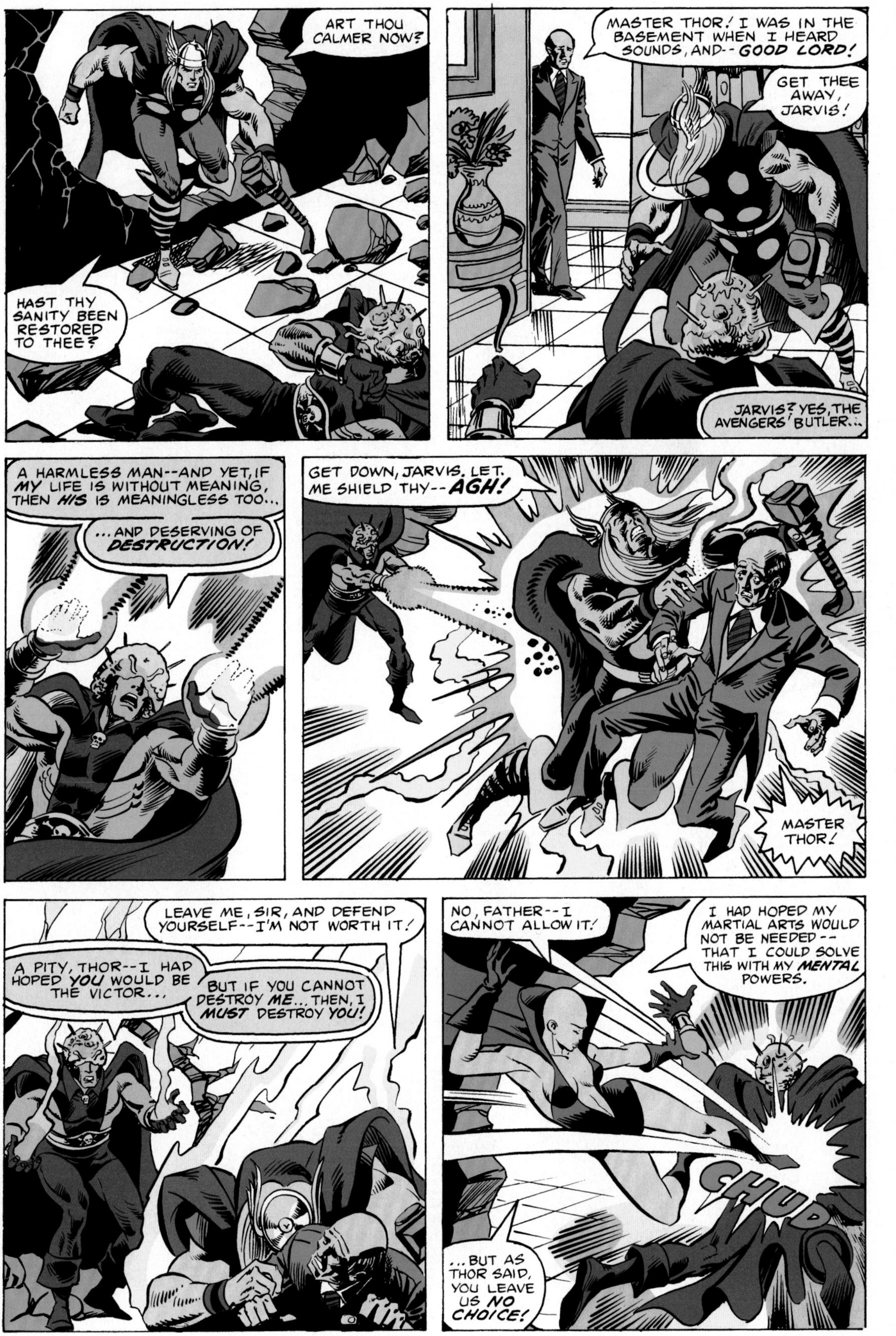
ART THOU CALMER NOW?
HAST THY SANITY BEEN RESTORED TO THEE?
MASTER THOR! I WAS IN THE BASEMENT WHEN I HEARD SOUNDS, AND--GOOD LORD!
GET THEE AWAY, JARVIS!
JARVIS? YES, THE AVENGERS' BUTLER...
A HARMLESS MAN--AND YET, IF MY LIFE IS WITHOUT MEANING, THEN HIS IS MEANINGLESS TOO...
...AND DESERVING OF DESTRUCTION!
GET DOWN, JARVIS. LET ME SHIELD THY--AGH!
MASTER THOR!
LEAVE ME, SIR, AND DEFEND YOURSELF--I'M NOT WORTH IT!
A PITY, THOR--I HAD HOPED YOU WOULD BE THE VICTOR...
BUT IF YOU CANNOT DESTROY ME... THEN, I MUST DESTROY YOU!
NO, FATHER--I CANNOT ALLOW IT!
I HAD HOPED MY MARTIAL ARTS WOULD NOT BE NEEDED--THAT I COULD SOLVE THIS WITH MY MENTAL POWERS.
CHUD
...BUT AS THOR SAID, YOU LEAVE US NO CHOICE!

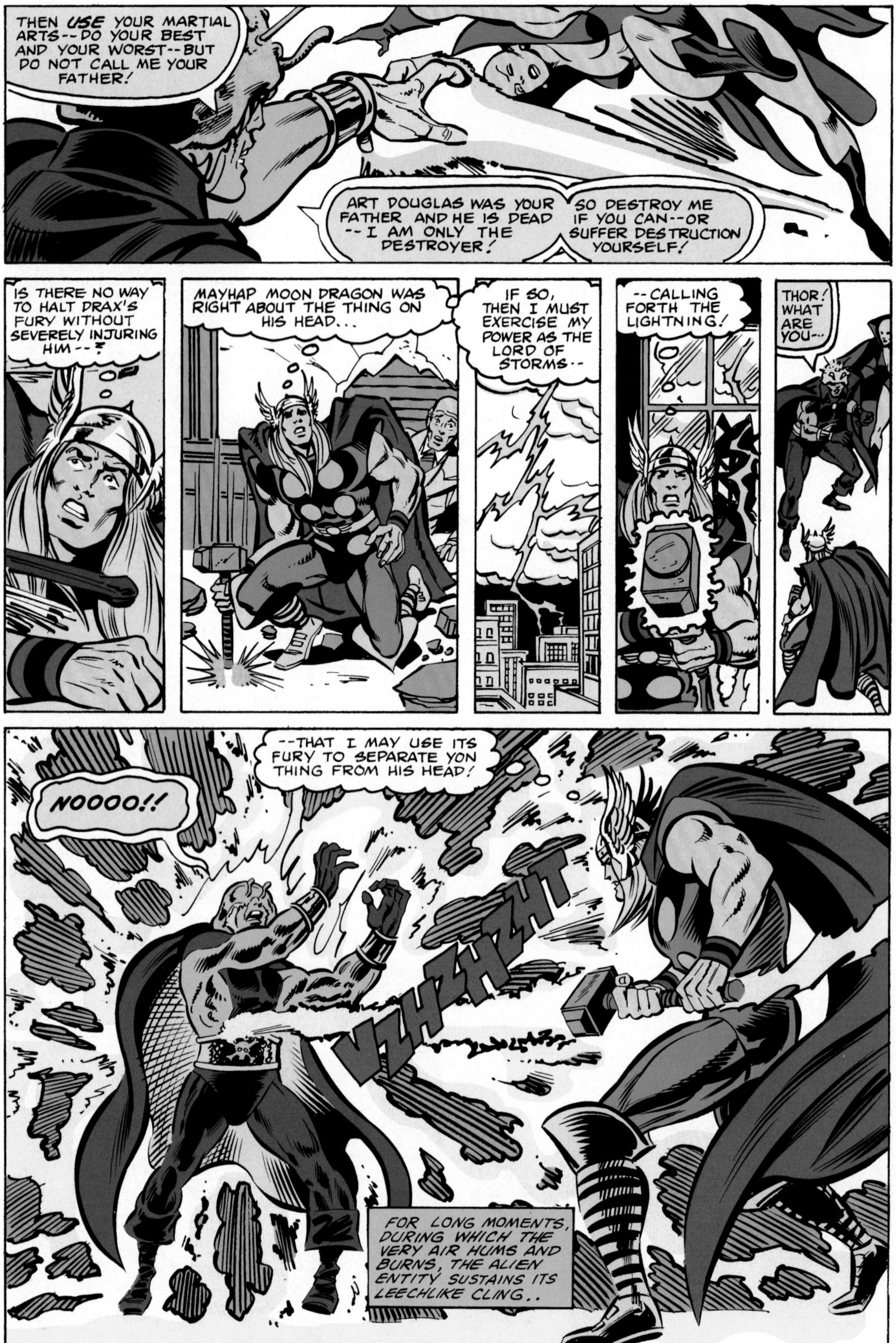
THEN USE YOUR MARTIAL ARTS--DO YOUR BEST AND YOUR WORST--BUT DO NOT CALL ME YOUR FATHER!
ART DOUGLAS WAS YOUR FATHER AND HE IS DEAD --I AM ONLY THE DESTROYER!
SO DESTROY ME IF YOU CAN--OR SUFFER DESTRUCTION YOURSELF!
IS THERE NO WAY TO HALT DRAX'S FURY WITHOUT SEVERELY INJURING HIM--?
MAYHAP MOON DRAGON WAS RIGHT ABOUT THE THING ON HIS HEAD...
IF SO, THEN I MUST EXERCISE MY POWER AS THE LORD OF STORMS--
--CALLING FORTH THE LIGHTNING!
THOR! WHAT ARE YOU--
--THAT I MAY USE ITS FURY TO SEPARATE YON THING FROM HIS HEAD!
NOOOO!!
VZHZHZHZHT
FOR LONG MOMENTS, DURING WHICH THE VERY AIR HUMS AND BURNS, THE ALIEN ENTITY SUSTAINS ITS LEECHLIKE CLING..

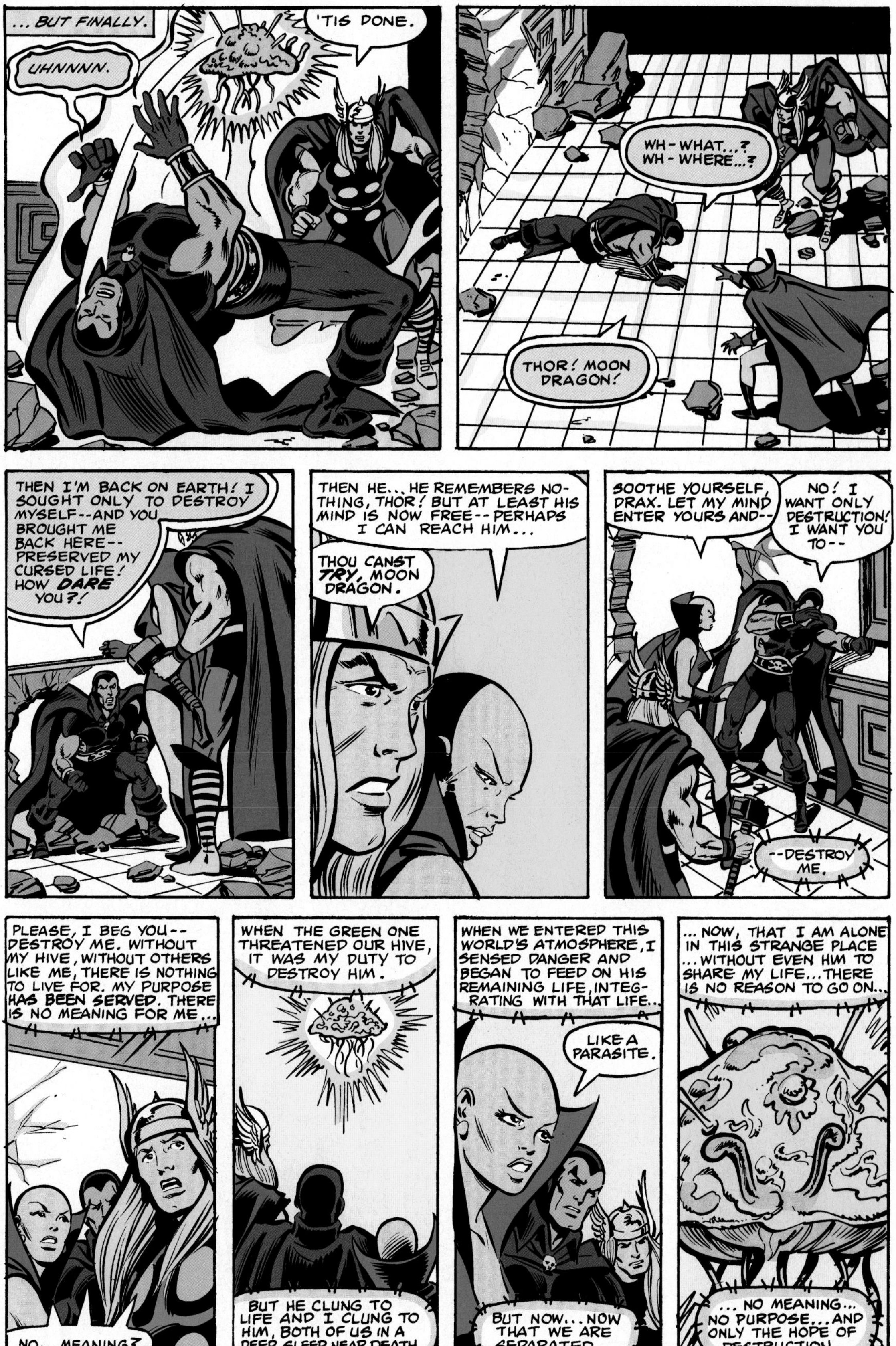

... BUT FINALLY.
UHNNNN.
'TIS DONE.
WH-WHAT...? WH-WHERE...?
THOR! MOON DRAGON!
THEN I'M BACK ON EARTH! I SOUGHT ONLY TO DESTROY MYSELF--AND YOU BROUGHT ME BACK HERE--PRESERVED MY CURSED LIFE! HOW DARE YOU?!
THEN HE... HE REMEMBERS NOTHING, THOR! BUT AT LEAST HIS MIND IS NOW FREE--PERHAPS I CAN REACH HIM...
THOU CANST TRY, MOON DRAGON.
SOOTHE YOURSELF, DRAX. LET MY MIND ENTER YOURS AND--
NO! I WANT ONLY DESTRUCTION! I WANT YOU TO--
--DESTROY ME.
PLEASE, I BEG YOU--DESTROY ME. WITHOUT MY HIVE, WITHOUT OTHERS LIKE ME, THERE IS NOTHING TO LIVE FOR. MY PURPOSE HAS BEEN SERVED. THERE IS NO MEANING FOR ME...
NO... MEANING?
WHEN THE GREEN ONE THREATENED OUR HIVE, IT WAS MY DUTY TO DESTROY HIM.
BUT HE CLUNG TO LIFE AND I CLUNG TO HIM, BOTH OF US IN A DEEP SLEEP NEAR DEATH.
WHEN WE ENTERED THIS WORLD'S ATMOSPHERE, I SENSED DANGER AND BEGAN TO FEED ON HIS REMAINING LIFE, INTEGRATING WITH THAT LIFE...
LIKE A PARASITE.
BUT NOW... NOW THAT WE ARE SEPARATED...
... NOW, THAT I AM ALONE IN THIS STRANGE PLACE ...WITHOUT EVEN HIM TO SHARE MY LIFE...THERE IS NO REASON TO GO ON...
... NO MEANING... NO PURPOSE... AND ONLY THE HOPE OF DESTRUCTION.

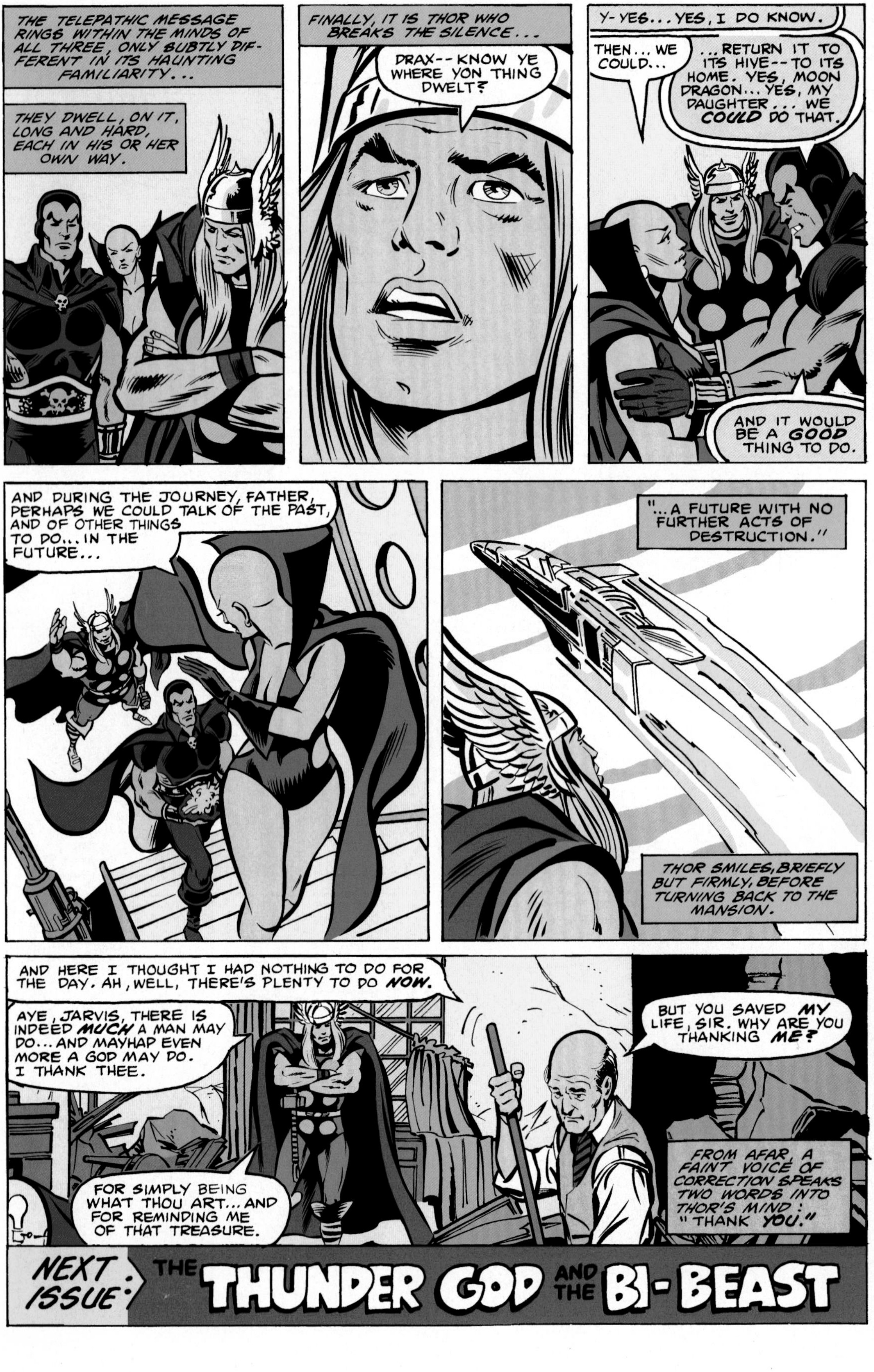
THE TELEPATHIC MESSAGE RINGS WITHIN THE MINDS OF ALL THREE, ONLY SUBTLY DIFFERENT IN ITS HAUNTING FAMILIARITY...
THEY DWELL, ON IT, LONG AND HARD, EACH IN HIS OR HER OWN WAY.
FINALLY, IT IS THOR WHO BREAKS THE SILENCE...
DRAX--KNOW YE WHERE YON THING DWELT?
Y-YES... YES, I DO KNOW.
THEN... WE COULD...
...RETURN IT TO ITS HIVE--TO ITS HOME. YES, MOON DRAGON... YES, MY DAUGHTER... WE COULD DO THAT.
AND IT WOULD BE A GOOD THING TO DO.
AND DURING THE JOURNEY, FATHER, PERHAPS WE COULD TALK OF THE PAST, AND OF OTHER THINGS TO DO... IN THE FUTURE...
"...A FUTURE WITH NO FURTHER ACTS OF DESTRUCTION."
THOR SMILES, BRIEFLY BUT FIRMLY, BEFORE TURNING BACK TO THE MANSION.
AND HERE I THOUGHT I HAD NOTHING TO DO FOR THE DAY. AH, WELL, THERE'S PLENTY TO DO NOW.
AYE, JARVIS, THERE IS INDEED MUCH A MAN MAY DO... AND MAYHAP EVEN MORE A GOD MAY DO. I THANK THEE.
BUT YOU SAVED MY LIFE, SIR. WHY ARE YOU THANKING ME?
FOR SIMPLY BEING WHAT THOU ART... AND FOR REMINDING ME OF THAT TREASURE.
FROM AFAR, A FAINT VOICE OF CORRECTION SPEAKS TWO WORDS INTO THOR'S MIND: "THANK YOU."
NEXT ISSUE: THE THUNDER GOD AND THE BI-BEAST

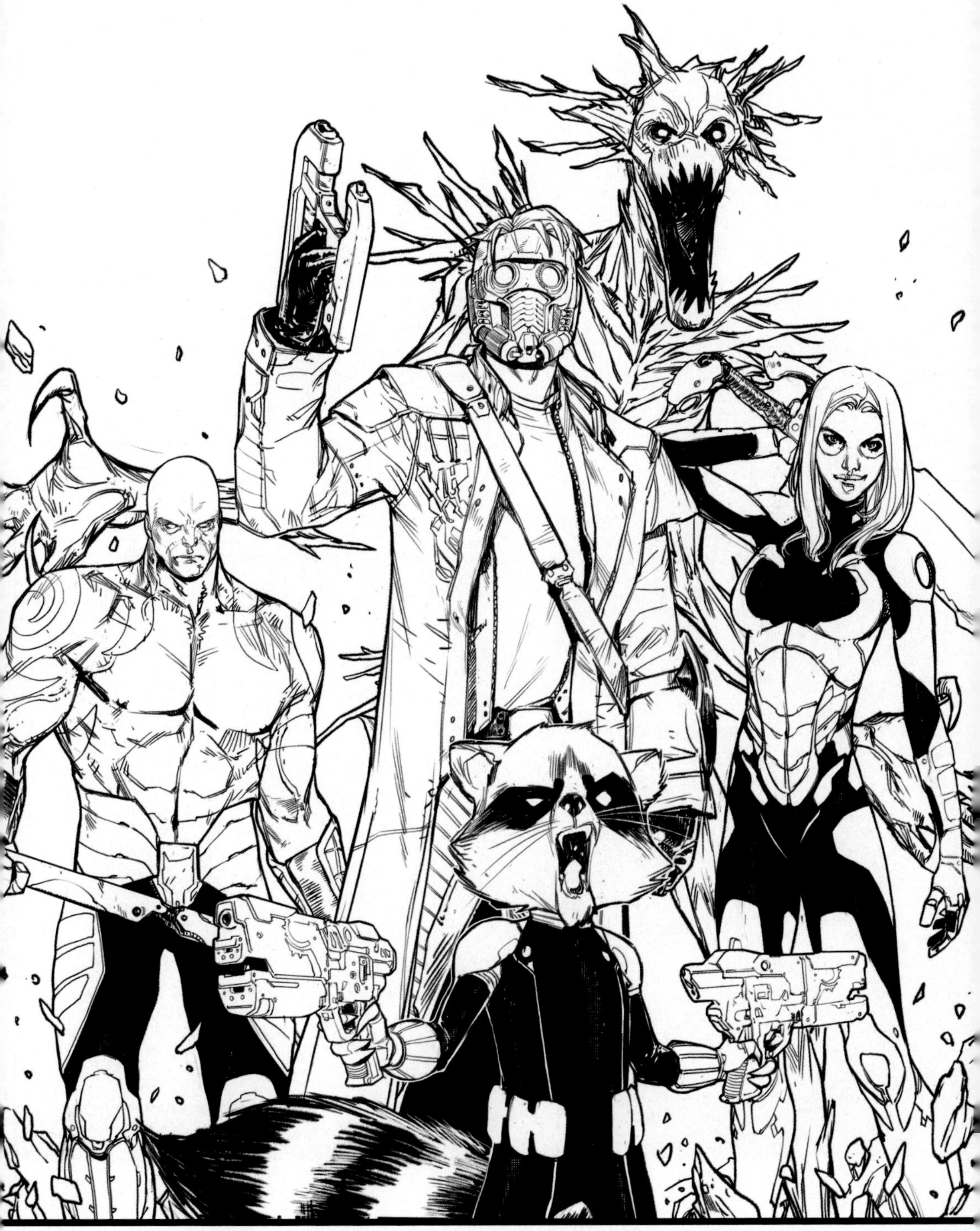

GUARDIANS OF THE GALAXY: GALAXY'S MOST WANTED #1 VARIANT BY SARA PICHELL

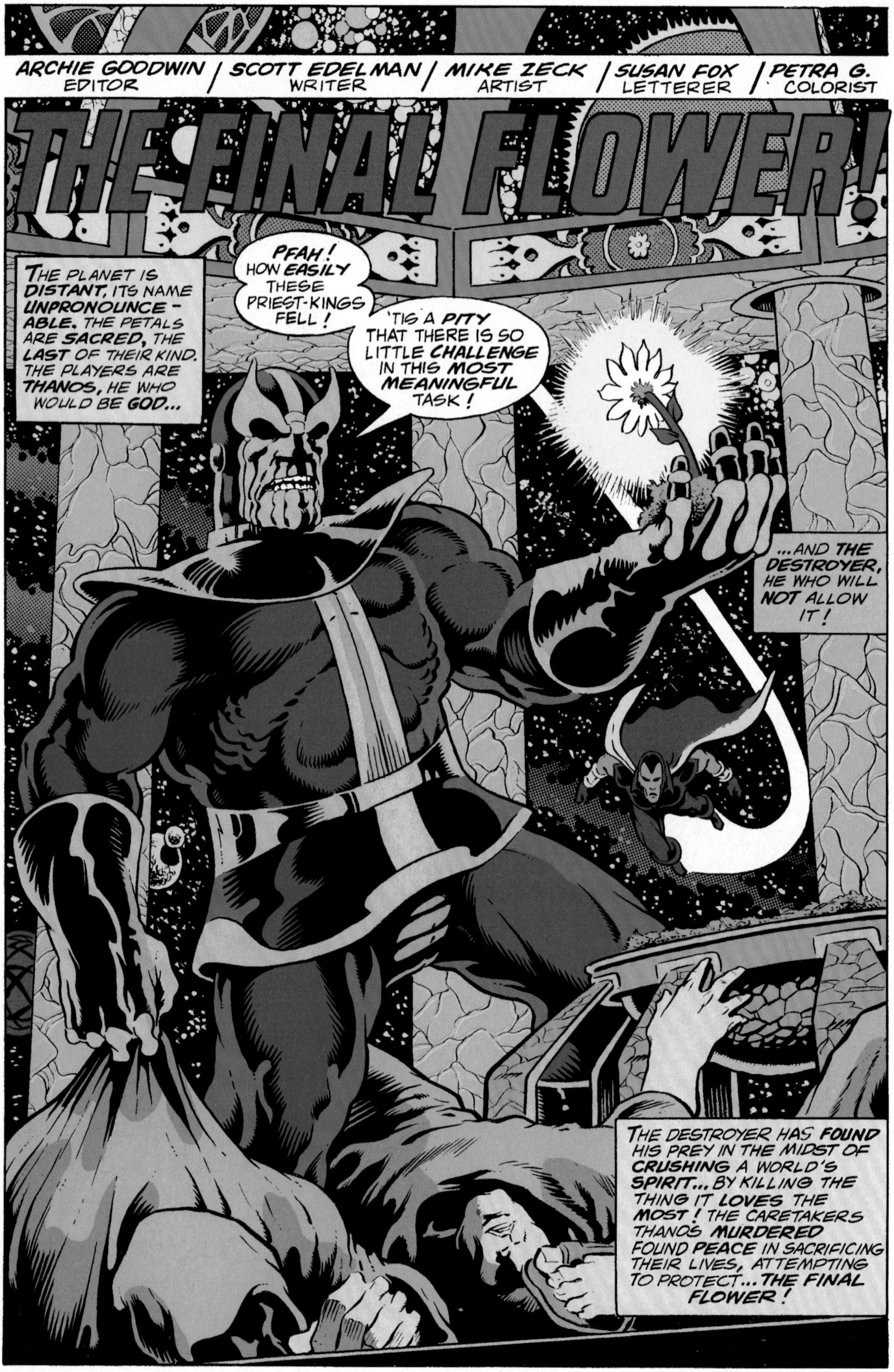
ARCHIE GOODWIN EDITOR / SCOTT EDELMAN WRITER / MIKE ZECK ARTIST / SUSAN FOX LETTERER / PETRA G. COLORIST
THE FINAL FLOWER!
THE PLANET IS DISTANT, ITS NAME UNPRONOUNCE-ABLE. THE PETALS ARE SACRED, THE LAST OF THEIR KIND. THE PLAYERS ARE THANOS, HE WHO WOULD BE GOD...
PFAH! HOW EASILY THESE PRIEST-KINGS FELL!
'TIS A PITY THAT THERE IS SO LITTLE CHALLENGE IN THIS MOST MEANINGFUL TASK!
...AND THE DESTROYER, HE WHO WILL NOT ALLOW IT!
THE DESTROYER HAS FOUND HIS PREY IN THE MIDST OF CRUSHING A WORLD'S SPIRIT... BY KILLING THE THING IT LOVES THE MOST! THE CARETAKERS THANOS MURDERED FOUND PEACE IN SACRIFICING THEIR LIVES, ATTEMPTING TO PROTECT... THE FINAL FLOWER!

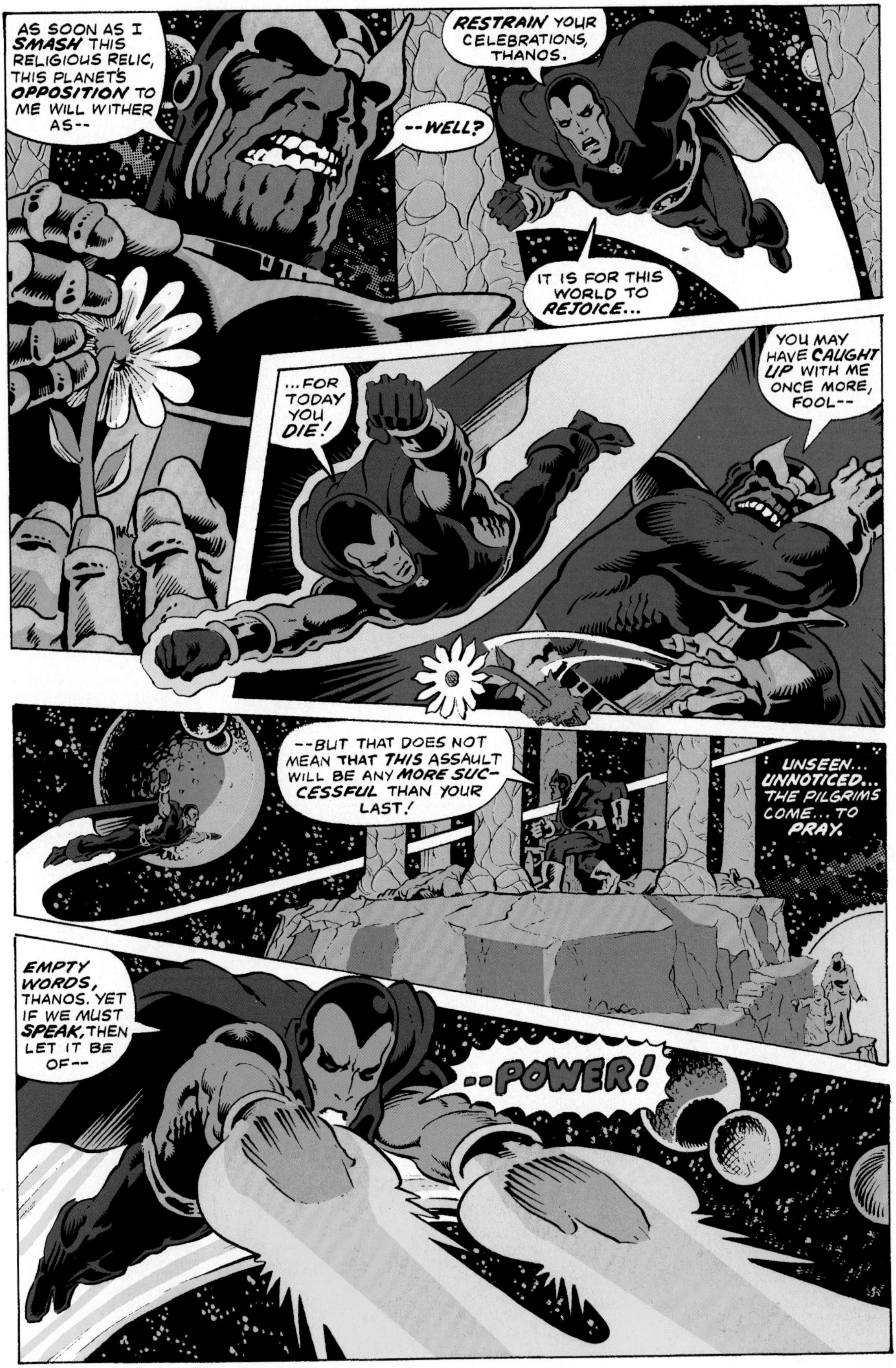
AS SOON AS I SMASH THIS RELIGIOUS RELIC, THIS PLANET'S OPPOSITION TO ME WILL WITHER AS--
RESTRAIN YOUR CELEBRATIONS, THANOS.
--WELL?
IT IS FOR THIS WORLD TO REJOICE...
...FOR TODAY YOU DIE!
YOU MAY HAVE CAUGHT UP WITH ME ONCE MORE, FOOL--
--BUT THAT DOES NOT MEAN THAT THIS ASSAULT WILL BE ANY MORE SUCCESSFUL THAN YOUR LAST!
UNSEEN... UNNOTICED... THE PILGRIMS COME... TO PRAY.
EMPTY WORDS, THANOS. YET IF WE MUST SPEAK, THEN LET IT BE OF--
..POWER!

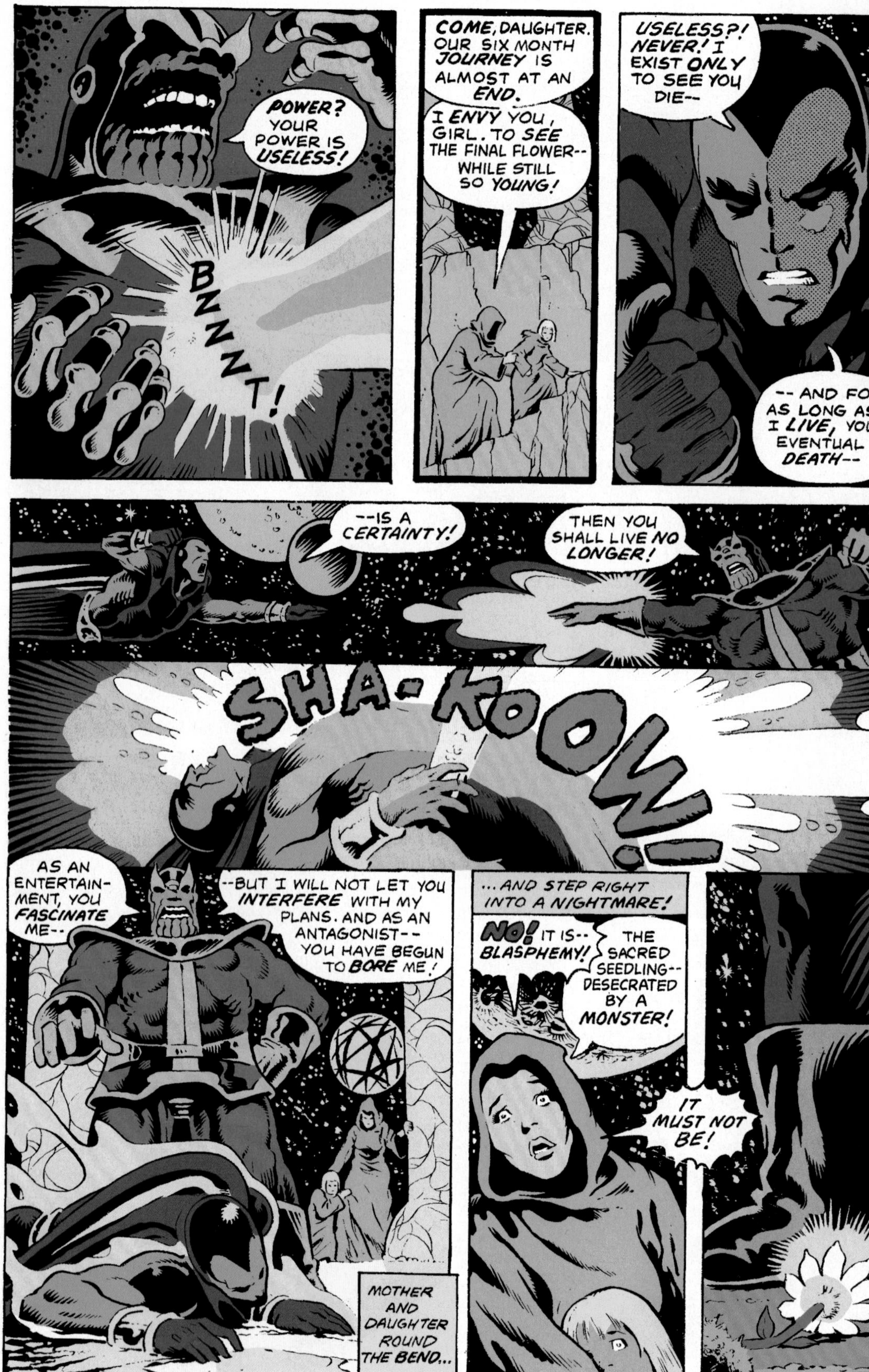
POWER? YOUR POWER IS USELESS!
BZZZT!
COME, DAUGHTER. OUR SIX MONTH JOURNEY IS ALMOST AT AN END.
I ENVY YOU, GIRL. TO SEE THE FINAL FLOWER-- WHILE STILL SO YOUNG!
USELESS?! NEVER! I EXIST ONLY TO SEE YOU DIE--
-- AND FOR AS LONG AS I LIVE, YOUR EVENTUAL DEATH--
--IS A CERTAINTY!
THEN YOU SHALL LIVE NO LONGER!
SHA-KOOOW!
AS AN ENTERTAINMENT, YOU FASCINATE ME--
--BUT I WILL NOT LET YOU INTERFERE WITH MY PLANS. AND AS AN ANTAGONIST-- YOU HAVE BEGUN TO BORE ME!
MOTHER AND DAUGHTER ROUND THE BEND...
...AND STEP RIGHT INTO A NIGHTMARE!
NO! IT IS-- BLASPHEMY!
THE SACRED SEEDLING-- DESECRATED BY A MONSTER!
IT MUST NOT BE!

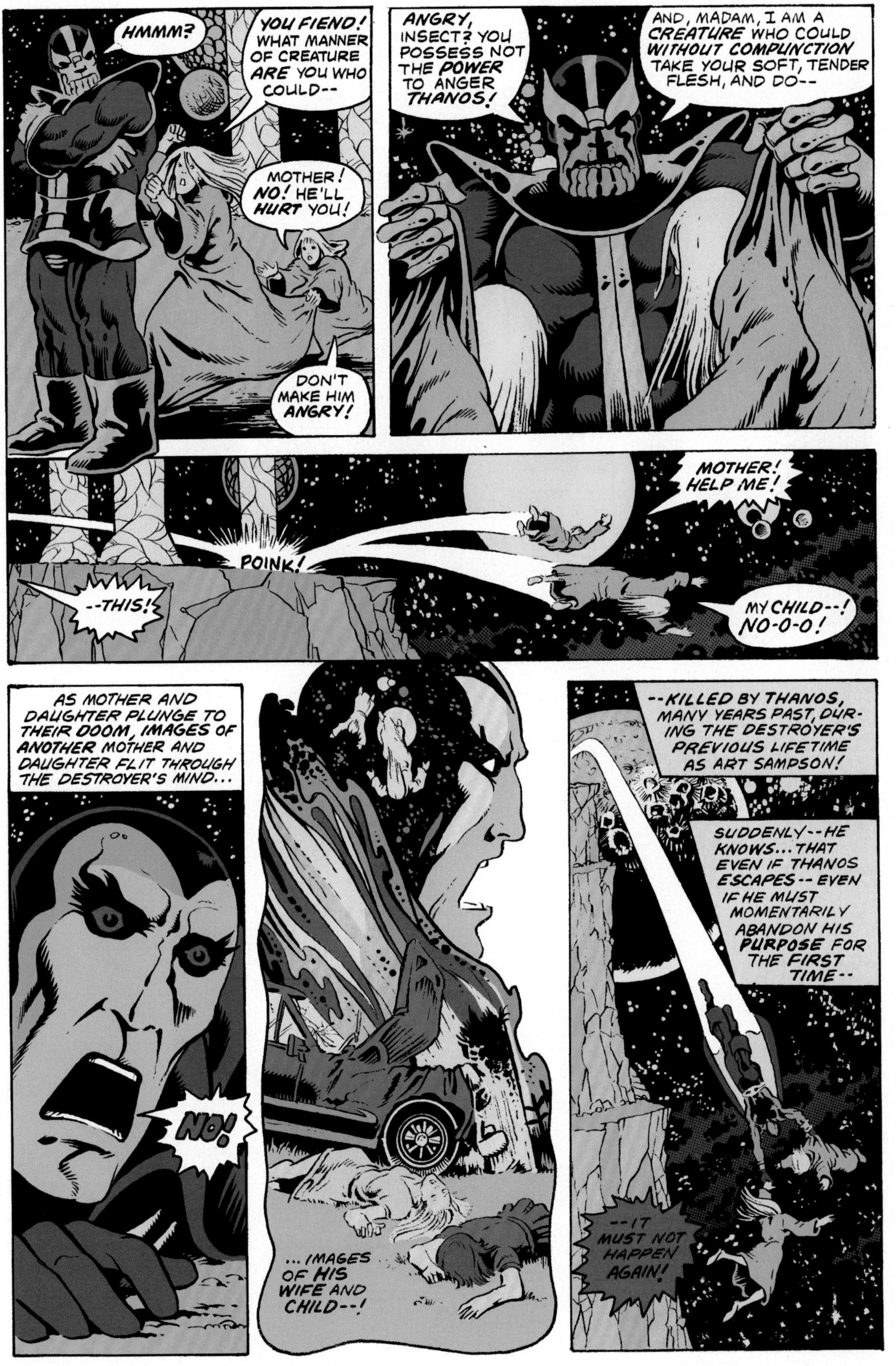
HMMM?
YOU FIEND! WHAT MANNER OF CREATURE ARE YOU WHO COULD--
MOTHER! NO! HE'LL HURT YOU!
DON'T MAKE HIM ANGRY!
ANGRY, INSECT? YOU POSSESS NOT THE POWER TO ANGER THANOS!
AND, MADAM, I AM A CREATURE WHO COULD WITHOUT COMPUNCTION TAKE YOUR SOFT, TENDER FLESH, AND DO--
--THIS!
POINK!
MOTHER! HELP ME!
MY CHILD--! NO-O-O!
AS MOTHER AND DAUGHTER PLUNGE TO THEIR DOOM, IMAGES OF ANOTHER MOTHER AND DAUGHTER FLIT THROUGH THE DESTROYER'S MIND...
NO!
...IMAGES OF HIS WIFE AND CHILD--!
--KILLED BY THANOS, MANY YEARS PAST, DURING THE DESTROYER'S PREVIOUS LIFETIME AS ART SAMPSON!
SUDDENLY--HE KNOWS...THAT EVEN IF THANOS ESCAPES--EVEN IF HE MUST MOMENTARILY ABANDON HIS PURPOSE FOR THE FIRST TIME--
--IT MUST NOT HAPPEN AGAIN!

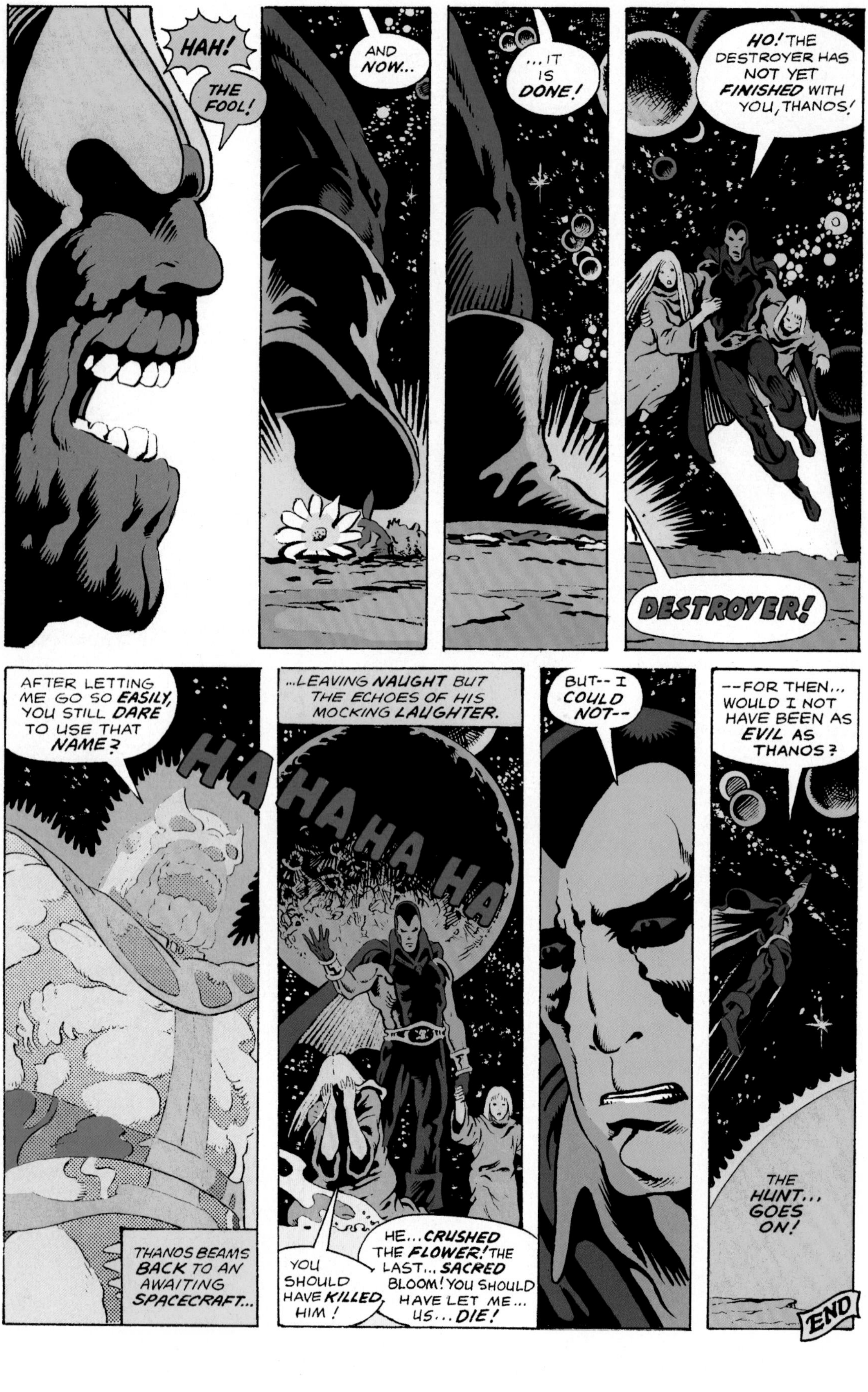
HAH!
THE FOOL!
AND NOW...
...IT IS DONE!
HO! THE DESTROYER HAS NOT YET FINISHED WITH YOU, THANOS!
DESTROYER!
AFTER LETTING ME GO SO EASILY, YOU STILL DARE TO USE THAT NAME?
HA
THANOS BEAMS BACK TO AN AWAITING SPACECRAFT...
...LEAVING NAUGHT BUT THE ECHOES OF HIS MOCKING LAUGHTER.
HAHAHA HA
YOU SHOULD HAVE KILLED HIM!
HE... CRUSHED THE FLOWER! THE LAST... SACRED BLOOM! YOU SHOULD HAVE LET ME... US... DIE!
BUT-- I COULD NOT--
--FOR THEN... WOULD I NOT HAVE BEEN AS EVIL AS THANOS?
THE HUNT... GOES ON!
END

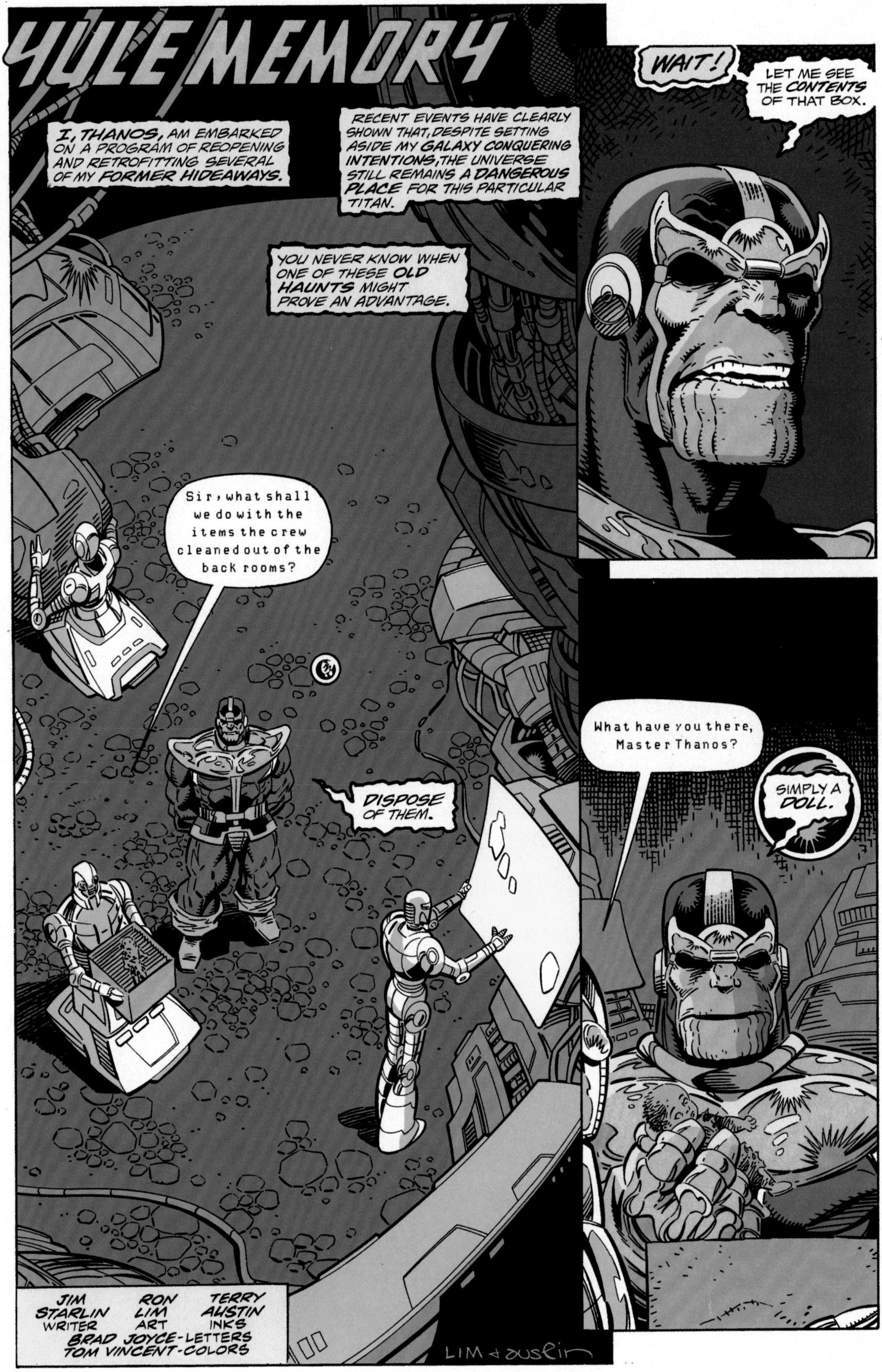

YULE MEMORY
I, THANOS, AM EMBARKED ON A PROGRAM OF REOPENING AND RETROFITTING SEVERAL OF MY FORMER HIDEAWAYS.
RECENT EVENTS HAVE CLEARLY SHOWN THAT, DESPITE SETTING ASIDE MY GALAXY CONQUERING INTENTIONS, THE UNIVERSE STILL REMAINS A DANGEROUS PLACE FOR THIS PARTICULAR TITAN.
YOU NEVER KNOW WHEN ONE OF THESE OLD HAUNTS MIGHT PROVE AN ADVANTAGE.
Sir, what shall we do with the items the crew cleaned out of the back rooms?
DISPOSE OF THEM.
JIM STARLIN WRITER
RON LIM ART
TERRY AUSTIN INKS
BRAD JOYCE-LETTERS
TOM VINCENT-COLORS
LIM + austin
WAIT!
LET ME SEE THE CONTENTS OF THAT BOX.
What have you there, Master Thanos?
SIMPLY A DOLL.

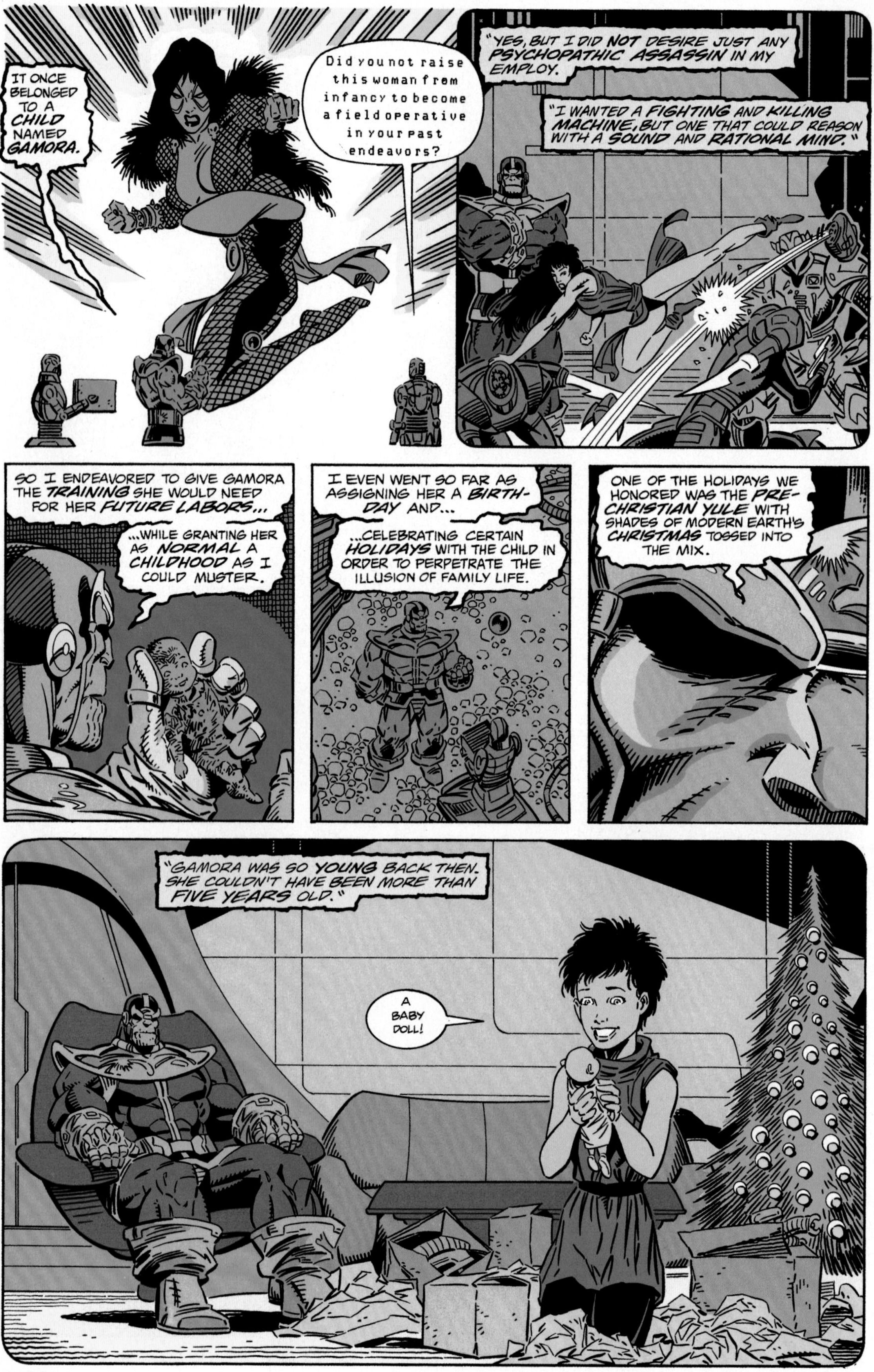
IT ONCE BELONGED TO A CHILD NAMED GAMORA.
Did you not raise this woman from infancy to become a field operative in your past endeavors?
"YES, BUT I DID NOT DESIRE JUST ANY PSYCHOPATHIC ASSASSIN IN MY EMPLOY.
"I WANTED A FIGHTING AND KILLING MACHINE. BUT ONE THAT COULD REASON WITH A SOUND AND RATIONAL MIND."
SO I ENDEAVORED TO GIVE GAMORA THE TRAINING SHE WOULD NEED FOR HER FUTURE LABORS...
...WHILE GRANTING HER AS NORMAL A CHILDHOOD AS I COULD MUSTER.
I EVEN WENT SO FAR AS ASSIGNING HER A BIRTH-DAY AND...
...CELEBRATING CERTAIN HOLIDAYS WITH THE CHILD IN ORDER TO PERPETRATE THE ILLUSION OF FAMILY LIFE.
ONE OF THE HOLIDAYS WE HONORED WAS THE PRE-CHRISTIAN YULE WITH SHADES OF MODERN EARTH'S CHRISTMAS TOSSED INTO THE MIX.
"GAMORA WAS SO YOUNG BACK THEN. SHE COULDN'T HAVE BEEN MORE THAN FIVE YEARS OLD."
A BABY DOLL!

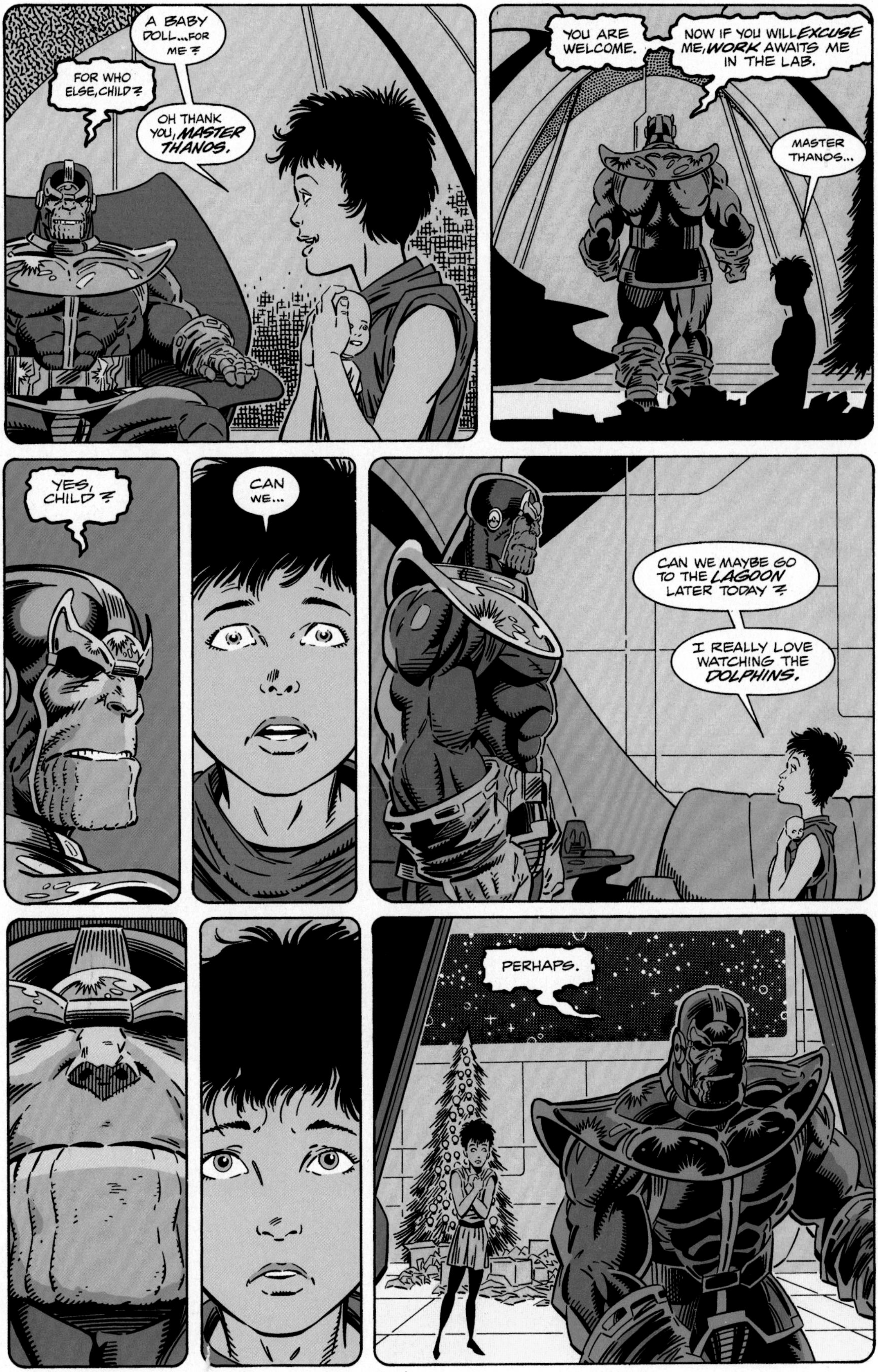
A BABY DOLL...FOR ME?
FOR WHO ELSE, CHILD?
OH THANK YOU, MASTER THANOS.
YOU ARE WELCOME.
NOW IF YOU WILL EXCUSE ME, WORK AWAITS ME IN THE LAB.
MASTER THANOS...
YES, CHILD?
CAN WE...
CAN WE MAYBE GO TO THE LAGOON LATER TODAY?
I REALLY LOVE WATCHING THE DOLPHINS.
PERHAPS.

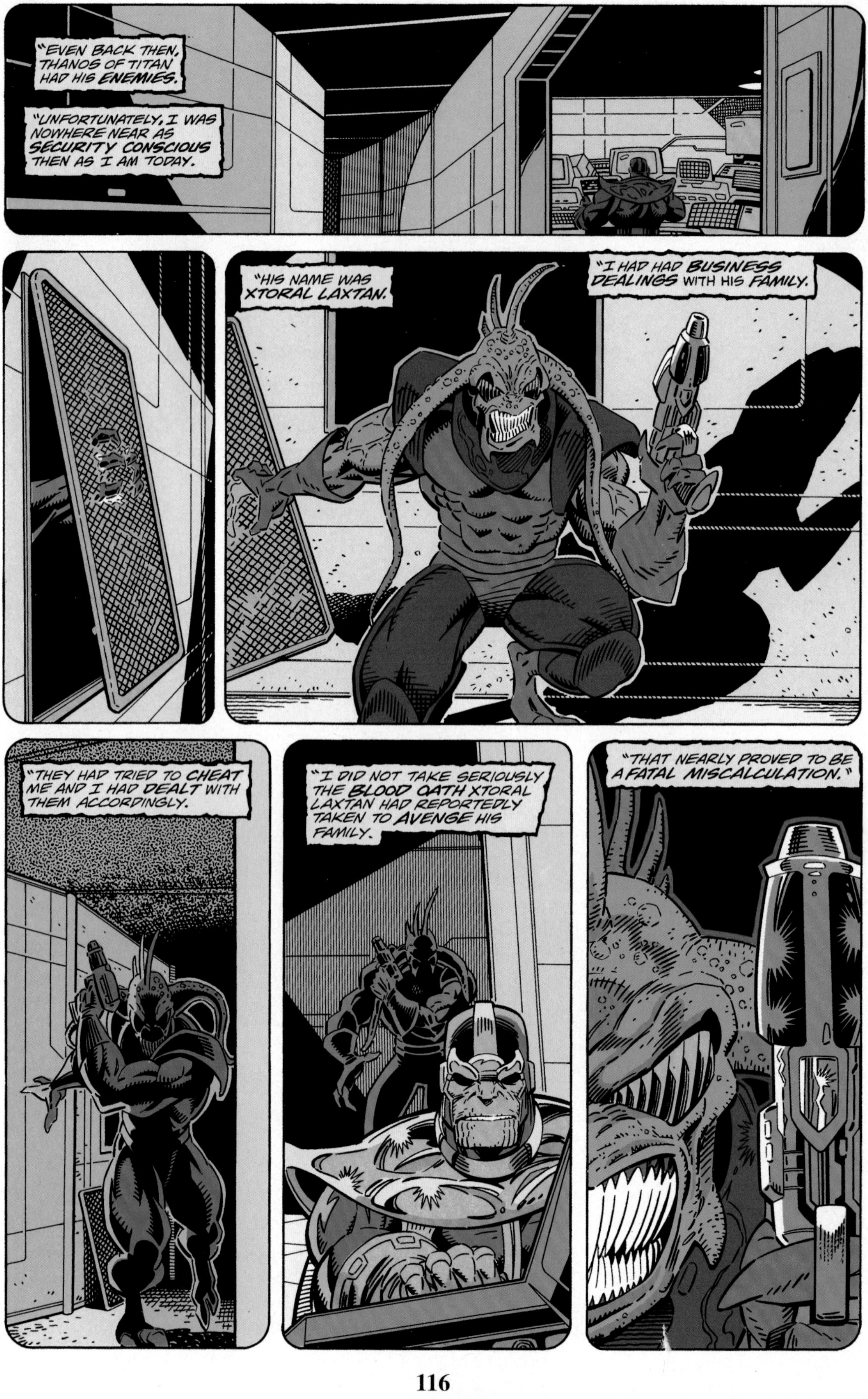
"EVEN BACK THEN, THANOS OF TITAN HAD HIS ENEMIES.
"UNFORTUNATELY, I WAS NOWHERE NEAR AS SECURITY CONSCIOUS THEN AS I AM TODAY.
"HIS NAME WAS XTORAL LAXTAN.
"I HAD HAD BUSINESS DEALINGS WITH HIS FAMILY.
"THEY HAD TRIED TO CHEAT ME AND I HAD DEALT WITH THEM ACCORDINGLY.
"I DID NOT TAKE SERIOUSLY THE BLOOD OATH XTORAL LAXTAN HAD REPORTEDLY TAKEN TO AVENGE HIS FAMILY.
"THAT NEARLY PROVED TO BE A FATAL MISCALCULATION."

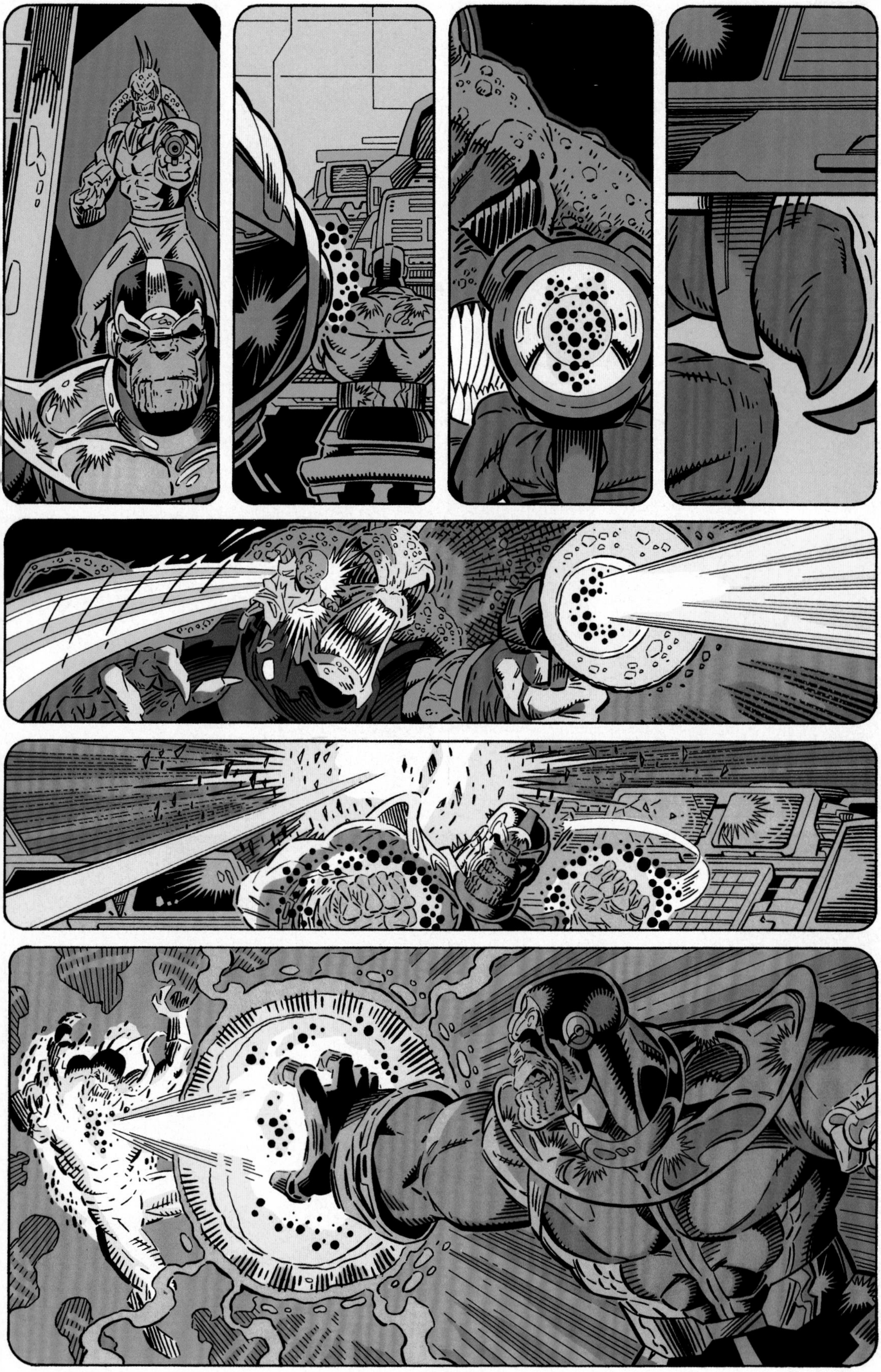

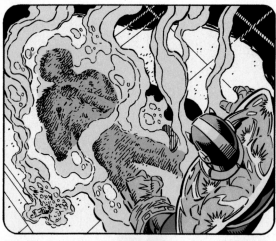

YOU...

YOU...

I KNOW.

YOUR DOLL WAS *SCORCHED* IN THE BLAST.

I WILL *REPLACE* IT.

THERE'S *NO NEED* FOR YOU TO BOTHER, MASTER THANOS.

I'LL MAKE DOLLY *ALL BETTER*.

DOLLY WILL BE OKAY.

118

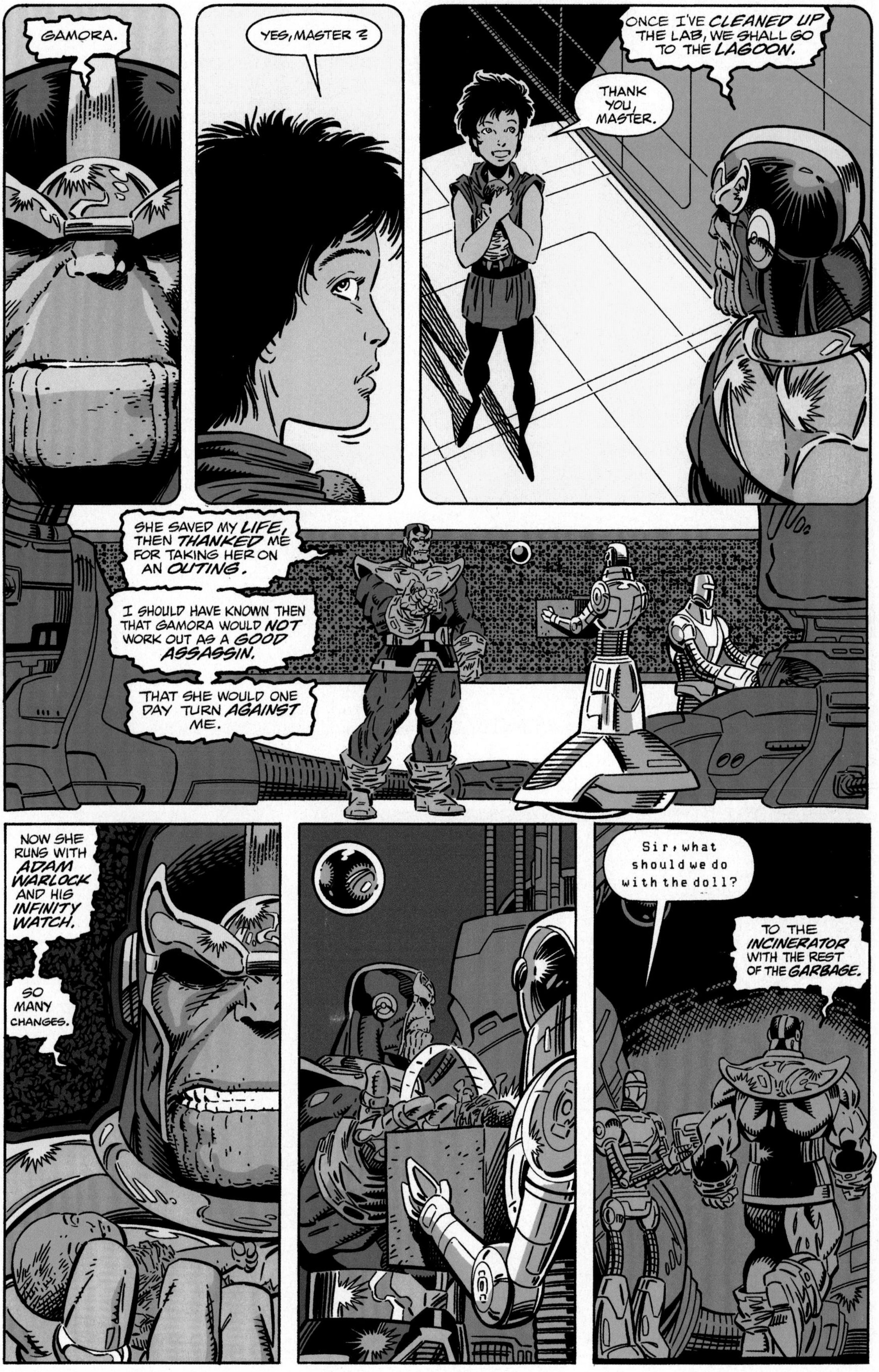
GAMORA.
YES, MASTER ?
ONCE I'VE CLEANED UP THE LAB, WE SHALL GO TO THE LAGOON.
THANK YOU, MASTER.
SHE SAVED MY LIFE, THEN THANKED ME FOR TAKING HER ON AN OUTING.
I SHOULD HAVE KNOWN THEN THAT GAMORA WOULD NOT WORK OUT AS A GOOD ASSASSIN.
THAT SHE WOULD ONE DAY TURN AGAINST ME.
NOW SHE RUNS WITH ADAM WARLOCK AND HIS INFINITY WATCH.
SO MANY CHANGES.
Sir, what should we do with the doll?
TO THE INCINERATOR WITH THE REST OF THE GARBAGE.

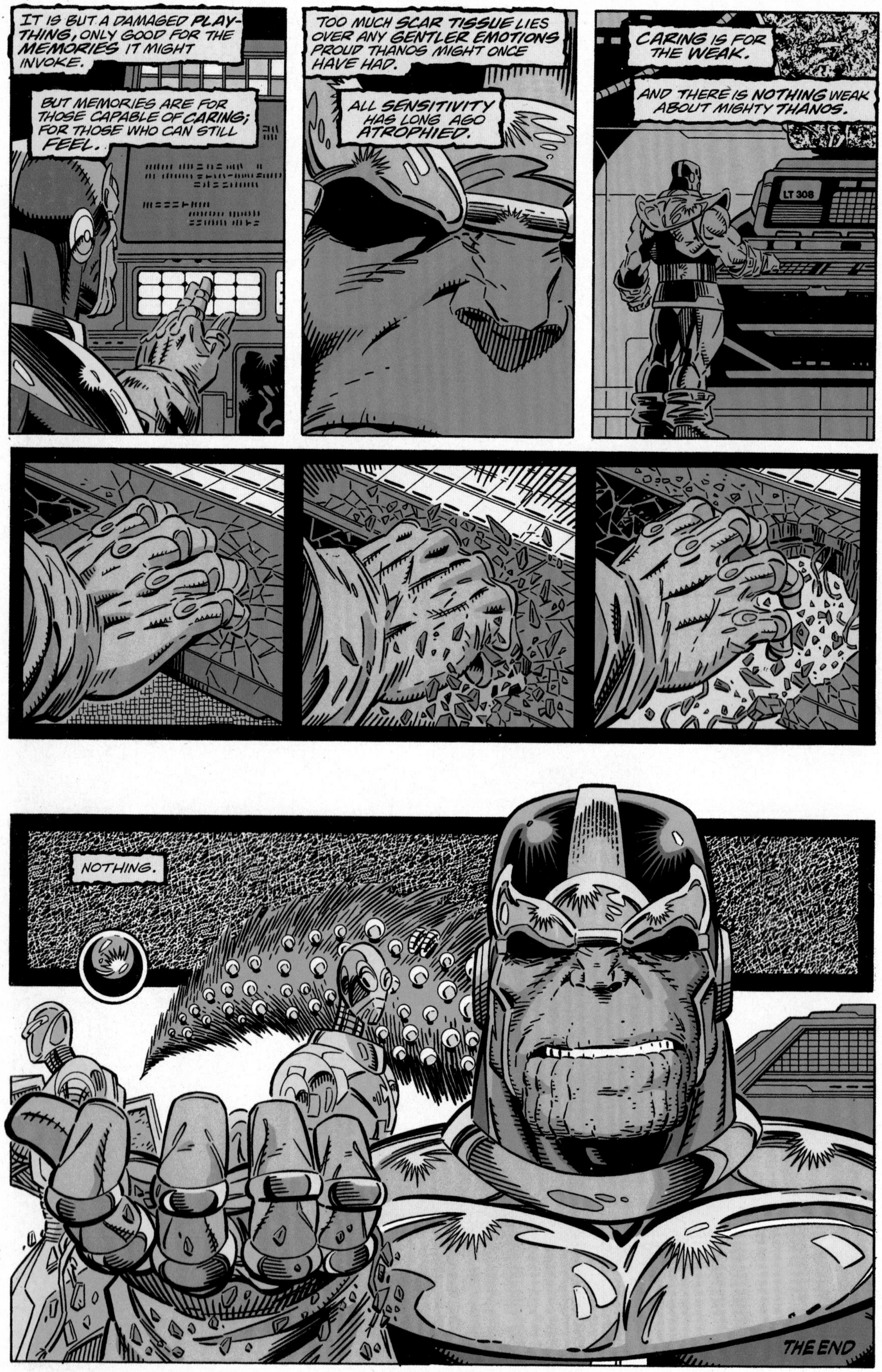
IT IS BUT A DAMAGED PLAYTHING, ONLY GOOD FOR THE MEMORIES IT MIGHT INVOKE.
BUT MEMORIES ARE FOR THOSE CAPABLE OF CARING; FOR THOSE WHO CAN STILL FEEL.
TOO MUCH SCAR TISSUE LIES OVER ANY GENTLER EMOTIONS PROUD THANOS MIGHT ONCE HAVE HAD.
ALL SENSITIVITY HAS LONG AGO ATROPHIED.
CARING IS FOR THE WEAK.
AND THERE IS NOTHING WEAK ABOUT MIGHTY THANOS.
LT 308
NOTHING.
THE END